Ron Silliman The Age of Huts (compleat)

UNIVERSITY OF CALIFORNIA PRESS BERKELEY LOS ANGELES LONDON

University of California Press, one of the most distinguished university presses in the United States, enriches lives around the world by advancing scholarship in the humanities, social sciences, and natural sciences. Its activities are supported by the UC Press Foundation and by philanthropic contributions from individuals and institutions. For more information, visit www.ucpress.edu.

University of California Press
Berkeley and Los Angeles, California

University of California Press, Ltd.
London, England

Library of Congress Cataloging-in-Publication Data

Silliman, Ronald, 1946–.
[Age of huts]
The age of huts (compleat) / Ron Silliman.
    p.   cm.   —   (New California poetry ; 21)
This title is one of a four-part poem cycle, which is entitled Ketjak. The parts are: The age of huts, Tjanting, The alphabet, & Universe.
    ISBN: 978-0-520-25014-7 (cloth : alk. paper)
    ISBN: 978-0-520-25016-1 (pbk. : alk. paper)
    I. Silliman, Ronald, 1946– Ketjak. II. Title.
PS3569.I445A7   2007
811'.54—dc22   2006025507

Manufactured in Canada

16 15 14 13 12 11 10 09 08 07
10 9 8 7 6 5 4 3 2 1

This book is printed on New Leaf EcoBook 50, a 100% recycled fiber of which 50% is de-inked post-consumer waste, processed chlorine-free. EcoBook 50 is acid-free and meets the minimum requirements of ANSI/ASTM D5634–01 (*Permanence of Paper*).

for Krishna Evans

Contents

Since 1974, I have been at work on a single poem, which I call *Ketjak*. This project in turn is composed of four works: *The Age of Huts, Tjanting, The Alphabet,* & *Universe*. With the exception of *Tjanting,* a book-length poem in its own right, each of these incorporated projects is itself a compilation of texts. This is the first opportunity I have had to present *The Age of Huts* in its complete form, a cycle of four poems with two satellite texts. In keeping with the sort of Russian-doll structure that I seem to keep reinventing, it may come as no surprise that one of the four poems in the *Age of Huts* cycle is itself composed of a series of poems.

Acknowledgments

My thanks to This, Roof Books, Tuumba Press, Potes & Poets Press, the Walt Whitman Cultural Arts Center, & Ubu Editions for publishing portions of *The Age of Huts* in book, chapbook, & ebook form. My thanks also to the many journals & periodicals in which these poems first appeared, as well as to the various anthologies that republished sections, both in English & in translation.

Ketjak

for Rae Armantrout

Revolving door.

Revolving door. A sequence of objects which to him appears to be a caravan of fellaheen, a circus, begins a slow migration to the right vanishing point on the horizon line.

Revolving door. Fountains of the financial district. Houseboats beached at the point of low tide, only to float again when the sunset is reflected in the water. A sequence of objects which to him appears to be a caravan of fellaheen, a circus, camels pulling wagons of bear cages, tamed ostriches in toy hats, begins a slow migration to the right vanishing point on the horizon line.

Revolving door. First flies of summer. Fountains of the financial district spout. She was a unit in a bum space, she was a damaged child. Dark brown houseboats beached at the point of low tide— men atop their cabin roofs, idle, play a Dobro, a jaw's harp, a 12-string guitar—only to float again when the sunset is reflected in the water. I want the grey-blue grain of western summer. A cardboard box of wool sweaters on top of the bookcase to indicate Home. A sequence of objects, silhouettes, which to him appears to be a caravan of fellaheen, a circus, dromedaries pulling wagons bearing tiger cages, tamed ostriches in toy hats, begins a slow migration to the right vanishing point on the horizon line.

Revolving door. Earth science. Fountains of the financial district spout soft water in a hard wind. How the heel rises and the ankle bends to carry the body from one stair to the next. She was a unit in a bum space, she was a damaged child. The fishermen's cormorants wear rings around their necks to keep them from swallowing, to force them to surrender the catch. Dark brown houseboats beached at the point of low tide—men atop their cabin roofs, idle, play a Dobro, a jaw's harp, a 12-string guitar—only to float again when the sunset is reflected in the water. Silverfish, potato bugs. What I want is the gray-blue grain of western summer. The nurse, by a subtle shift of weight, moves in front of the student in order to more rapidly board the bus. A cardboard box of wool sweaters on top of the bookcase to indicate Home. A day of rain in the middle of June. A sequence of objects, silhouettes, which to him appears to be a caravan of fellaheen, a circus, dromedaries pulling wagons bearing tiger cages, fringed surreys, tamed ostriches in toy hats, begins a slow migration to the right vanishing point on the horizon line. We ate them.

Revolving door. The garbage barge at the bridge. Earth science. Resemblance. Fountains of the financial district spout soft water in a hard wind. The bear flag in the plaza. How the heel rises and the ankle bends to carry the body from one stair to the next. A tenor sax is a toy. She was a unit in a bum space, she was a damaged child, sitting in her rocker by the window. I'm unable to find just the right straw hat. The fishermen's cormorants wear rings around their necks to keep them from swallowing, to force them to surrender the catch. We drove through fields of artichokes. Dark brown houseboats beached at the point of low tide—men atop their cabin roofs, idle, play a Dobro, a jaw's harp, a 12-string guitar—only to float again when the sunset is reflected in the water of Richardson Bay. Write this down in a green notebook. Silverfish, potato bugs. A tenor sax is a weapon. What I want is the gray-blue grain of western summer. Mention sex. The nurse, by a subtle redistribution of weight, shift of gravity's center, moves in front of the student of oriental porcelain in order to more rapidly board the bus. Awake, but still in bed, I listen to cars pass, doors, birds, children are day's first voices. A cardboard box of wool sweaters on top of the bookcase to indicate Home. Attention is all. A day of rain in the middle of June. Modal rounders. A sequence of objects, silhouettes, which to him appears to be a caravan of fellaheen, a circus, dromedaries pulling wagons bearing tiger cages, fringed surreys, tamed ostriches in toy hats, begins a slow migration to the right vanishing point on the horizon line. The implications of power within the ability to draw a single, vertical straight line. Look at that room filled with fleshy babies. We ate them.

Revolving door. How will I know when I make a mistake. The garbage barge at the bridge. The throb in the wrist. Earth science. Their first goal was to separate the workers from their means of production. He bears a resemblance. A drawing of a Balinese spirit with its face in its stomach. Fountains of the financial district spout soft water in a hard wind. In a far room of the apartment I can hear music and a hammer. The bear flag in the black marble plaza. Rapid transit. How the heel rises and the ankle bends to carry the body from one stair to the next. The desire for coffee. A tenor sax is a toy. Snow is remarkable to one not accustomed to it. She was a unit in a bum space, she was a damaged child, sitting in her rocker by the window. The formal beauty of a back porch. I'm unable to find just the right straw hat. He hit the bricks, took a vacation, got rolled up, popped, as they say. The fishermen's cormorants wear rings around their necks to keep them from swallowing, to force them to surrender their catch. She had only the slightest pubic hair. We drove through fields of artichokes. Feet, do your stuff. Dark brown houseboats beached at the point of low tide—men atop their cabin roofs, idle, play a Dobro, a jaw's harp, a 12-string guitar—only to float again when the sunset is reflected in the water of Richardson

Bay. Frying yellow squash in the wok. Write this down in a green notebook. Television in the 1950s. Silverfish, potato bugs. We stopped for hot chocolate topped with whipped cream and to discuss the Sicilian Defense. A tenor sax is a weapon. The Main Library was a grey weight in a white rain. What I want is the gray-blue grain of western summer. Subtitles lower your focus. Mention sex, fruit. Drip candles kept atop old, empty bottles of wine. The young nurse in sunglasses, by a subtle redistribution of weight, shift of gravity's center, moves in front of the black student of oriental porcelain in order to more rapidly board the bus home, before all the seats are taken. Are pears form. Awake, but still in bed, I listen to cars pass, doors, birds, children are day's first voices. Eventually the scratches became scabs. A cardboard box of wool sweaters on top of the bookcase to indicate Home. Bedlingtons were at first meant to hunt rats in coal mines. Attention is all. He knew how to hold an adz. A day of rain in the middle of June. The gamelan is not simple. Modal rounders. A sequence of objects, silhouettes, which to him appears to be a caravan of fellaheen, a circus, drome-daries pulling wagons bearing tiger cages, fringed surreys, tamed ostriches in toy hats, begins a slow migration to the right vanishing point on the horizon line. Slag iron. The implicit power within the ability to draw a single, vertical straight line. That was when my nose began to peel. Look at that room filled with fleshy babies, incubating. A tall glass of tawny port. We ate them.

Revolving door. Song of the garbage collectors beneath the bedroom window. How will I know when I make a mistake. Soap. The gar-bage barge at the bridge. The Japanese floor manager. Throb in the wrist. Terms imply domains. Earth science. Steam pours from the alley sewers. Their first goal was to separate the workers from their means of production. No hurry, no hassle. He bears a resemblance to Lee. Clap hands. A drawing of a Balinese spirit with its face in its stomach. This new arc is wider, more gradual. Fountains of the financial district spout soft water in a hard wind. Little moons of my thumbnail grow. In a far room of the apartment I can hear music and a hammer. Gray clouds to give the sky weight. The bear flag in the black marble plaza. A white bowl of split pea soup is set upon the table. Rapid transit. Those curtains which I like above the kitchen sink. How the heel rises and the ankle bends to carry the body from one stair to the next. Chalk dust. The desire for coffee. Animal crackers. The tenor sax is a toy. Watching her hand to see if there is a ring. Snow is remarkable to one not accustomed to it. Gives names to his typewriter, car, chairs. She was a unit in a bum space, she was a damaged child, sitting in her rocker by the window. The raised highway through the flood plain. The formal beauty of a back porch. Fuchsias fall and stick to the walk. I'm unable to find just the right straw hat. Pineapple slices. He hit the bricks, took a vacation, got rolled up, popped, as they say. A blue flame. The fishermen's cormorants wear rings around their necks to keep them from swallowing, to force them to surrender their catch. The word I want is "shampoo." She had only the slightest pubic hair. Playing with the pilot light. We drove through fields of artichokes. Women, smelling of ammonia, board the bus. Feet, do your stuff. On the reparsing of names. Dark brown houseboats beached at the point of low tide—men atop their cabin roofs, idle, play a Dobro, a jaw's harp, a 12-string guitar—only to float again when the sunset is reflected in the water of Richardson Bay. Prose like a garden. Frying yellow squash in the wok, with string beans, bell pepper, tofu, sprouts. Normal discourse. Write this down in a green notebook. Power curtain. Television in the 1950s. A deliberate refusal to perform the normal chores of verse. Silverfish, potato bugs. His friend forgot her sandals. We stopped for hot chocolate topped with whipped cream and to discuss the Sicilian Defense. The odor in towels. A tenor sax is a weapon. Linoleum story. The Main Library was a grey weight in a white rain. The knot is not the rope. What I want is the gray-blue grain of western summer. In the beach night, campfires lit up the city of dune buggies. Subtitles lower your focus. You wake in waves, each new day's small tides of attention. Mention sex, fruit, candy, cities, books. Glossed lines. Drip candles kept atop old, empty wine bottles, a canister full of pennies. A clock talks ticking. The young nurse in blue sunglasses, by a subtle redistribution of weight, shift of gravity's center, moves in front of the black lanky graduate student of oriental porcelain in order to more rapidly board the bus, before all of the seats are taken. The urinary habits of Dr. Williams. Are pears form. Summer morning foghorn. Awake, but still in bed, I listen to cars pass, doors, birds, children are day's first voices. Surrogate information. Eventually the scratches become scabs. Rattle of water in pipes. A cardboard box of wool sweaters on top of the bookcase to indicate Home. Broken shoelace. Bedlingtons were at first meant to hunt rats in coal mines, later they were bred to show. Caffeine enjambment of the nervous system. Attention is all. Varieties of helicopter filled the sky. He knew how to hold an adz, to till. Because accumulation is not conscious, we walk around in circles, becoming gradually heavier, weighted and slower, until finally we begin to discard or toss off hats, greatcoats, muffs, gloves, blazers, vests, ties, galoshes, shoes, cufflinks, belt, etc. A day of rain in the middle of June, the weather stickier than would have been usual in some other month. How could one ever hope to have known prose. The gamelan is not simple. Great urge to sneeze, mouth full of banana. Modal rounders. Between the television and the bed was an ironing board, half-finished bottles of lager atop it. A sequence of objects, silhouettes, which to him appears to be a caravan of fellaheen, a circus, dromedaries pulling wagons bearing tiger cages, fringed surreys, tamed ostriches in toy hats, begins a slow migration to the right vanishing point on the horizon line signified by a palm tree. I want to tell you the tales of lint. Slag iron. Unable to read a book for any great length of time, for to abandon himself thus threatened him. The implicit power within the ability to draw a single, vertical straight line. This posit is not altogether the philosopher's doing. That was when my nose began to peel. Get aboard. Look at that room filled with fleshy babies, incubating. Points of transfer. A tall glass of tawny port. The shadows between houses leave the earth cool and damp. A slick gaggle of ambassadors. We ate them.

Revolving door. Dry blood. Song of the garbage collectors beneath the bedroom window. Seeds of the fig. How will I know when I make a mistake. Presentness. Soap. The half-formed friendship before he died left her with a taste of unfinished business. The garbage barge at the bridge. I tugged at the cord to coax the plug from the socket. The Japanese floor manager in a red sport coat, red trousers, white shoes. Those rural boys are bulky, mean, that get called the Bulls. Throb in the wrist or knee joint. We climbed three flights of stairs to arrive at the door, then two floors up and through to the back porch, old boards that held a couch and a rocker, for to view the city from that great height gave the sky place or weight, fog wedged amid rooftops but still the clear view, the Big Dipper. Terms imply domains. Meridian mass murder. Earth science. The tapestry

concerns the mass capture of rabbits. Steam pours from the alley
sewers, corridor of fire escapes, loading docks, dumpsters. Capable
of sitting in the chair for hours, quiet, watching her sleep. Their
first goal was to separate the workers from their means of produc-
tion. Notational process, musical juncture. No hurry, no hassle.
Thought is a labyrinth. He bears a resemblance to Lee Oswald.
Speech of no word and word of no speech. Clap hands. A lather
for shaving. A drawing of a Balinese spirit with its face in its stom-
ach. The sun rose undetected behind the sculpted clouds, the air
humid in the eucalyptus grove or up over the Mormon Temple, or
the Greek Church. This new arc is wider, more gradual. Portrait of
the best worker in Auto Plant 7. Fountains of the financial district
spout soft water in a hard wind. Repeating on paper that stanza
one hundred times, each with a new pen, watching how the width
of the ink's path shifted the weight and intention of reference,
penumbra of signification, from act to act. Little moons of my
thumbnail grow. I see that young woman each morning as she
jogs in a blue sweatsuit, trailed by her four small dogs. In a far
room of the apartment I can hear music and a hammer. The asym-
metry in any face. Grey clouds to give the sky weight. Layers of
bandage about the ankle. The bear flag in the black marble plaza.
Roundness is an ideal embodied in the nostril. A white bowl of split
pea soup is set upon the table. It's cold. Rapid transit information.
Doors open, footsteps, faucets, people are waking up. Those cur-
tains which I like above the kitchen sink. Stood there broke and
rapidly becoming hungry, staring at nickels and pennies at the
bottom of the fountain. How the heel rises and the ankle bends
to carry the body from one stair to the next. Forced outside first
thing, just to purchase food for one's breakfast. Chalk dust. Hun-

kered down against a cyclone fence to write words in a sequence concerning the movement of a chair to a room's center for the purpose of changing a lightbulb. The desire for coffee. Lighting a cigarette because it will make the bus come. Animal crackers. The young man with long eyelashes. The tenor sax is a toy. Felt thought. Watching her hand to see if there is a ring amid long, thin fingers. Putting my shoes on last and then standing, dressed. Snow is remarkable to one not accustomed to it. The gentle knocking of a sock filled with sand on my forehead. Gives names to his type-writer, car, chairs. We want coherence. She was a unit in a bum space, she was a damaged child, sitting in her rocker by the window. Yellowing gauze curtains. The raised highway through the flood plain. White wings of a magpie. The formal beauty of a back porch. One's age is best seen on the back of one's hand. Fuchsias fall and stick to the walk. Red shingle roof. I'm unable to find just the right straw hat. Primal soup. Pineapple slices. Extra paper money was kept in the closet, rolled by my grandmother into the shade of the small window there, behind the coat hanger heavy with old ties. He hit the bricks, took a vacation, got rolled up, popped, as they say. Bulky tale, pointless as it is long. A blue flame. Western movies. The fishermen's cormorants wear rings around their necks to keep them from swallowing, to force them to surren-der their catch. Monday morning. The word I want is Shampoo. Cat sleeps on the hood of parked car. She had only the slightest pubic hair, light brown. I was swimming in a clear pool. Playing with the pilot light. Infinite expansion. We drove through fields of artichokes. One does not shiver here, one shudders. Women, smelling of ammonia, board the bus. These emotions have been proposed. Feet, do your stuff. Green tint to the shit. On the reparsing of names. Instances return, thought to have been lost. Dark brown houseboats beached at low tide—men atop their cabin roofs, shirtless and in overalls, idle, play a Dobro, a jaw's harp, a 12-string guitar—only to float again, anchored, when the sunset is reflected in Richardson Bay. One wants a place to locate events of the mind. Prose like a garden. Solid object. Frying yellow squash in the wok, with string beans, bell pepper, tofu, sprouts. An old spool for cable made into a table. Normal discourse. Prefers instruments of percussion, for discreteness. Write this down in a green note-book. Piano man. Power curtain. Interest is something you impose. Television in the 1950s. Evolution of the mailbox. A deliberate refusal to perform the normal chores of verse. A kick in the coccyx for good luck. Silverfish, potato bugs. Deliberate sentimentalism perceived as description. His friend forgot her sandals. Tiger balm. We stopped for hot chocolate topped with whipped cream and to discuss the Sicilian Defense. A book of short poems to be called Spare Parts. The odor in towels. Early morning mental system. The tenor sax is a weapon. We stood or sat on the deck, breaking oranges into slices, watching the four-masted prison ship cross the bay. Linoleum story. Bob's bitter days. The Main Library was a grey weight in a white rain. What is to be taken as no information, de-cisions we make each time we cross the street. The knot is not the rope. Lots of exercise, little thought. What I want is the gray-blue grain of western summer. Sea cucumber. In the beach night, camp-fires lit up the city of dune buggies, surfboards pitched vertically into the sand bearing a presence as of clan shields. One could pro-pose, for example, the inclusion of anything. Subtitles lower your focus. Old sentences heard new carry a different purpose. You wake in waves, each new day's small tides of attention. Such poems are like keystones in need of a monument. Mention sex, fruit, candy, cities, books, the cinema, or geology. Necrotizing association with laryngotracheobronchitis. Glossed lines. Passed ball. Drip candles kept atop old, empty wine bottles, a canister full of pennies. Tuesday noon. A clock talks ticking. Eggshells in the flower bed for the calcium. The young nurse in blue sunglasses, by a subtle redistribution of weight, shift of gravity's center, moves in front of the black lanky graduate student of oriental porcelain in order to more rapidly board the bus, before all of the seats are taken. Mould forms in old coffee. The urinary habits of Dr. Williams. Traits of verbal form do not extend to their objects. Are pears form. Tumor press on the optic chiasma. Summer morning foghorn. Heard "my ancestors" as "Hawaiian sisters." Awake, but still in bed, I listen to cars pass, doors, birds, children are day's first voices. From under the eave pigeons pour. Surrogate information. Necessitation and contingency. Eventually the scratches become scabs. It'll keep your ego going for a few days. Rattle of water in pipes. We cannot in conscience blame these varied sorrows of modality on the notion of analyticity. A cardboard box of wool sweaters on top of the bookcase to indicate Home. Kids who ride shopping carts down the street. Broken shoelace. Sentences do not designate. Bedlingtons were at first meant to hunt rats in coal mines, later they were bred to show. Urban bourbon. Caffeine enjambment of the nervous system. Chinese fire drill. Attention is all. Writing the white lines. Varieties of helicopter filled the sky. Fucked in the head. He knew how to hold an adz, to till. Always, across the bay, there was Oakland. Because accumulation is not conscious, we shuffle about in circles, in hot rooms with the windows shut, becoming gradually heavier, weighted and slower, until finally we begin to discard, to shed, to toss off, panama hat, white blazer with wide lapel, cufflinks, black shirt and white tie until we stand, arms "akimbo," in white bells, see-thru net tee shirt, feet wrapped in sandals. E for Edgar. A day of rain in the middle of June. Friday night. How could one ever hope to have known prose. The intensionalism of crewcuts. The gamelan is not simple. Brushing the drums. Great urge to sneeze, mouth full of banana. You sap. Modal rounders. Every word is either current, or strange, or metaphorical, or ornamental, or newly coined, or lengthened, or contracted, or altered. Between the television and the bed was an ironing board, half-finished bottles of lager atop it. Narwhale, I confront you. A sequence of objects, silhouettes, which to him appears to be a caravan of fellaheen, a circus, dromedaries pulling wagons bearing tiger cages, fringed surreys, tamed ostriches in toy hats, begins a slow migration to the right vanishing point, signified by a palm tree on the horizon line. Refuse connectedness. I want to tell you tales of lint. Smashed watermelon sidewalk. Slag iron. Then we found the testes in the scrotal sac. Unable to read a book for any great length of time, for to abandon himself thus threatened him. Sad dream of gas pain. The implicit power within the ability to draw a single, vertical straight line. Opposed to the image. This posit is not altogether the philosopher's doing. Small kids swarm the porch. That was when my nose began to peel. Axiology, or Value Systems I have seen. Get aboard. Time was real to him, but not linear, more a sensation of gravity, of falling from some precipice forward until, thousands of feet above the valley floor with its chalked concentric circles, acceleration approximated weightlessness. Look at that white room, filled with fleshy babies. Peach pits. Point of transfer. When, as I hunkered down to turn over the small shells, shaking them free of sand, she asked me what it was I was doing, I said "Looking for the good ones." A tall glass of tawny port. A pleasure and discomfort in the knowledge of having become, by the fact of your absence, the focal point. Shadows between houses leave earth cool and damp. Retina burn. A slick gaggle of ambassadors. Astronauts hold hands, adrift in the sky. We ate them. The flag.

Revolving door. Over farm fields in a glider. Dry blood. Like a pitcher's kick, t'ai chi. Chorus of the garbage collectors beneath the bedroom window, chewing cabbage discards, smashing bottles. Elongated motion, emotion slowed him, brought the oncoming traffic out gradually from about the turn, blind mountain road. Seeds of the fig. Kareem and the skyhook. How will I know when I make a mistake. Alice and the sky boat. Presentness. The first day of July. Soap. His love of the border, of the instant in irrevocable acts, the hammer of the trigger changing the powder, a completion even if a move of only an inch is required. The half-formed friendship before he died left her with a taste of unfinished business. Sea plane. The garbage barge at the bridge. These reflections count only against hoping to base identity of propositions on some sort of intensional isomorphism derived from the broad sort of sentence synonymy which is interdefinable with analyticity. I tugged at the cord to coax the plug from the socket. We watched him punch, repeatedly, the garage door. The Japanese floor manager in a red sport coat, red trousers, white shoes. Cold coffee. Those rural boys are bulky, mean, what get called the Bulls. Alter the order of prints on the wall, inexpensive reproduction. Throb in the wrist or knee joint. Cheapo keeno. We climbed three flights of stairs to arrive at the door, then two flights up and through to the back porch, old boards that held a couch and rocker, for to view the city from that

great height gave the sky place or weight, fog wedged amid roof-
tops but still the clear view, the Big Dipper. To keep warm burn the
news. Terms imply domains. It was only when the trash bag crashed
into the middle of the kitchen that we realized it bore the weight
of ants. Meridian mass murder. Odor of old orange in the compost.
Earth science. Basic speed law. This tapestry concerns the mass cap-
ture of rabbits. Because my room faces west I watch the sun rise "in
the windows" across the street. Steam pours from alley sewers, cor-
ridor of fire escapes, loading docks, dumpsters. Sky soup. Capable
of sitting in the chair for hours, quiet, watching her sleep. Emulsi-
fied memory. Their first goal was to separate the workers from their
means of production. You come at last into the realization as into
a banquet room, domed perhaps but with chandeliers, that a lush
ordering of events is no different than any other so that one might
as well eat squid or tripe or plums, dressed in the regalia of tennis,
tho perceiving in the punchbowl reflection a costume as clownish
as it is offensive. Notational process, musical juncture. How pro-
pose to release the fly from the bottle. No hurry, no hassle. Honey-
dew head, hair of bean sprouts. Thought is a labyrinth. Shelves of
neatly folded linen. He bears a resemblance to Lee Harvey Oswald.
Who do you do. Speech of no word and word of no speech. Excuses.
Clap hands. Wild dog packs roam that part of the city. A lather
for shaving with a rum scent. A writing that grows out of itself,
a poetry of mould. Drawing of a Balinese spirit with its face in its
stomach. Ives jives. The sun rose undetected behind the sculpted
clouds, the air humid in the eucalyptus grove or up over the Mor-
mon Temple, or the Greek Church. If words were bells. This arc
is wider, more gradual. Torn tendon. Portrait of the best worker
in Auto Plant 7. Left his emotional options open. Fountains of the

financial district spout soft water in a hard wind. At six, rise up, sun threatens day. Repeating on paper that stanza one hundred times, each with a new pen, watching how the width of the ink's path shifted the weight and intentions of reference, penumbra of signification, from act to act. The enormous comedy of the emotion imposed on the peasant's bent shoulders. Little moons of my thumbnail grow. Were these true events. I see that young woman each morning as she jogs in a blue sweatsuit, trailed by her four small dogs. The hill blackens in a controlled burn. In a far room of the apartment I can hear music and a hammer. Poem took the form of the Ice Age. The asymmetry in any face. Fat man at the bus stop. Grey clouds to give the sky weight. Night light. Layers of bandage about the ankle. Anchovy. The bear flag in the black marble plaza. Straw shoes from Japan. Roundness is an ideal embodied in the nostril. The aardwolf. A white bowl of split pea soup is set upon the table. Thursday noon. It's cold. Patterns of possibility come together, intersect, disperse. Rapid transit information. My childhood passed in contemplation of Ichabod Crane. Doors open, footsteps, faucets, people are waking up. Feel the stress in day's recesses. Those curtains which I like above the kitchen sink. Imagined lives we posit in the bungalows, passing, counting, with another part of the mind, the phone poles. Stood there broke and rapidly becoming hungry, staring at nickels and pennies at the bottom of the fountain. Dear Quine, sentences are not synonymous when they mean the same proposition. How the heel rises and ankle bends to carry the body from one stair to the next. This page is slower. Forced outside first thing, just to purchase food for one's breakfast. The even keel. Chalk dust. Write and sunbathe at the same time, or ride the bus, or eat dry cereal in a bowl of milk on the upended cable spool you use for a table. Hunkered down against a cyclone fence to write words in a sequence concerning the movement of a chair to a room's center for the purpose of changing the lightbulb. Cigarette butt in clovered grass. The desire for coffee. Ships, arriving or leaving the harbor, stir water, leave wakes as we also, walking a trail to the hilltop, displace the air. Lighting a cigarette because it will make the bus come. Cherry bomb. Animal crackers. Drums accelerate before bells begin, then flutes and I am walking on the dusty forest floor, wearing trousers held by suspenders, bare foot and chest, searching for my hat again where caterpillars weave homes upon its wet, white wide brim. The young man with long eyelashes. Imbalance in the body compass. The tenor sax is a toy. Three teeth in a pill bottle kept on the mantel. Felt thought. Sparklers, or incense, it's all the same principle. Watching her hand to see if there is a ring amid long, thin fingers. Piano clusters. Putting my shoes on last, then standing, dressed. Bloody Thursday. Snow is remarkable to one not accustomed to it. To view from the porch the whole bay was not the point, but to stand there, drink in hand, perceiving oneself in relation to all visible lives, much like the pine ridge, each in the midst of a personal navigation, so that this interlude was itself a form of carrying forward, was what it meant to be drunk. The gentle knocking of a sock filled with sand on my forehead. Each term bears its purpose. Gives names to his typewriter, car, chair. Terrorism courts respect. We want coherence. Epic of doodling. She was a unit in a bum space, she was a damaged child, sitting in her rocker by the window. Carry, if you can, the proposition to its limit. Yellowing gauze curtains. Listening to the seals on the dark beach, not able to see them. The raised highway through the flood plain. We came upon the god of the starfish.

White wings of a magpie. At possibility's edge occurs limit. The formal beauty of a back porch. A learned solitude, constantly in the head looking out. One's age is seen best in the back of one's hand. Sentiment is memory confused with desire. Fuchsias fall and stick to the walk. That he was not brutal enough for her confused him. Red shingle roof. Waiting for the phone to ring at the far end, I could hear voices, whole muted conversations. I'm unable to find just the right straw hat. Tuba booms. Primal soup. Forms from nouns are known. Pineapple slices. Agents, he noticed, once removed from their jobs, were the dullest ones of all. Extra paper money was kept in the closet, rolled by my grandmother into the shade of the small window there, behind the coat hanger heavy with old ties. Said of her organization that it was the third largest tendency, but held to the correct line. He hit the bricks, took a vacation, got rolled up, popped, as they say. Luggage. Bulky tale, pointless as it is long. It is not as though our lives bear intended meaning, but that it gathers about us like fallen leaves that someone has failed to sweep away. A blue flame. All talk. Western movies. I hate speech. The fishermen's cormorants wear rings around their necks to keep them from swallowing, to force them to surrender their catch. Tales from the crypt. Monday morning. In the fog I saw the great grass boats float toward the delta. The word I want is Shampoo. A procedure by which they stick a metal device up one's prick. Cat sleeps on the hood of the parked car. Linear accelerator. She had only the slightest pubic hair, light brown. What if one killed one, never to be caught, constantly alive with that information. I was swimming in a clear pool. What does it mean to know, sleeping, that you sleep in Idaho. Playing with the pilot light. A clear thing. Infinite expansion. She threw her legs back, up, over my shoulders, and with my ass I shoved in. We drove through fields of artichokes. Primed canvas. One does not shiver here, one shudders. A key ring raps on the glass. Women, smelling of ammonia, board the bus. The throat, hearing the toilet flush, invariably swallows. These emotions have been proposed. Manifest destiny. Feet, do your stuff. That woman new to the building seemed interesting, until the night she brought home the man who clearly was not, so curiosity drained away. Green tint to the shit. The water in the pipes does not wake me, but keeps me from sleep, unable to determine the source, the user, the time of night. On the reparsing of names. Grew up, she said, able to hear Chiang's firing squads by the river at dawn. Instances return, thought to have been lost. Waking wasted. Dark brown houseboats beached at low tide—men atop their cabin roofs, shirtless and in overalls, idle, play a Dobro, a jaw's harp, a 12-string guitar—only to float again, anchored, when the sunset is reflected in Richardson Bay. Words in a line pass time. One wants a place to locate mind's events. Tourists from Taiwan. Prose like a garden. Diminishing world where the head dwells, avoidance of which is the test. Solid object. She makes constructions to sit in, whose common form implies the electric chair. Frying yellow squash in the wok, with string beans, bell pepper, tofu, sprouts. Bone bruise. An old spool for cable made into a table, made home for a garden in an old wine jug. Each morning geese circle the lake until they refind day's forms. Normal discourse. What in the wall whistles. Prefers instruments of percussion, for discreteness. Raw mush-rooms. Write this down in a green notebook. Celery. Piano man. Almonds. Power curtain. Each day new vistas become possible, yesterday's earlobe, today's toenail, a radio on a mantel one had forgotten to think of, a flashlight. Interest is something you impose.

Cohn's loans. Television in the 1950s. Lone Star Hotel. Evolution of the mailbox. Until I myself became trapped in the Bermuda Triangle of the heart. A deliberate refusal to perform the normal chores of verse. Xylophones. A kick in the coccyx for good luck. This day's reaches features peaches. Silverfish, potato bugs. Everybody balls everybody, eventually, and nothing changes. Deliberate sentimental-ism perceived as description. Calling out, as though after a large dog. His friend forgot her sandals. The map is not the territory. Tiger balm. Man on the bus, scavenger, sips cough medicine. We stopped for hot chocolate topped with whipped cream, and to discuss the Sicilian Defense. Acres wake, bugs of the soil shivering about their business, day's light precedes its heat. A book of short poems to be called Spare Parts. Yonder. The odor in towels, the oil in skin. Exorcise your monkey. Early morning mental system. The poem as a form sensed prior to the writing, as the act thereof, as a text fixed upon paper, as the act of reading, as the memory of one of the above. The tenor sax is a weapon. Posits of new information not like cars recently attached to a train, but like memory, embed-ded in the presences. We stood or sat on the deck, breaking oranges into slices, watching the four-masted prison ship cross the bay. Her sense of the distance within families is American, but beyond that, Chinese. Linoleum story. Men eating burgers in silence, at a drug-store counter, wearing t-shirts and short hair, staring at their food. Bob's bitter days. The bottle of white wine is empty. The Main Library was a grey weight in a white rain. He sat under the kitchen table, writing furiously into a notebook every word we said, Emily scolding, the bright light of a bare bulb on dark painted walls, the Kelly green fridge, the rest of us drinking or smoking dope, but it was his kitchen. What is to be taken as no information, decisions

made each time we cross the street. Mucous membrane. The knot
is not the rope. The signs sing. Lots of exercise, little thought. These
roofs, their angles, give the hill texture, houses packed together,
cramped yards, kids on porches, dog sounds, mowers, web of the
clotheslines. What I want is the grey-blue grain of western summer.
Yellow beach, pink sky, pink beach, yellow sky. Sea cucumber.
Burma Shave parataxis. In the beach night, campfires lit up the city
of dune buggies, surfboards pitched vertically into the sand bearing
a presence as of clan shields. How the press of information, the first
time you walk down a new street, cannot be repeated. One could
propose, for example, the inclusion of anything. With such atten-
tion the mind can follow the act of her washing in the next room,
it knows hands from neck from cheeks. Subtitles lower your focus.
When Zukofsky debuted Reich's Violin Phase on the west coast,
the first person to stomp out was Mario Savio. Old sentences heard
new carry a different purpose. Rhodochrosite, tourmaline. You
wake in waves, each new day's small tides of attention. Analysanda
and their analysantia. Such poems are like keystones in need of a
monument. Barnwood ash. Mention sex, fruit, candy, cities, books,
the cinema or geology. The air in its fair layers. Necrotizing laryngo-
tracheobronchitis, consequent of a chemical irritant, CS. Employ-
ment gainful of what. Glossed lines. Special weapons and tactics.
Passed ball. Weary of waking, talking, faking it. Drip candles kept
atop old, empty wine bottles, a canister full of pennies. The stric-
tures against propositions apply with equal force to attributes and
relations. Tuesday noon. Nails that glow in burning wood. A clock
talks ticking. From what they did, he will not recover. Eggshells
in the flower bed for calcium. Consumption of wood by fire. The
young nurse in blue sunglasses, by a subtle redistribution of weight,

shift of gravity's center, moves in front of the black lanky graduate
student of oriental porcelain in order to more rapidly board the
bus, before all of the seats are taken. Three days of July rain. Mould
forms in old coffee. As the heat of the hand will draw the leaves up
to it, so thought's pressure folds the flower. The urinary habits of
Dr. Williams. You thought somehow to copy Rodia not having seen
the work. Traits of verbal form do not extend to their objects. Leav-
ing out. Are pears form. Thursday dawn. Tumor press on the optic
chiasma. Mouthful of crab meat. Summer morning foghorn. The
light caught in the gauzy curtains, beyond which the terrace and the
city of verticals. Heard "my ancestors" as "Hawaiian sisters." Wine
glasses in rows, in a cabinet. Awake, but still in bed, I listen to cars
pass, doors, birds, children are day's first voices. Mole on her ass.
From under the eave pigeons pour. Watercress. Surrogate informa-
tion. The great seagull would have come inside, but my mother
went at it with a broom. Necessitation and contingency. Troll
bridge. Eventually the scratches become scabs. The brown paint
yellows. It'll keep your ego going for a few days. On Treat Street.
Rattle of water in pipes. As classes to attributes, ordered pairs to
relations. We cannot in conscience blame these varied sorrows of
modality on the notion of analyticity. In a room, on a warm night,
music on, over voices, a spoon scrapes a pot. A cardboard box of
wool sweaters on top of the bookcase to indicate Home. Bob takes
Barry to the airport. Kids who ride shopping carts down the street.
The form I saw in South Orange Sonnets. Broken shoelace. Fatal
framer. Sentences do not designate. Insert opaque erotic data,
stimulate focus. Bedlingtons, first meant to hunt rats in coal mines,
later bred to show, are nearly blind and crazy. This this this this.
Urban bourbon. Neither the present nor past hold for you the

attractive indeterminacy of the future, the elaborate half-finished contraption of the yacht in the yard, tho you live in an apartment, waking from the sweating nightmare of hair starting to grow on all the walls and the great sound of breathing. Caffeine enjambment of the nervous system. Gross national poet. Chinese fire drill. Folds her toilet paper into perfect squares. Attention is all. Older music. Writing the white lines. Earliest imaginings of the married life, the chiropractor's daughter washing dishes. Varieties of helicopter filled the sky. Marjorie Daw. Fucked in the head. He does not write so much as his impatience does, the scribble. He knew how to hold an adz, to till. This sort of sentence. Always, across the bay, there was Oakland. The playground north of the coffee plant roils with soccer, kites, sunbathers. Because accumulation is not conscious, we shuffle about in circles, in hot rooms with the windows shut, becoming gradually heavier, weighted and slower, until finally we begin to discard, to shed, to toss off, panama hat, white blazer with wide lapel, cufflinks, black shirt and white tie, until we stand, arms "akimbo," in white bells, see-thru net tee shirt, feet wrapped in sandals. Compared to, say, Chile, where Santiago's higher elevations support the poor. E for Edgar. Theoretical framework for pudding. A day of rain in the middle of June. This is the alphabet. Friday night. The Ferris wheel. How could one ever hope to have known prose. So that it rains light. The intensionalism of crewcuts. Shopper's world, a whole store for quilts. The gamelan is not simple. That one could become a cop, to enforce the forms partially, the Highway Patrol. Brushing the drums. Thought as a boy to swallow all seeds, that the tree in the belly could become one. Great urge to sneeze, mouth full of banana. A mouse's fear of a cat is counted as his fearing true a certain English sentence. You sap. Butterflies churn the air. Modal rounders. The sharp shadows of a low sun, the light smack against the white housefronts. Every word is either current, or strange, or metaphorical, or ornamental, or newly coined, or lengthened, or contracted, or altered. Weathercock, scrimshaw. Between the television and the bed was an ironing board, half-finished bottles of lager atop it. When, looking out the window, you no longer see what is there, it's time to move. Narwhale, I confront you. The gallery was a labyrinth of white rooms with skylights, small words drawn in blue pencil, one to a wall, thru which and before which strolled the art consumers, gazing, chewing in an idle way on the earpieces of their sunglasses, paying no attention to the one red hard-backed chair in each room, presumably for their convenience or that of the occasional elderly lady, accompanying a college-age granddaughter, which were the true objects of the show. A sequence of objects, silhouettes, which to him appears to be a caravan of fellaheen, a circus, dromedaries pulling wagons bearing tiger cages, fringed surreys, tamed ostriches in toy hats, begins a slow migration to the right vanishing point, signified by a palm tree on the horizon line. Small boy shouts at the dog, insistent, scolding. Refuse connectedness. I hear the hose in the tomato plants. I want to tell you tales of lint. Feeling my fingernail bend back, pushing it against my front tooth, to signal thought. Smashed watermelon sidewalk. A park upon a hilltop, below which the city, its hills and verticals jammed together, and beyond that not the bay but rather the hills on the far side, as tho near, brown now in August with a light sky, rippling planet crust. Slag iron. Asleep in the sun is all peace there is. Then we found the testes in the scrotal sac. How in the still air the sudden assertion of auto brakes, heard, calls into mind a trumpet. Unable to read a book for any great

length of time, for to abandon himself thus threatened him. A big
she St. Bernard. Sad dream of gas pain. Not asleep, I lay in the
grass, still, while the ladybug crossed my chest. The implicit power
within the ability to draw a single, vertical straight line. Presences
I thought dust in the air came closer now, had wings to move them.
Opposed to the image. The hill would fill with people bathing in
the sun. This posit is not altogether the philosopher's doing. Of
all these faces seen as spaces, which are you. Small kids swarm
the porch. Knowing it changes it. That was when my nose began
 to peel. Straw flowers. Axiology, or Value Systems I have seen. A
world of routines, of returns to small forms, insistently. Get aboard.
It was a summer of few hot nights. Time was real to him, but not
linear, more a sensation of gravity, of falling from some precipice
forward until, thousands of feet above the valley floor with its
chalked concentric circles, acceleration approximated weightless-
ness. It was his smaller toes that hurt. Look at that white room,
filled with fleshy babies. The words, as in a boat, float. Peach pits.
Driving freeway over San Bruno mountains in night fog, exhaustion
registering in the body as force, pressure, partial "G." Point of
transfer. Tenderness in that wicked man. When, as I hunkered down
to turn over the small shells, shaking them free of sand, she asked
me what it was I was doing, I said "Looking for the good ones."
Short glass of tequila. Tall glass of tawny port. Headlights, street-
lights, lit living rooms. A pleasure and discomfort in the knowledge
of having become, by the fact of your absence, the focal point.
Borate bomber's song. Shadows between houses leave earth cool
and damp. A scaffold around light. Retina burn. A tooth gone in
the root. A slick gaggle of ambassadors. Tension manager's domain.

Astronauts holding hands, adrift in the sky. Caves of the tuna. We ate them. Each ear pierced in four places. The flag. Log fort.

Revolving door. Clear lake. Over farm fields in a glider. Finally, there was nothing to turn you aside, the crowd's bustle as tho at your own momentum, the voices would ebb and echo, as you push at last thru lobby after lobby. Dry blood. Stretched canvas. Like a pitcher's kick, t'ai chi. Each day's particulars conjoined, a morning habit, raising the shade, say, as the coffee steeps. Chorus of the garbage collectors beneath the bedroom window, chewing cabbage discards, smashing bottles, the odor from the cud of their great truck. You are not certain which reality to hold constant. Elongated motion, emotion slowed him, brought the oncoming traffic out gradually from about the turn, blind mountain road. Trunk of the palm snapped where the truck hit, fibers about. Seeds of the fig. If we are limning the true and ultimate structure of reality, the canonical scheme for us is the austere scheme that knows no quotation but direct quotation and no propositional attitudes but only the physical constitution and behavior of organisms. Kareem and the sky-hook. That the thing which you thought possible is not, which, having once made the assumption, governed your days until the fault this morning showed, the wall's weak rock, which, tho it has not made itself felt, shall, is not, since you must carry it now to its conclusion, rubble, to be acknowledged. How will I know when I make a mistake. Ladders, propped up against the walls of act. Alice and the sky boat. Manhattan itself a form of definition. Presentness. The eye is the limit. The first day of July. Only way he could know what occurred in their heads would be to put words down in a sequence, and that would be their thought. Soap. The curious literal

meaning of vacation. His love of the border, of the instant in irrevo-
cable acts, the hammer of the trigger changing the powder, a com-
pletion even if a move of only an inch is required. Wind in the
chimney would scatter ashes back into the room. The half-formed
friendship before he died left her with a taste of unfinished business.
Game for a chessboard, pennies doubling square by square. Sea
plane. Ontic antics in the attic. The garbage barge at the bridge.
Brushing dry leaves off dead poets. These reflections count only
against hoping to base identity of propositions on some sort of
intensional isomorphism derived from the broad sort of sentence
synonymy which is interdefinable with analyticity. Scratches his
ass, then sniffs his fingers. I tugged at the cord to coax the plug
from the socket. As tho speech nailed to the wall would be writing.
We watched him punch, repeatedly, the garage door, slowly, with
his head down, a blunt precision. The dream deepens. The Japanese
floor manager in a red sport coat, red trousers, white shoes. The
bones of the foot, the veins. Cold coffee. When our objective is
an austere canonical form for the system of the world. Those rural
boys are bulky, mean, what get called the Bulls. The calculus of
predicates. Alter the order of prints on the wall, inexpensive repro-
duction. This stone is thinking about Vienna. Throb in the wrist
or knee joint. Quadruplicity drinks procrastination. Cheapo
keeno. Tolerance of the don't-care is a major source of simplicity.
We climbed three flights of stairs, slope of a eucalyptus grove, to
arrive at the door, then two flights up through dark rooms of music,
shadowy shuffle of dancers, and through to the back porch, old
boards that held a couch and rocker, for to view the city from that
great height gave the night sky place or weight, fog wedged amid
rooftops but still the clear view, the Big Dipper. A single unparti-

tioned universe of values of bound variables, a simple grammar
of predication which admits general terms all on an equal footing.
To keep warm burn the news. The type of old man who wears
his white hair in a crewcut and keeps small, fat dogs. Terms imply
domains. Art as habit merges with the renewal of solutions which
constitute it. It was only when the trash bag crashed into the middle
of the kitchen that we realized it bore the weight of ants. Objects
whose terms are learned only in deep context. Meridian mass mur-
der. Intervening neural activity goes on, but the claim is that noth-
ing is clarified, nothing but excess baggage is added, by positing
intermediary subjective objects of apprehension anterior to the
physical objects overtly alleged in the spoken sentences themselves.
Odor of old orange in the compost. Unwashed pot. Earth science.
Soap dish. Basic speed law. Proof of termhood. This tapestry con-
cerns the mass capture of rabbits. The operator of class abstraction
can be reduced to description, and description to quantifiers. Be-
cause my room faces west I watch the sun rise "in the windows"
across the street. This sentence has five words. Steam pours from
alley sewers, corridor of fire escapes, loading docks, dumpsters.
I resented seeing History and Nature confused at every turn. Sky
soup. Each dawn a return to an eternal conclusion, the lemon tree
in flower, the sun amid the dissolving fog to warm the porch, this
day's proposition. Capable of sitting in the chair for hours, quiet,
watching her sleep. The squeal in the tone of a clothesline pulley.
Emulsified memory. Reflective persons unswayed by wishful think-
ing can themselves now and again have cause to wonder what, if
anything, they are talking about. Their first goal was to separate
the workers from their means of production. Numbers, Mind, and
Body. You come at last into the realization as into a banquet room,

domed perhaps but with chandeliers, that a lush ordering of events is no different than any other so that one might as well eat squid as tripe or plums, dressed in the regalia of tennis, tho perceiving in the punchbowl reflection a costume as clownish as it is offensive. Red eye. Notational process, musical juncture. That language fails to share the object-positing pattern of our own. How propose to release the fly from the bottle. The moth that destroyed Cleveland. No hurry, no hassle. Heat ripples the air rising from the street, reshaping houses on the hill's other peak. Honeydew head, hair of bean sprouts. Subvention of the usual capital outlay process. Thought is a labyrinth. The boys play at war atop washers, amid dryers. Shelves of neatly folded linen. Her roommate remarked casually she could tell he had stayed the night, that the toilet seat would be vertical in the morning. He bears a resemblance to Lee Harvey Oswald, aiming. Whipped at by branches, duck and run. Who do you do. The beautiful dump truck. Speech of no word and word of no speech. Are miles alike. Excuses. Iced tea as a system. Clap hands. Amid shouting, could write of silence and believe it. Wild dog packs roam that part of the city. Erotic insert. A lather for shaving with a rum scent. A child saw me write that, asking what it was. Writing that grows out of itself, poetry of mould. Dusty sill or wainscot. Drawing of a Balinese spirit with its face in its stomach. Would you know if this was prose. Ives jives. The wives that weave the home together. The sun rose undetected be-hind the sculpted clouds, the air humid in the eucalyptus grove or up over the Mormon Temple, or the Greek Church. Stretch marks on her body. If words were bells. Positing facts in the image of sentences as intermediaries for what is. This arc is wider, more gradual. The hard press of her fingers about the pen as she wrote into her diary while I watched. Torn tendon. Vandalism is folk art. Portrait of the best worker in Auto Plant 7. Flowering milkweed through the cracks in the sidewalk, around which what hand drew stars in colored chalk. Left his emotional options open. Balloons, having gotten loose from children, would rise up steadily, yellow discs diminishing on a blue plane. Fountains of the financial district spout soft water in a hard wind. Half asleep on the hillside, the breeze would pass over this part of my body, that one. At six, rise up, sun threatens day. This before, this after. Repeating on paper that stanza one hundred times, each with a new pen, watching how the width of the ink's path shifted the weight and intentions of reference, penumbra of signification, from act to act. He stood over them, alternately shouting and drinking from a bottle of bourbon. The enormous comedy of the emotion imposed on the image of the peasant's bent shoulders. Geometry as the theory of relative position. Little moons of my thumbnail grow. Writing in public as a form of performance, on buses, say, or here amid sunbathers, not paid attention to, looking up, myself, to watch the jugglers. Were these true events. This used to be a nice place. I see that young woman each morning as she jogs in a blue sweatsuit, trailed by her four small dogs, bringing to mind Darrell's tale, the poet dyed blond, jogging through the mourners of an evangelist, bishop of a black church. Each morning I rise to praise these faces. The hill blackens in a controlled burn. Pulling at my toenails. In a far room of the apartment I can hear music and a hammer. Whether to speak of geometrical objects as bypassed or as reconstrued is a matter of indifference. Poem took the form of the Ice Age. Elimination can often be allowed the gentler air of explication. The asymmetry in any face. Sperm count. Fat man at the bus stop. Morning in the gauzy curtains. Gray clouds to give the sky weight. It was here the poem spoke of itself, casual, dissembling, remarking of its admiration for the great Watts Towers, tho it had never seen them. Night light. A metal table, round, whose center is a large beach umbrella placed instead upon concrete, at the pool's edge, for us to set our drinks upon while we gaze at the divers. Layers of bandage about the ankle. People are starving. Anchovy. How do I know if this is page or wall. The bear flag in the black marble plaza. Hand lotion, bandages, rainbows of toilet paper. Straw shoes from Japan. Bus routes constitute a sculpture, with density of lines, frequency of units, the pleasure to be taken in slashed seats. Roundness is an ideal embodied in the nostril. Transfer points. The aardwolf. The external is simply proposed. A white bowl of split pea soup is set upon the table. The yellow house, the beige house, the blue one, the block. Thursday noon. Monday morning on Joe's steps, filling the notebook. It's cold. Muslims idle in front of their temple. Patterns of possibility come together, intersect, disperse. Dream of a great air tragedy, the neighborhood smoldering, lit by floodlights atop police cars and fire trucks, damp night fog, everybody dazed on their porches, odor of meat. Rapid transit information. One knows how to receive this because it is a poem, because it bears that family resemblance, because one gradually understood how to receive the last one and the one prior, because one has learned how to receive them in general without seeming conspicuous. My childhood passed in contemplation of Ichabod Crane. Dream breaks up sleep. Doors open, footsteps, faucets: people are waking up. Crash city. Feel the stress in day's recesses. Anticipation specifically an extension of memory, so that one salt flat cracked into pentagonal patterns will become another. Those curtains which I

like above the kitchen sink. Beeswax mixed with paraffin. Imagined
lives we posit in the bungalows, passing, counting, with another
part of the mind, the phone poles. Wasp adheres to flesh. Stood
there broke and rapidly becoming hungry, staring at nickels and
pennies at the bottom of the fountain. A walk through the railroad
yards, a rainbow out of gray-brown. Dear Quine, sentences are not
synonymous when they mean the same proposition. Kids, with
nothing better to do than ride about in an old car, shining a flash-
light in the eyes of night drivers. How the heel rises and ankle bends
to carry the body from one stair to the next. The feminine way men
fold their hands when, say, they ride the bus. This page is slower.
Hotels for old single men. Forced outside first thing, just to pur-
chase food for one's breakfast. Each sentence is a solution. The
even keel. The fight quietly going on in the back of the bus. Chalk
dust. We walked through the financial district at midnight, the
street deep between these buildings, a film crew working down
an alley, pausing as we passed to stare at great tapestries in bank
lobbies. Write and sunbathe at the same time, or ride the bus, or
eat dry cereal in a bowl of milk on the upended cable spool you
use for a table. Great whistling anus. Hunkered down against a
cyclone fence to write words in a sequence concerning the move-
ment of a chair to a room's center for the purpose of changing the
lightbulb. What if it were cancer. Cigarette butt in clovered grass.
Morning of the middle. The desire for coffee. Designated art words
here. Ships, arriving or leaving the harbor, stir water, leave wakes as
we also, walking a trail to the hilltop, displace the air. Eat what you
kill. Lighting the cigarette because it will make the bus come. Bruise
in the banana. Cherry bomb. The cranes in the gray dawn fog over
the holds of the boats. Animal crackers. Leaves of lettuce, formless,

left in a bowl of salad oil. Drums accelerate before bells begin, then flutes and I am walking on the dusty forest floor, wearing trousers held by suspenders, bare foot and chest, searching for my hat again where caterpillars weave homes upon its wet, white, wide brim. Liner notes to a Dylan album. The young man with long eyelashes. Swarm of carpenters within the burned-out house. Imbalance in the body compass. We are well within the made place. The tenor sax is a toy. The slower, deeper heat of August days. Three teeth in a pill bottle kept on the mantel. Of pores as eyes as they open. Felt thought. Xerox days. Sparklers, or incense, it's all the same principle. White or white-gray or gray, cream call it, fade away. Watching her hand to see if there is a ring amid long, thin fingers. The possibility of terms like rooms in a house, huge Hillsborough home, doors of syntax, windows of nuance, a long, carpeted hall-way lined with Persian mirrors, doors ajar through which you see, a guest in the place tho not thoroughly welcome, the furniture of usage. Piano clusters. The song of the Cessna, its propellers. Putting my shoes on last, then standing, dressed. This is or is not an object, its words as bricks. Bloody Thursday. Kill what you eat. Snow is remarkable to one not accustomed to it. A sign within the diesel's whine. To view from the porch the whole bay was not the point, but to stand there, drink in hand, perceiving oneself in relation to all visible lives, much like the pine ridge, each in the midst of a per-sonal navigation, so that this interlude was itself a form of carrying forward, was what it meant to be drunk. Piss smell of eggs. The gentle knocking of a sock filled with sand on my forehead. Just the way I wrote when I was twelve years old. Each term bears its purpose. The form itself is the model of a city, extension, addition, modification. Gives names to his typewriter, car, chairs. (1) Sound

of an electric saw from the (temporarily) closed-off gallery, or
(2) sound of a film projector rewinding. Terrorism courts respect.
Writes better when he wears his hat. We want coherence. An
expensive sundae carefully constructed around three mounds
of French vanilla, entitled Hobo. Epic of doodling. The page is
only the documentation, or the page is more, the field, resistance.
She was a unit in a bum space, she was a damaged child, sitting in
her rocker by the window. This emptying out of interiority to the
benefit of its exterior signs, this exhaustion of content by its form,
is the principle. Carry, if you can, the proposition to its limit. The
particularly thick nail of the big toe. Yellowing gauze curtains.
Waking, sleeping, days bleed one into the other, so that it is this
unrelenting need to rest that breeds image of discontinuity, line,
cycle, circle, line. Listening to seals on that dark beach, not able
to see them. Listening patiently, until one is able to hear the one
watch in the room, perfectly. The raised highway through the flood
plain. Each time this path is taken, its distances shift. We came
upon the god of the starfish. We bring to the encounter what we
choose to see, so that of all the terms picked to describe that dog,
only one, proper name so-called, defines a category that has but
one member, yet, not knowing it, the next time we saw him we
would recognize him, we would greet him, we would be correct.
White wings of a magpie. Great jolt of travel. At possibility's edge
occurs limit. Each day as I lie here, I hear her rise and wash. The
formal beauty of a back porch. Spider bites. A learned solitude,
constantly in the head looking out. Constantly waking, new day.
One's age is best seen in the back of one's hand. Void is what's left
when the cosmos breaks down as the interesting evidence of order.
Sentiment is memory confused with desire. Mexican blue hammock

to write in. Fuchsias fall and stick to the walk. Wind chimes. That he was not brutal enough for her confused him. Across the empty states to Chicago if at all possible. Red shingle roof. The naval air base across the still bay water, behind which the hills rise, houses crowding the lower slopes, United States. Waiting for the phone to ring at the far end, for her to pick it up, I could hear voices, whole muted conversations. Jack rabbit's fatal dive across the blacktop. I'm unable to find just the right straw hat. Slept by the roadside to wake in a vast flat space. Tuba booms. A slope filled with soldiers sifting through the large charred green debris, explosion of a helicopter. Primal soup. Red sky above a dry land. Forms from nouns are known. Red dirt hills. Pineapple slices. Nevada into Utah as tho through conditions of the mind. Agents, he noticed, once removed from their jobs, were the dullest ones of all. Day's first sky was a fan of blues. Extra paper money was kept in the closet, rolled by my grandmother into the shade of the small window there, behind the coat hanger heavy with old ties. Writing, riding. Said of her organization that it was the third largest tendency, but held to the correct line. From the house where Trotsky died they caught a ride with a man who worked for the World Bank. He hit the bricks, took a vacation, got rolled up, popped, as they say. You read this sentence before. Bulky tale, pointless as it is long. The true sign of agriculture is the small plane. Luggage. Where ranch hands would wander in daily for coffee or breakfast. It is not as though our lives bear intended meaning, but that it gathers about us like fallen leaves which someone has failed to sweep away. Occasionally a dirt road will curl out of the mountains to come up to the freeway, tho you never know what fact it extends from, house, mine, town. A blue flame. Drop City. All talk. On holiday, I read Barthes' "The Writer on Holiday." Western movies. We are, each of us, somehow, given to a realization of the possibility of disaster, but when the slowed traffic took us around the curve into view of the scattered remains of the helicopter, engine at the road's edge, amid a crowd of soldiers, police, hearses, pushing us immediately onward, away, it was an image we saw, no more. I hate speech. Child's form. The fishermen's cormorants wear rings around their necks to keep them from swallowing, to force them to surrender their catch. Home of the curator of Africana, room in the attic, breeze of Lake Michigan turned this page. Tales from the crypt. House of red brick. Monday morning. Cowbell doorbell. In the fog I saw the great grass boats floating toward the delta. The truck had burned, now, at road's edge, merely glowed. The word I want is Shampoo. The young children of the wife of my friend's brother. A procedure by which they stick a metal device up one's prick. How the roads wrap around the town. Cat sleeps on the hood of the parked car. An Italian love song played on the accordion. Linear accelerator. If for every window there were a person. She had only the slightest pubic hair, light brown. At home amid engineers, on a patio, with chicken and gin and tonic. What if one killed never to be caught, constantly alive with that information. Large, evenly hard beds. I was swimming in a clear pool. Here also were buried the soldiers killed at the Battle of Lake Erie, 1813. What does it mean to know, sleeping, that you sleep in Idaho. The fountain forms a geometry of the particular, five waterfalls, six spouts, all of which arrive in the general pool. Playing with the pilot light. Each event will be its own name. A clear thing. This is the fable of objects. Infinite expansion. Sulphur, the hanged man, I swing between realms. She threw her legs back, up, over my shoulders, and with my ass I shoved in. This line written in Windsor, once the way out, as, say, Guatemala now is, sitting on a park bench, river's edge, facing Detroit. We drove through fields of artichokes. Green water, gray sky. Primed canvas. Canadian cactus. One does not shiver here, one shudders. They invented logic and classification. A key ring raps on the glass. Form is to seize the time. Women, smelling of ammonia, board the bus. Form is the tame cat. The throat, hearing the toilet flush, invariably swallows. Form is the minute hand. These emotions have been proposed. Form is the structure of character, what. Manifest destiny. BFTP of the Apes. Feet, do your stuff. Wanted no limits, only possibility. Woman new to the building seemed interesting, until the night she brought home the man who clearly was not, so curiosity drained away. Table with a black top. Green tint to the shit. Filling the yellow cup with coffee. Water in the pipes does not wake me, but keeps me from sleep, unable to determine the source, the user, the time of night. A sentence begun on the green page is completed on the yellow. On the reparsing of names. Sat in the Ford World Headquarters lobby, reading Olson. Grew up, she said, able to hear Chiang's firing squads by the river at dawn. Dark glasses on the black desk, their blue tint. Instances return, thought to have been lost. To kill the clock. Waking wasted. Assertion, not journal, in a house with four bathrooms, on a two-acre lot. Dark brown houseboats beached at low tide—men atop their cabin roofs, shirtless and in overalls, idle, play a Dobro, a jaw's harp, a 12-string guitar—only to float again, anchored, when the sunset is reflected in Richardson Bay. The particular, the particular. Words in a line pass time. Autogyro. One wants a place to locate mind's events. If you go wider, deeper. Tourists from Taiwan. Later they send for their wives. Prose like a garden. Globe is the lower. Diminishing world where the head dwells, avoidance of which is the test. A light that I saw, that mountain road, that passed. Solid object. Alone in a stranger's house. She makes constructions to sit in, whose common form implies the electric chair. Only in the flats is the fat of the green gone. Frying yellow squash in the wok, with string beans, bell pepper, tofu, sprouts. Intermittent as it is, the process of refrigeration sets up a hum in the wall, non-specific, not to be avoided, not precisely heard, felt rather by the wake in the belly's fluids. Bone bruise. Rose of china embedded in the lamp. An old spool for cable made into a table, made home for a garden in an old wine jug. The alimentary life. Each morning geese circle the lake until they refind day's forms. Feta cheese. Normal discourse. You are not the most complicated of men eating an English muffin. What in the wall whistles. Exploration in closure. Prefers instruments of percussion, for discreteness. Fat dimpled thighs. Raw mushrooms. The waitress looms over the table, pot of coffee in hand. Write this down in a green notebook. The rectangular geometry of the tiles, the plane of floor held stories above the ground, which flows under the metal door into this cubicle of the john. Celery, salary. Auto-dactyl dream. Piano man. He gave the impression that very many cities rubbed him smooth. Almonds. The warm blood of rain, say, such image as proposes an aesthetic. Power curtain. So it seemed I woke in a castle, or, rather, its inner court, whose walls of yellow and brown brick supported vines of ivy, until, standing, shaking off dead leaves, I could see into the windows of the rooms, the classes going on there. Each day new vistas become possible, yesterday's earlobe, today's toenail, a radio on a mantel one had forgotten to think of, a flashlight. Would pour pigment directly on the canvas, then manipulate that. Interest is something you impose. Endless possibility, drifting from campus to campus, hanging out. Cohn's loans. So muggy it seemed there was no oxygen in the air, how was it the cigar burned. Television in the 1950s. The mountains, more by darkness visible and their own size. Could you trace this to its source, particular, iridescent, useful only as it disappears. Lone Star Hotel. An harbor, Ann Arbor. Evolution of the mailbox, professionalism of cops. The poem as long as California, or summer. Until I myself became trapped in the Bermuda Triangle of the heart. Technographic typography. A calculated refusal to perform the normal chores of verse. From the barracks of the Wilcox Mansion, where he took the oath, saw only the offices of doctors. Xylophones. Mountain View Cemetery equal to Central Park. A kick in the coccyx for good luck. The way the open hands hang limp at the wrists and the elbows swing out when he runs. This day's reaches features peaches. That jay imitates the cricket. Silverfish, potato bugs. From the veranda of a mansion above the Russian River, I first heard this music. Everybody balls everybody, eventually, and nothing changes. Wept, swept, slept. Deliberate sentimentalism perceived as description. Dense red meat. Call out, as though after a large dog. Antelope bites, watermelon fever. His friend forgot her sandals. There the drab girl sat, hair dryer in her lap, awaiting the airport limousine. The map is not the territory. Does it contradict action. Tiger balm. Sheet lightning in Michigan hills. Man on the bus, scavenger, sips cough medicine. Of speed as experience, gobbled space. We stopped for hot choco- late topped with whipped cream, and to discuss the Sicilian Defense. Motion is a vertical disorder. Acres wake, bugs of the soil shivering about their business, day's light precedes heat. The nice man. A book of short poems to be called Spare Parts. The private lives of kinder- garten teachers, a party about the clubhouse of an apartment complex, one who by the pool shows the young woman an appropriate way to drive a golf ball, or strangers stare confusedly at the sauna, read instructions, implies to the newcomer, engaged now in a contest of pocket billiards, chalking his cue in that harder light, high beamed ceiling, aligning in the mind ball to pocket, a world of repose, of a stasis that includes activity, sailboats decked in a garage, as, what is the word, he can't find it, as something as the light which each night is turned upon the garden. Yonder. History is not a good bourgeois. The odor in towels, the oil in skin. Repressed behavior, a small grin upon gin and tonic. Exorcise your monkey. The abruptness of seafood. Early morning mental system. Doors here are more complex, framed panes of glass interlocking with one of wire mesh. The poem as a form sensed prior to the writing, as the act thereof, as a text fixed upon paper, as the act of reading, as the memory of one of the above. The usual dead people most parents are. The tenor sax is a weapon. Our lives in the mineral world. Posits of new information not like cars recently attached to a train, but like memory, embedded in the presences. Pleistocene statements. We stood or sat on the deck, breaking oranges into slices, watching the four-masted prison ship cross the bay. A tractor necessary to care for this lawn. Her sense of the distance within families is American, but beyond that, Chinese. The beginnings of a new phenomenology of assembling. Linoleum story. Void in, void out. Men eating burgers in silence, at a drugstore counter, wearing t-shirts and short hair, staring at their food. Greased lady. Bob's bitter days. The last dance, the end of dancing. The bottle of white wine is empty. The eyes, forced to focus. The Main Library was a grey weight in a white rain. Against the hearth leans a line drawing framed in glass, in which the apple tree with its too-small fruit is reflected, whipped by what must soon become rain. He sat under the kitchen table, writing furiously into a notebook every word we said, Emily scolding, the bright light of a bare bulb on dark-painted walls, the Kelly green fridge, the rest of us drinking or smoking dope, but it was his kitchen. The competition of these realities, as tho any of us were of a mobile, spinning, each point the view in a rotating geometry. What is to be taken as no information, decisions made each time we cross the street. Gradually these pages fill, an intentionality like mass. Mucous membrane. Cool clouded sanity. The knot is not the rope. Amelia naps. The signs sing. The after-noon curls about me or I wrap myself in it, folds of attention aired with movement to a pot of coffee or the john. Lots of exercise, little thought. Twang in the rope, what holds the new apple tree to such wind as this. These roofs, their angles, give the hill texture, houses packed tight, cramped yards, kids on porches, dog growls, mowers, yelps, web of clothesline. Eye as sponge to day's light. What I want is the grey-blue grain of western summer. Attempted to confront her explosion at such arrogance, but did not, could not, transfer the smell, mould in the meat about whoever might ski or skate, that she herself was so circled by. Yellow beach, pink sky, pink beach, yellow sky. Eye is spine. Sea cucumber. Air more active, clouds pil-ing, folding into themselves, rolling. Burma shave parataxis. Who needs not a lover but a tennis partner. In the beach night, campfires lit up the city of dune buggies, surfboards pitched vertically into the sand, a presence as of clan shields. As if those words not written remained locked in ink. How the press of information, that first time you walk down a new street, cannot be repeated. Quills and crackers, jewels or miracles. One could propose, for example, the inclusion of anything. Cigar-shaped art object would hover near the

highway then quickly fly away. With such attention the mind can
follow the act of her washing in the next room, it knows hands
from neck from cheeks. Haul ass, kitten. Subtitles lower your focus.
Such, of. The first person to stomp out, when Zukofsky debuted
Reich's Violin Phase in the west, was Mario Savio. Yoyo's alibi,
the way back. Old sentences heard new carry a different purpose.
Weight in the line. Rhodochrosite, tourmaline. Motor city farewell.
You wake in waves, each new day's small tides of attention. The
road, the rug, fading dawn moon. Analysanda and their analy-
santia. A field of corn, green, in a plain of dry grass. Such poems
are like keystones in need of a monument. Learn the art of seizing
control. Barnwood ash. They live in condos. Mention sex, fruit,
candy, cities, books, the cinema, geology. Water towers with happy
faces. The air in its fair layers. Jet trails between clouds would
disperse. Necrotizing laryngotracheobronchitis, consequent of
a chemical irritant, CS. Not the sick, strict, slick legalisms. Employ-
ment gainful of what. Iowa clay, that slight planes do sculpt place,
the red west horizon bearing night. Glossed lines. I am meat in
motion only, all other is construct, Pinto going west. Special weap-
ons and tactics. The signifier is empty, the sign is full. Passed ball.
Eroded mesa. Weary of waking, talking, faking it. Night rodeo.
Drip candles kept atop old, empty wine bottles, a canister full
of pennies. Mountain lightning. The strictures against propositions
apply with equal force to attributes and relations. A man who
lurched suddenly toward us on the road, his hair filled with blood.
Tuesday noon. Somehow fog on the desert floor. Nails that glow in
burning wood. Myth is a language. A clock talks ticking. In Great
Salt Desert one is the vertical, located. From what they did, he will
not recover. Morning moon over mountains. Eggshells in the flower

bed for the calcium. The road, a line, to define the canvas. Consumption of wood by fire. Because my name is lion. The young nurse in blue sunglasses, by a subtle redistribution of weight, shift of gravity's center, moves in front of the black lanky graduate student of oriental porcelain in order to more rapidly board the bus, before all of the seats are taken. Watched, each day as we traveled west, the moon dissolve. Three days of July rain. Reassert older orders. Mould forms in old coffee. The bells return. As the heat of the hand will draw the leaves up to it, so thought's pressure folds the flower. Andy has leukemia, needs blood. The urinary habits of Dr. Williams. The flat was empty, the lights on, dishes in the sink, books about the floor, the shower torn to pieces. You thought somehow to copy Rodia not having seen the work. Today's embraces. Traits of verbal form do not extend to their objects. The white room, as you waken, begins to fill with the objects of perception, open suitcase, rumpled blankets, etc., events in discrete sequence, the chair, table, stereo, until, the world nearly completed, they begin to cohere, come into focus, new form, not as individuals, but each in relation, one to the other. Leaving out. The blood bank. Are pears form. The uncomplicated tyranny of punctuation, the residual aspect of print, to fix spelling, phuque it. Thursday dawn. Mobile of leaves called a tree. Tumor press on the optic chiasma. Through misuse arrive at important information. Mouthful of crab meat. You knew, you were certain, you were sure. Summer morning foghorn. Fool's toes. The light caught in the gauzy curtain, beyond which the terrace and the city of verticals. There is a hand here. Heard "my ancestors" as "Hawaiian sisters." I think that I know that I think, etc., infinite regression. Wine glasses in rows, in a cabinet. Provisional existence of the external world. Awake, but still in

bed, I listen to cars pass, doors, birds, children are day's first voices.
The poem is all that is the case. Mole on her ass, or prefer to call it
butt. To demonstrate the hand, prove the existence of fingers, possi-
bly, or Saturn, pain, roundness. From under the eave pigeons pour.
Doubt about existence works only in a language game. Watercress.
What use is a rule here. Surrogate information. One has to keep
reminding oneself of the unimportance of the inner process or state.
The great seagull would have come inside but my mother went at
it with a broom. I am forced, each time I write, to reinvent language
and form. Necessitation and contingency. That content does not
intrude. Troll bridge. Residue of sinus condition. Eventually the
scratches become scabs. Random sample. The brown paint yellows.
The end of the freeway in the middle of the country. It'll keep your
ego going for a few days. You could start almost anywhere and find
anything. On Treat Street. Signification extends the sign. Rattle
of water in pipes. Architect, schoolteacher, poet, the trio wandered
through Old Town, sobered by the evident despair. As classes to
attributes, ordered pairs to relations. A vocabulary for grammar
school lacking verbs of change. We cannot in conscience blame
these varied sources of modality on the notion of analyticity. Yellow
is the color of mental activity. In a room, on a warm night, music
on, over voices, a spoon scrapes a pot. Headhunter. A cardboard
box of wool sweaters on top of the bookcase to indicate Home.
We link together our various perceptual spaces whose contents
vary from person to person and from time to time, as parts of
one public spacio-temporal order. Bob takes Barry to the airport.
The ignorance surface from North Dakota. Kids who ride shopping
carts down the street. The confusion matrix, the travel field. The
form I saw in South Orange Sonnets. Ecumeniopolis. Broken shoe-

lace. Desire to replicate speech as thought is silly, great grinding hum of language in head. Fatal framer. Would play a piano on the beach. Sentences do not designate. The octoroon, the octillion. The signifier of myth presents itself in an ambiguous way. Insert opaque erotic data, stimulate focus. Would put a lit match to his thumbnail, because he liked the smell. Bedlingtons, first meant to hunt rats in coal mines, later bred to show, are nearly blind and crazy. Phantom Czechoslovak. This this this this. This is here if you think it is. Urban bourbon. If I am in a car and look through the window at the scenery, I can, at will, look at the countryside or the pane, and, if at the latter, at other worlds reflected there, the view, say, from a window on the far side, a small town lodged on the hillside. Neither present nor past hold for you the attractive indeterminacy of the future, the elaborate half-finished contraption of the yacht in the yard, tho you live in an apartment, waking from the sweating nightmare of hair starting to grow on all the walls and the great sound of breathing. There is no myth without motivated form. Caffeine enjambment of the nervous system. It is a speech justified in excess. Gross national poet. Why, over a valley this size, the white-grey sky becomes a great dome. Chinese fire drill. This sentence is not what I intended. Folds her toilet paper into perfect squares. It was a language robbery. Attention is all. The language is never anything but a system of forms, and the meaning is a form. Older music. The net, the fog, two alphabets. Writing the white lines. Mathematics is a finished language, deriving its perfection from this acceptance of death. Earliest imaginings of the married life, the chiropractor's daughter doing dishes. Drums under water. Varieties of helicopter filled the sky. A kind of spatial, tangible analogue of silence. Marjorie Daw. Give historical intention a natural justification, make contingency appear eternal. Fucked in the head. If you have an interest in the page, say, as a form of preservation. He does not write so much as his impatience does. Essence and scale. He knew how to hold an adz, to till. Between reality and men, between description and explanation, between object and knowledge. This sort of sentence. Identify the assumptions, define them. Always, across the bay, there was Oakland. Political because it must be, but at what level. The playground north of the coffee plant roils with soccer, kites, sunbathers. All good ideas are simple. Because accumulation is not conscious, we shuffle about in circles, in hot rooms with the windows shut, becoming gradually heavier, weighted and slower, until finally we begin to discard, to shed, to toss off, panama hat, white blazer with wide lapel, cufflinks, black shirt and white tie, until we stand, arms "akimbo," in white cuffed flares, see-thru net tee shirt, feet wrapped in sandals. If it needs more than one performer, that's an ideology, equipment, that's another. Compared to, say, Chile, where Santiago's higher elevations support the poor. Rumor that R beat one performer up. E is for Edgar. Entangled in a language, whose syntax leads you to multiple murder, political kidnap or an ashram in Colorado. Theoretical framework for pudding. Our colonies are the last proletariat. A day of rain in the middle of June. This sentence in August. This is the alphabet. These are the trees. Friday night. A cigar purchased in Vera Cruz, but smoked in Windsor. The Ferris wheel. Prepare to turn this record over. How could one ever hope to have known prose. The hidden assumption is that once the novel lived. So that it rains light. Adoration of my own two feet. The intensionalism of crewcuts. Single string of marine trumpet. Shopper's world, a whole store for quilts. Film of each of eighty victims, over Tubular Bells, called news. The gamelan is not simple. Who first refined petrol. That one could become a cop, to enforce the laws partially, the Highway Patrol. Magnetic tape to Patty Hearst, to Richard Nixon. Brushing the drums. The dawn light is before us, let us rise up and act. Thought as a boy to swallow all seeds, that the tree in the belly could become one. The death of heat is the birth of steam. Great urge to sneeze, mouth full of banana. But the grass spider eats only violets. A mouse's fear of a cat is counted as his fearing true a certain English sentence. They control insects and enemies of the trout. You sap. If we imagine the facts otherwise than as they are, certain language games lose some of their importance, while others become more important. Butterflies churn the air. The meaning of a word like the function of an official. Modal rounders. One could be wrong intentionally, but without deceit. The sharp shadows of a low sun, the light smack against the white housefronts. Each day there's the bridge. Every word is either current, or strange, or metaphorical, or ornamental, or newly coined, or lengthened, or contracted, or altered. The salute of the fireboats. Weathercock, scrimshaw. Panama Exposition. Between the television and the bed was an ironing board, half-finished bottles of lager atop it. Throttle's glottal stop. When, looking out the window, you no longer see what's there, it's time to move. Not every false belief is a mistake. Narwhale, I confront you. The quick brown fox jumped over the lazy revisionist running dog. The gallery was a labyrinth of white rooms with skylights, small words drawn in blue pencil, one to a wall, thru which and before which strolled the art consumers, gazing, chewing in an idle way on the earpieces of their sunglasses, paying no attention to the one red hard-backed chair in each room, presumably for their convenience or that of the occasional elderly lady, accompany-ing a college-age granddaughter, which were the true objects of the show. Implicitly or explicitly, all environmental planning and action reflects a particular view of society and the groups that compose it. A sequence of objects, silhouettes, which to him appears to be a caravan of fellaheen, a circus, dromedaries pulling wagons bear-ing tiger cages, fringed surreys, tamed ostriches in toy hats, begins a slow migration to the right vanishing point, signified by a palm tree on the horizon line. Here is Spain, that is Africa, this the water. Small boy shouts at the dog, insistent, scolding. A teller, she said of him, of moral tales. Refuse connectedness. Music for marimbas, voice and organ. I hear the hose in the tomato plants. What dura-tion does to the meaning of any word. I want to tell you tales of lint. Clapping music. Feeling my fingernail bend back, pushing it against my front tooth, to signal thought. All research is so set as to exempt certain propositions from doubt. Smashed watermelon sidewalk. A belief is what it is whether it has any practical effects or not. A park upon a hilltop, below which the city, its hills and verticals jammed together, and beyond that not the bay but rather the hills on the far side, as tho near, brown now in August with a light sky, rippling planet crust. How do I verify the imagination. Slag iron. As tho each bus route were a specific syntax. Asleep in the sun is all peace there is. Why should not a king be brought up with the belief that the world began with him. Then we found the testes in the scrotal sac. The proposition that you have spent your whole life in close proximity to the earth. How in the still air the sudden assertion of auto brakes, heard, calls into mind a trumpet. Whose boats dwell in the bay. Unable to read a book for any great length of time, for to abandon himself thus threatened him. I did not get my picture of the world by satisfying myself of its correctness. A big she St. Bernard. The truths of which he says he knows are such as all of us know, if he knows them. Sad dream of gas pain. My convictions do form a system. Not asleep, I lay in the grass, still, while the ladybug crossed my chest. I don't make the language, I enforce it. The power implicit within the ability to draw a single, vertical straight line. Thousands lavishing, thousands starving, intrigues, wars, flatteries, envyings, hypocrisies, lying vanities, hollow amusements, exhaustion, dissipation, death. Presences I thought dust in the air came closer now, had wings to move them. Twenty loose sheets of lined foolscap, undated. Opposed to the image. I am for example also convinced that the sun is not a hole in the vault of heaven. The hill would fill with people bathing in the sun. Climate replaces weather. This posit is not altogether the philosopher's doing. Laundry boat. Of all these faces seen as spaces, which are you. No one ever taught me that my hands don't disappear when I am not paying attention to them. Small kids swarm the porch. Display of the corpse of Che Guevara as bourgeois sculpture. Knowing it changes it. Solitary line of a sea lute. That was when my nose began to peel. Blue genes. Straw flowers. This is an exhibit for the prosecution. Axiology, or Value Systems I have seen. Talking heads of television. A world of routines, of returns to small forms, insistently. As astronauts enter the outer air. Get aboard. Symbols cramp the temple. It was a summer of few hot nights. Zoo caw caw of the sky. Time was real to him, but not linear, more a sensation of gravity, of falling from some precipice forward until, thousands of feet above the valley floor with its chalked concentric circles, acceleration approximated weightlessness. Garbage mind pearl diver. It was his smaller toes that hurt. Wittgenstein and the moon.

Look at that white room, filled with fleshy babies. Attempt, between poems, to be charming. The words, as in a boat, float. Any project large enough to capsize. Peach pits. Endless intimate detail ultimately bores. Driving freeway over San Bruno mountains in night fog, exhaustion registering in body as force, pressure, partial "G." Words, where you are, as in a trail, not forest but thicket, briar, pine needle modifiers, shingles of a pine cone on which to focus, but syntax, syntax was the half-light. Point of transfer. The abnormal mind is quick to detect and attach itself to this quality. Tenderness in that wicked man. Grandfather robed in white, horizontal in grey-green shadows of Intensive Care, would not look up, tubes in nose, waiting. When, as I hunkered down to overturn the small shells, shaking sand off, she asked what it was, I said "Looking for the good ones." Is this winter or is this morning. Short glass of tequila. Personality is an unbroken series of successful gestures. Tall glass of tawny port. Glide on through the sea change of faces and voices and color. Headlights, streetlights, lit living rooms. Ideological basis of sleep. A pleasure and discomfort in the knowledge of having become, by the fact of your absence, the focal point. Blond body hair. Borate bomber's song. Hyperventilation. Shadows between houses leave earth cool and damp. Molding my senselessness into forms. A scaffold around light. The last hot day of summer. Retina burn. There is no confusion like the confusion of a simple mind. A tooth gone in the root. Suffering succotash. A slick gaggle of ambassadors. The flat black hills beyond which summer's form, the sun, would rise. Tension manager's domain. The city is a thing mingled. Astronauts holding hands, adrift in the sky. There is no content here, only dailiness, the driver education car poised in the intersection by the playground, around which a jogger orbits, all in the hill's shadow at sunset. Caves of the tuna. Bowl in which map of world was etched. We ate them. Couple at next table, over coffee, discuss power relations of their home. Each ear pierced in four places. Question of sexuality. The flag. I told him I was tired, bored by sense of his misuse, my voice the line drawn. Log fort. As map could extend beyond the margin.

Revolving door. Splinters or slivers, sofa or couch. Clear lake. The east is red, the west is ready. Over farm fields in a hang glider. Memories of underdevelopment. Finally, there was nothing to turn you aside, the crowd's bustle as tho at your own momentum, the voices would ebb and echo, as you push at last thru lobby after lobby. Now I am on the moon, now in Death Valley. Dry blood. The tenor sax is a tool. Stretched canvas. This is no more than an hypothesis, haltingly proposed. Like a pitcher's kick, t'ai chi. Serial numbness. Each day's particulars conjoined, a morning habit, raising the shade, say, as the coffee steeps. Radio ideology. Chorus of the garbage collectors beneath the bedroom window, chewing cabbage discards, smashing bottles, the odor from the cud of their great truck. Eventually empties into a lonely logic, projects that will not resolve, locked in, terms providing terms, endless consequence of equation, until final factors fail to cross out. You are not certain which reality to hold constant. Signifies change, clay fear, with no substantive modification. Elongated motion, emotion slowed him, brought the oncoming traffic out gradually from about the turn, blind mountain road. Laura Riding, say, to have stopped writing, act not complete until old poems back into print. Trunk of the palm snapped where the truck hit, fibers about. Questions of distribution here. Seeds of the fig. Economics or language or where are these the same, value as speech. If we are limning the true and ultimate structure of reality, the canonical scheme for us is the austere scheme that knows no quotation but direct quotation and no propositional attitudes but only the physical constitution and behavior of organisms. We are preparing to start over and start over and have started over. Kareem and the skyhook. Morning of the mossback. That the thing which you thought possible is not, which, having once made the assumption, governed your days until the fault this morning showed, the wall's weak rock, which, tho it has not made itself felt, shall, is not, since you must carry it now to its conclusion, rubble, to be acknowledged. The skaters were a kind of solution. How will I know when I make a mistake, that, says, your hand as I shake it, fleshy palm, pudgy fingers, is not my imagination. The yellow rose of civic concern. Ladders, propped up against the walls of act. Disturbed that your approvers seem oblique to the intention, unaware that the concentric circles expanding about the stone thrown into the lake will extend to the shore, that the flute's vibrations form an act that yet others will be consequent to, as your own presence was predicated on the odor of pine in the air, you turn the orders of your attention to your fingers in relation to the stops along the bamboo shaft, a fix on precision, aware without saying so that evasive action cannot solve it. Alice and the sky boat. Tonto's memo to the effect that life is hard, pard. Manhattan itself a form of definition. As we loitered, waiting for the bus, I overheard her whispering to herself, a furious conversation. Presentness. City of nurses. The eye is the limit. City of stenographers. The first day of July. Underpass at Division Street. Only way he could know what occurred in their heads would be to put words down in a sequence, and that would be their thought. City of busboys, of administrative assistants. Soap. Here is an empirical fact, this word is used like this. The curious literal meaning of vacation. As he stood at the intersection, we stared at the young Persian whose face was bruised. His love of the border, of the instant in irrevocable acts, the hammer of the trigger changing the powder, a completion even if only a move of an inch is required. King of cornflakes, conference of the birds. Wind in the chimney would scatter ashes back into the room. Here a vast terminal murrain. The half-formed friendship before he died left her with a taste of unfinished business. The unceasing effort to force this to reveal its absolute self-existing quality of mass. Game for a chessboard, pennies doubling square by square. This is the city that never went to town. Sea plane. Oranges dislodge time. Ontic antics in the attic. Adventures of the dialectic. The garbage barge at the bridge. This list. Brushing dry leaves off dead poets. A woman dressed to polka. These reflections count only against hoping to base identity of propositions on some sort of intensional isomorphism derived from the broad sort of sentence synonymy which is interdefinable with analyticity. It was my racism causing me to hear these blacks in the cafe discussing Heisenberg. Scratches his ass, then sniffs his fingers. Vocabulary of dinner in the syntax of my mouth. I tugged at the cord to coax the plug from the socket. Suddenly he rose from our table, then left. As tho speech nailed to the wall would be writing. As Berkeley nears September. We watched him punch, repeatedly, the garage door, slowly, with his head down, a blunt precision. Words drain. The dream deepens. Who put the bob in the Baba Ram Dass. The Japanese floor manager in a red sport coat, red trousers, white shoes. The sign of the seven-headed cobra. The bones of the foot, the veins. This resolve. Cold coffee. Would I read this. When our objective is an austere

canonical form for the system of the world. I felt I was trapped
within the restaurant, moving from table to table, to sit down,
to write this sentence, that one. Those rural boys are bulky, mean,
what get called the Bulls. Art is not not art. The calculus of predi-
cates. It has the particular turnings, springs, shutters, the weavings
and the riding away. Alter the order of prints on the wall, inexpen-
sive reproduction. A treasure of trash. This stone is thinking about
Vienna. Interest in exact sequence, dating, calendars, chronology,
clocks, time wages, time graphs, time as used in physics, annals, his-
tories, the historical attitude, interest in the past, attitudes of intro-
jection toward past periods. Throb in the wrist or knee joint. Wide
range of ideation in practice. Quadruplicity drinks procrastination.
History is the confidence of limit. Cheapo keeno. Unfixed gaze.
Tolerance of the don't-care is a major source of simplicity. Quarts
of weather. We climbed three flights of stairs, slope of a eucalyptus
grove, to arrive at the door, then two flights up through dark rooms
of music, shadow dance shuffle, and thru to the back porch, old
boards holding couch and rocker, for to view the city from that
great height gave the night sky place or weight, fog wedged amid
rooftops but still the clear view, the Big Dipper. If a lion could
speak, we could not understand him. A single unpartitioned uni-
verse of values of bound variables, a simple grammar of predication
which admits general terms all on an equal footing. As tho one
were searching for an object in a room, opening a drawer and
not finding it, closing the drawer, waiting, opening it again, closing,
waits. To keep warm burn the news. Neckerchief. The type of old
man who wears his white hair in a crewcut and keeps small, fat
dogs. The pressure artist or the pressured. Terms imply domains.
Don't try to cold me up on this bridge now. Art as a habit merges

with the renewal of solutions which constitute it. Tier-tender's
tale. It was only when the trash bag crashed into the middle of
the kitchen that we realized it bore the weight of ants. Day's era-
sures perception traces. Objects whose terms are learned only in
deep context. Sudden failure of the mails. Meridian mass murder.
Blue-brown. Intervening neural activity goes on, but the claim is
that nothing is clarified, nothing but excess baggage is added, by
positing intermediary subjective objects of apprehension anterior
to the physical objects overtly alleged in the spoken sentences them-
selves. Personal antagonism toward art. Odor of old orange in the
compost. The culture of children. Unwashed pot. Attention directed
to directed attention. Earth science. Carbonated water. Soap dish.
Fastidious women have unwanted hair removed. Basic speed law.
Six into eight now, explained by page size. Proof of termhood.
Indeterminate gray pile of undershirts, shorts. This tapestry con-
cerns the mass capture of rabbits. Platform rocker. The operator
of class abstraction can be reduced to description, and description
to quantifiers. Ache in my bones awakens groans. Because my room
faces west I watch the sun rise "in the windows" across the street.
By now we have made the far turn. This sentence has five words.
My baby she has no shoes. Steam pours from alley sewers, corridor
of fire escapes, loading docks, dumpsters. Two ducks rocked in. I
resented seeing History and Nature confused at every turn. Yellow
leather vest. Sky soup. Too fond of bondage. Each dawn a return
to an eternal conclusion, the lemon tree in flower, the sun amid the
dissolving fog to warm the porch, this day's proposition. Autumn
now. Capable of sitting in the chair for hours, quiet, watching her
sleep. Pinball in the Greek cafe. The squeal in the tone of a clothes-
line pulley. Presence of stool in the tract forces the gas out. Emulsi-

fied memory. Was what I saw in her true deterioration or merely my own awakening. Reflective persons unswayed by wishful thinking can themselves now and again have cause to wonder what, if anything, they are talking about. Earth herself is inorganic, where fire is literally itself. Their first goal was to separate the workers from their means of production. Waking in the dark now, more so each day, the year's slide. Numbers, Mind, and Body. The partial function in the connective touch. You come at last into the realization as into a banquet room, domed perhaps but with chandeliers, that a lush ordering of events is no different than any other so that one might as well eat squid as tripe or plums, dressed in the regalia of tennis, the perceiving in the punchbowl reflection a costume as clownish as it is offensive. What is here. Red eye. The light has no right. Notational process, musical juncture. Do not denigrate the history of solitude. That language fails to share the object-positing pattern of our own. But trees are not orderly. How propose to release the fly from the bottle. Bigger, to serve you better. The moth that destroyed Cleveland. Close cover before striking. No hurry, no hassle. Only a thorough historical-materialist analysis, piercing the ideological fog maintained by the dominant coalition of interests and destroying the fetishes continually produced and reproduced by those concerned with the preservation of the status quo, only such historical-materialist analysis can hope to disentangle the snarl of tendencies and counter-tendencies, forces, influences, convictions and opinions, drives and resistances which account for the pattern of economic and social development. Heat ripples the air rising from the street, reshaping houses on the hill's other peak. Have these words a meaning. Honeydew head, hair of bean sprouts. It comes out here that knowledge is related to a prior decision.

Subvention of the usual capital outlay process. Waterways of Marin. Thought is a labyrinth. This is due process. The boys play at war atop washers, amid dryers. Diphtheria of the larynx. Shelves of neatly folded linen. California. Her roommate remarked casually she could tell he had stayed the night, that the toilet seat would be vertical in the morning. Oboe hobo. He bears a resemblance to Lee Harvey Oswald, aiming from the window, silent, not alone. This is about this. Whipped at by branches, duck and run. Badwater. Who do you do. Is boredom seriousness coming of age. The beautiful dump truck. Red sky at night. Speech of no word, word of no speech. When you get a value judgment that's all you've got. Are miles alike. You may remember. Excuses. Nothing was authentic except sensibility, and so sensibility became the very substance of my life. Iced tea as a system. Metabolic imbalance, called a cold. Clap hands. "If you are heading for the outdoors," as if that were not everywhere present. Amid shouting, could write of silence and believe it. State time. Wild dog packs roam that part of the city. Ska. Erotic insert. The concern with quality in writing can only be another form of consumer research. A lather for shaving with a rum scent. Fast karma outrage. A child saw me write that, asking what it was. Strategy against personal starvation. Writing that grows out of itself, poetry of mould. Fear that tooth will just drop out. Dusty sill or wainscot. Percussion as such. Drawing of a Balinese spirit with its face in its stomach. Dog would stand on the porch and not permit us to pass. Would you know if this was prose. Scissor with broken blade. Ives jives. Was my intention clear. The wives that weave the homes together. First day of September. The sun rose undetected behind the sculpted clouds, the air humid in the eucalyptus grove or up over the Mormon Temple, or the Greek Church.

Great sinus swell. Stretch marks on her body. There has been a hierarchy of languages headed by the "direct read-out from the object" language, which has served as the creative core, and then various support languages acting as explicative and elucidatory tools to the central creative core. If words were bells. Copyright is theft. Positing facts in the image of sentences as intermediaries for what is. On why this is a poem. This arc is wider, more gradual. A form of art could not maintain itself outside a society of language users. The hard press of her fingers about the pen as she wrote into her diary while I watched. The poetry component is merely specified. Torn tendon. Black burro. Vandalism is folk art. As a result a mistake becomes something forbidden. Portrait of the best worker in Auto Plant 7. Absence of doubt belongs to the essence of the language game. Flowering milkweed through the cracks in the sidewalk, around which to draw stars in colored chalk. Knowledge in the end is based on acknowledgment. Left his emotional options open. If I am dreaming, this remark is dreamed as well, as I dream that these words carry meaning towards you. Balloons, having gotten loose from children, would rise up steadily, yellow discs diminishing on a blue plane. Art language. Fountains of the financial district spout soft water in a hard wind. Taking off shoes like removing knot from balloon. Half asleep on the hillside, the breeze would pass over this part of my body, that one. Friendship trumpet fade-out. At six, rise up, sun threatens day. Barnwood, in the fireplace, hisses as it burns, pops. This before, this after. Is jazz discourse. Repeating on paper that stanza one hundred times, each with a new pen, watching how the width of the ink's path shifted the weight and intention of reference, penumbra of signification, from act to act. Mathematical piano. He stood over them, alternately shouting and drinking from a bottle of bourbon. Detention garden. The enormous comedy of the emotion imposed on the image of the peasant's bent shoulders. The being towards which it spills over its signs is neither more nor less than the being of thought. Geometry as the theory of relative position. Months at the stanza. Little moons of my thumbnail grow. The torch bulb holder is connected to two stiff wires and inserted in a test tube which serves as a handle. Writing in public as a form of performance, on buses, say, or here amid sunbathers, not paid attention to, looking up, myself, to watch the jugglers. You have no adequate ordinary terminology for dealing with such things as lines of force. Were these true events. How this sentence could open to comment on itself, how these words, first written, swelled with intention, spilled meaning, later to have become so opaque certain terms, modifiers of the first purpose, expanded, redistributed value, took over. This used to be a nice place. The conditions of production corresponding to this specific, historically determined, mode of production have a specific, historical passing character. I see that young blonde woman each morning as she jogs in a green sweatsuit, trailed by her four small dogs, bring to mind Gray's tale, bleached-out poet trotting through a throng of mourners of an evangelist bishop to a black church. Poon tang. Each morning I rise to praise these faces. The desire to fix the point at which doubt and belief bleed into one another. The hill blackens in a controlled burn. Funereal disease. Pulling at my toenails. Truth defined as the unmoving foundation of any language game. In a far room of the apartment I can hear music and a hammer. Paratactics. Whether to speak of geometrical objects as bypassed or as reconstrued is a matter of indifference. Coordinated universal time. Poem took the form of the Ice Age. It is a wall that closes and does not. Elimination can often be allowed the gentler air of explication. It repeats and repeats, adding new lines without apparent relation, building with great visual and mental invention a tremendous formal beauty that carries no cargo at all. The asymmetry in any face. Words do, speech is. Sperm count. Balinese oral form. Fat man at the bus stop. Reality made an appearance. Morning in the gauzy curtains. Body like a bear. Grey clouds to give the sky weight. Neon and xenon, the so-called noble gases. It was here the poem spoke of itself, casual, dissembling, remarking of its admiration for the great Watts Towers, tho it had never visited them. How is doubt introduced. Night light. Warmest days were in September. A metal table, round, whose center is a large beach umbrella placed instead upon concrete, for us to set our drinks upon while we gaze at the divers' half-gainers. Space allocation. Layers of bandage about the ankle. Imagined life occurred at home. People are starving. Corporeal music, composing carpenter. Anchovy. He hoped the gift of the shirt would be the right size. How do I know if this is page or wall. At the cement works. The bear flag in the black marble plaza. We held sparklers on the porch or about the backyard's pine. Hand lotion, bandages, rainbows of toilet paper. Green brocade face cloth. Straw shoes from Japan. Sight itself is pre-logical and without constants. Bus routes constitute a sculpture, with density of lines, frequency of units, the pleasure to be taken in slashed seats. New, white, wide-brimmed denim hat. Roundness is an ideal embodied in the nostril. Gradually, debts decrease. Transfer points. Write this down in a yellow notebook. The aardwolf. Memories tend to be remains, not of past sensations but past verbalizations. The external is simply proposed. Pick up sticks. A white bowl of split pea soup is set upon the table.

Ballad of the ice cream vendor. The yellow house, the beige house, the blue one, the block. Poem like a towel wrapped around summer. Thursday noon. This is a piece of information directed at you. Monday morning on Joe's steps, filling the notebook. Great white belch. It's cold. You don't learn books, chair exist, but to fetch or sit in them. Muslims idle in front of their temple. Language did not emerge from ratiocination. Patterns of possibility come together, intersect, disperse. Day or page at a time. Dream of a great air tragedy, the neighborhood smoldering, lit by floodlights atop police cars and fire trucks, damp night fog, everybody dazed on their porches, odor of meat. Bus ride right to the ocean. Rapid transit information. Soup repair. One knows how to receive this because it is a poem, because it bears that family resemblance, this assertion, because one gradually understood how to receive the last one and the one prior, because one has learned how to receive them in general without seeming conspicuous. How many times have you read this. My childhood passed in contemplation of Ichabod Crane. Why should a language game rest on knowledge. Dream breaks up sleep. Fog, like a wedge of meringue on the bay. Doors open, footsteps, faucets: people are waking up. What if these words don't mean what I believe they do. Crash city. It is or is not your cup of tea. Feel the stress in day's recesses. Monetary units of Iraq. Anticipation specifically an extension of memory, so that one salt flat cracked into pentagonal patterns will be another. I saw houses gradually turn into steam without obvious cause. Those curtains which I like above the kitchen sink. Reading a page of print I see through the paper to words inverted on the far side, become conscious of the margin, begin to anticipate new paragraphs, etc. Beeswax mixed with paraffin. I is a predicate relation. Imagine lives we posit in the bungalows, passing, counting, with another part of the mind, the phone poles. Wide brown rim about the tit. Wasp adheres to flesh. Contempt that we felt as children for any other who was forced to have his/her mother present, just to cross the street. Stood there broke and rapidly becoming hungry, staring at nickels and pennies at the fountain's bottom. Soft pretzel, lemon ice. A walk through the railroad yards, rainbow out of gray-brown. Particular discourse. Dear Quine, sentences are not synonymous when they mean the same proposition. Analgesic. Kids, with nothing better to do than ride about in an old car, shining a flashlight in the eyes of night drivers. Advent of winter hinted. How the heel rises and the ankle bends to carry the body from one stair to the next. A decision not to permit his work to change, year after year several times each month to write the same poem, not copying, but each time working his way back through the identical process. The feminine way men fold their hands when, say, they ride the bus. Humidity of laundromat. This page is slower. Able to sunbathe in winter. Hotels for old single men. I want a form to cancel form. Forced outside first thing, just to purchase food for one's breakfast. A fact in fact. Each sentence is a solution. Theory: a specific form of practice. The even keel. The monkey hordes come to the aid of Prince Rama. The fight quietly going on in the back of the bus. Cupcake corral. Chalk dust. Either I will do this thing or I will not. We walked through the financial district at midnight, the street deep between these buildings, a film crew working down an alley, artificial twilights, pausing as we passed to stare at great tapestries in bank lobbies. Now I will ask the reverse questions. Write and sunbathe at the same time, or ride the bus, or eat dry cereal in a bowl of milk on the upended cable spool you use for a table. Golden rain in the morning of the world.

Great whistling anus. Sat on a stage behind a panel of gadgets and began to read. Hunkered down against a cyclone fence to write words in a sequence concerning the movement of a chair to a room's center for the purpose of changing the lightbulb. Skycycle. What if it were cancer. The evil king Ravana. Cigarette butt in clovered grass. It cannot be rushed, it must be steady. Morning of the middle. The history of all hitherto existing society is the history of class struggle. The desire for coffee. Personal density is directly proportional to temporal bandwidth. Designate art words here. Sign-oriented verbal behavior. Ships, arriving or leaving the harbor, stir water, leave wakes as we also, walking a trail to the hilltop, displace the air. Reported speech is speech within speech, message within message, and, at the same time, also speech about speech, message about message. Eat what you kill. Gum bichromate. Lighting the cigarette because it will make the bus come. In a garden of suspicious flowers. Bruise in the banana. When I speak these words you do not hear them, tho later you will, when, in your head, you will find their spaces formed and growing. Cherry bomb, prairie fire. Sunburnt kneecap. The cranes in the gray dawn fog over the holds of the boats. Subjection of nature's forces to man, machinery, application of chemistry to industry and agriculture, steam navigation, railways, electric telegraphs, clearing of whole continents for cultivation, canalization of rivers, whole populations conjured out of the ground. Animal crackers. Anything I do, anything I say. Leaves of lettuce, formless, left in a bowl of salad oil. Pleonastic spasm. Drums accelerate before bells begin, then flutes and I am walking on the dusty forest floor, wearing trousers held by suspenders, bare foot and chest, searching for my hat again where caterpillars weave homes upon its wet, white, wide brim. Like an old lady misplacing

constantly spectacles or keys, thus I words their meanings. Liner
notes to a Dylan album. Does it go for knowing as it does for col-
lecting. The young man with the long eyelashes. I hear the fire reels
charming out of the guardhouse. Swarm of carpenters within the
burned-out house. Sleeping, breathing, with my mouth open. Im-
balance in the body compass. Rise up before dawn, the whole hill
dark yet, wash, eyes adjusting, as colors begin to open up. We are
well within the made place. I will circle you as you more slowly
round our friend, X, as he walks an arc across the field, so as to
explain to ourselves more completely motions of the solar system.
The tenor sax is a toy. Trystero. The slower, deeper heat of August
days. We camped that night in a field so that, when day broke, a
whole valley lay before us. Three teeth in a pill bottle kept on the
mantel. The language in which the concept knowledge does not
exist. Of pores as eyes as they open. Divides the sky into cubes of
air. Felt thought. Woman next to me on bus pretends not to see what
is written. Xerox days. Waylaid by brigands on a voyage to get mil-
lions. Sparklers or incense, it's all the same principle. Gray rain on
the dark bay. White or white-gray or gray, cream call it, fade away.
There is always the danger of wanting to find an expression's mean-
ing by contemplating the expression itself, and the frame of mind in
which one uses it, instead of always thinking of the practice. Watch-
ing her hand to see if there is a ring amid long, thin fingers. Feel of
fever evenly spread throughout the body. The possibility of terms
like rooms in a house, huge Hillsborough home, doors of syntax,
windows of nuance, a long, carpeted hallway lined with Persian
mirrors, doors ajar through which you see, a guest in this place
tho not thoroughly welcome, the furniture of usage. This is taking
longer than I thought. Piano clusters. Very much please please send.

The song of the Cessna, its propellers. What do we mean, margins are justified. Putting my shoes on last, then standing, dressed. It must nestle itself everywhere, settle everywhere, establish connections everywhere. This is or is not an object. Now and then the workers are victorious, but only for a time. Blood Thursday. A musical composition is what the mind immediately reconstructs of the experience from the score or while listening, and by memory the whole effect of the experience, an intellectually reconstituted aesthetic consistency, which may differ in almost every way from the composer's intentions, and which may be supplemented by related and in many cases unrelated events that occur externally to the reading or performance, or by imagination or reverie while listening or while remembering. Kill what you eat. A similar movement is going on before our own eyes. Snow is remarkable to one not accustomed to it. What else does the history of ideas prove, than that intellectual production changes in character in proportion as material production is changed. A sign within the diesel's whine. The acoustics of emotion. To view from the porch the whole bay was not the point, but to stand there, drink in hand, perceiving oneself in relation to all visible lives, much like the pine ridge, each in the midst of a personal navigation, so that this interlude was itself a form of carrying forward, was what it meant to be drunk. This is logic. Piss smell of eggs. Revolving door. The gentle knocking of a sock filled with sand on my forehead. How will I know when I make a mistake. Just the way I wrote when I was twelve years old. The garbage barge at the bridge. Each term bears its purpose. The throb in the wrist. The form itself is the model of a city, extension, addition, modification. Earth science. Gives names to his typewriter, car, chairs. Their first goal was to separate the workers from their means of production. (1) Sound of an electric saw from the (temporarily) closed-off gallery, or (2) sound of a film projector rewinding. He bears a resemblance. Terrorism courts respect. A drawing of a Balinese spirit with its face in its stomach. Writes better when he wears his hat. Fountains of the financial district spout soft water in a hard wind. We want coherence. In a far room of the apartment I can hear music and a hammer. An expensive sundae carefully constructed around three mounds of French vanilla, entitled Hobo. The bear flag in the black marble plaza. Epic of doodling. Rapid transit. The page is only the documentation, or the page is more, the field, resistance. How the heel rises and the ankle bends to carry the body from one stair to the next. She was a unit in a bum space, she was a damaged child, sitting in her rocker by the window. The desire for coffee. This emptying out of interiority to the benefit of its exterior signs, this exhaustion of content by its form, is the principle. The tenor sax is a toy. Carry, if you can, the proposition to its limit. Snow is remarkable to one not accustomed to it. The particularly thick nail of the big toe. She was a unit in a bum space, she was a damaged child, sitting in her rocker by the window. Yellowing gauze curtains. The formal beauty of a back porch. Waking, sleeping, days bleed one into the other, so that it is this unrelenting need to rest breeds image of discontinuity, line, cycle, circle, line. I'm unable to find just the right straw hat. Listening to seals on that dark beach, not able to see them. He hit the bricks, took a vacation, got rolled up, popped, as they say. Listening patiently, until one is able to hear the one watch in the room, perfectly. The fishermen's cormorants wear rings around their necks to keep them from swallowing, to force them to surrender their catch. The raised highway through the flood plain. She had only the slightest pubic hair. Each time this path is taken, its distances shift. We drove through fields of artichokes. We came upon the god of the starfish. Feet, do your stuff. We bring to the encounter what we choose to see, so that of all the terms picked to describe the dog, only one, proper name so-called, defines a category that has but one member, yet, not knowing it, the next time we saw him, we would recognize, we would greet him, we would be correct. Dark brown houseboats beached at the point of low tide—men atop their cabin roofs, idle, play a Dobro, a jaw's harp, a 12-string guitar—only to float again when the sunset is reflected in the water of Richardson Bay. White wings of a magpie. Frying yellow squash in the wok. Great jolt of travel. Write this down in a green notebook. At possibility's edge occurs limit. Television in the 1950s. Each day as I lie here, I hear her rise and wash. Silverfish, potato bugs. The formal beauty of a back porch. We stopped for hot chocolate topped with whipped cream and to discuss the Sicilian Defense. Spider bites. A tenor sax is a weapon. A learned solitude, in the head looking out, constantly waking, new day. The Main Library was a grey weight in a white rain. One's age is best seen in the back of one's hand. What I want is the gray-blue grain of western summer. Void is what's left when the cosmos breaks down as the interesting evidence of order. Subtitles lower your focus. Sentiment is memory confused with desire. Mention sex, fruit. Mexican blue hammock to write in. Drip candles kept atop old, empty bottles of wine. Fuchsias fall and stick to the walk. The young nurse in sunglasses, by a subtle redistribution of weight, gravity's center, moves in front of the black student of oriental porcelain in order to more rapidly board the bus home, before all the seats are taken. Wind chimes. Are pears form. That he was not brutal enough for her confused him. Awake, but still in bed, I listen to cars pass, doors, birds, children are day's first voices. Across the empty states to Chicago if at all possible. Eventually scratches become scabs. Red shingle roof. A cardboard box of wool sweaters on top of the bookcase to indicate Home. The naval air base across the still bay water, behind which the hills rise, houses crowding the lower slopes, United States. Bedlingtons were at first meant to hunt rats in coal mines. Waiting for the phone to ring at the far end, for her to pick it up, I could hear voices, whole muted conversations. Attention is all. Jack rabbit's fatal dive across the blacktop. He knew how to hold an adz. I'm unable to find just the right straw hat. A day of rain in the middle of June. Slept by the roadside to wake in a vast flat space. The gamelan is not simple. Tuba booms. Modal rounders. A slope filled with soldiers sifting through the large charred green debris, explosion of a helicopter. A sequence of objects, silhouettes, which to him appears to be a caravan of fellaheen, a circus, dromedaries pulling wagons bearing tiger cages, fringed surreys, tamed ostriches in toy hats, begins a slow migration to the right vanishing point on the horizon line. Primal soup. Slag iron. Red sky above dry land. The implicit power within the ability to draw a single, vertical straight line. Forms from nouns are known. That was when my nose began to peel. Red dirt hills. Look at that room filled with fleshy babies, incubating. Pineapple slices. A tall glass of tawny port. Nevada into Utah as though through conditions of the mind. We ate them. Agents, he noticed, once removed from their jobs, were the dullest ones of all. Wanted to know what revision meant. Day's first sky was a fan of blues. Motown. Extra paper money was kept in the closet, rolled by my grandmother into the shade of the small window there, behind the coat hanger heavy with old ties. You are here now. Writing, riding. Graffitus. Said of her organization that it was the third largest tendency, but held to the correct line. Fish, fishes. From the house where Trotsky died they caught a ride with a man who worked for the World Bank. Increments of the familiar. He hit the bricks, took a vacation, got rolled up, popped, as they say. Nearer and farther. You read this sentence before. New bulge. Bulky tale, pointless as it is long. Vacancies. The true sign of agriculture is the small plane. This will be hell to type. Luggage. It was all over paper clips. Where ranch hands would wander in daily for coffee or breakfast. See how sane this is. It is not as though our lives bear intended meaning, but that it gathers about us like fallen leaves someone has failed to sweep away. What is the meaning of a single sentence. Occasionally, a dirt road will curl out of the mountains to come up to the freeway, tho you never know what fact it extends from, house, mine, town. After, before. A blue flame. This is a test. Drop City. All this only lately translated from the Korean. All talk. Face of a clown colored in. On holiday, I read Barthes' "The Writer on Holiday." The function of the paragraph is visual, to break the page into units, pre-logical intent. Western movies. Embedding. We are, each of us, somehow given to a realization of the possibility of disaster, but when the slowed traffic took us around the curve into view of the scattered remains of the helicopter, engine at the road's edge, amid a crowd of soldiers, police, hearses, pushing us immediately onward, away, it was an image we saw, no more. Got this from a fortune cookie. I hate speech. Geomagnetic. Child's form. This is not a new sentence. The fishermen's cormorants wear rings around their necks to keep them from swallowing, to force them to surrender their catch. They're good in all the violent spaces. Home of the curator of Africana, room in the attic, breeze off Lake Michigan turned this page. A doubt without an end is not even a doubt. Tales from the crypt. There is a difference between a mistake for which, as it were, a place is prepared in the game, and a complete irregularity that happens as an exception. House of red brick. We might speak of fundamental principles of human enquiry. Monday morning. Even if his dream were actually connected with the noise of the rain. Cowbell doorbell. Memory of not-well. In the fog I saw the great grass boats floating toward the delta. The first ring of the phone is short and, though we hear it, we feel frozen, unable to act. The truck had burned, now, at road's edge, glowed merely. He adds no figure to the atlas of the impossible. The word I want is Shampoo. To destroy syntax in advance. The young children of the wife of my friend's brother. A multiplicity of tiny, fragmented regions in which nameless resemblances agglutinate things into unconnected islets. A procedure by which they stick a metal device up one's prick. Superimposing different criteria. How the roads wrap around the town. Detention garden. Cat sleeps on the hood of the parked car. Why order exists in general, what universal law it obeys, what principle can account for it, and why this particular order has been established and not some other. An Italian love song played on the accordion. Employs, implies. Linear accelerator. As the ambulance passed, everyone stared to see if there was anyone in it. If for every window there were a person. Twenty-first century full of dumpy houses. She had only the slightest pubic hair, light brown. Riding buses on the weekend. At home amid engineers, on a patio, with chicken and gin and tonic. Next to last page in the green book now, deep in the yellow. What if one killed one, never to be caught, constantly alive with that information. These conditions of constant change demand the weapon of theory. Large, evenly hard beds. The meaning of this sentence resides in no one word. I was swimming in a clear pool. Moth, patiently, beating its wings on the window. Here also were buried the soldiers killed at the Battle of Lake Erie, 1813. Not urban but metropolitan culture now, city and suburb the single web. What does it mean to know, sleeping, that you sleep in Idaho. Seismograph and thermostat in the display case, gallery of imperial art. The fountain forms a geometry of the particular, five waterfalls, six spouts, all of which arrive in the general pool. Ozone park. Playing with the pilot light. Asleep in spurts, awake in starts. Each event will be its own name. Fabulous flab. A clear thing. Visitation Valley. This is the fable of objects. As if by special procedures at the pinball machines, free games without tilting, weeping and half singing, he could speak directly to that force he called the giants. Infinite expansion. Animalism of the garbage trucks. Sulphur, the hanged man, I swing between realms. Stem of steam from a kettle, cream in a small white cup. She threw her legs back up, over my shoulders, and with my ass I shoved in. That winter there were zeppelin alarms. This line written in Windsor, once the way out, as, say, Guatemala now is, sitting on a park bench, river's edge, facing Detroit. The mitigation of oranges. We drove through fields of artichokes. A great many notions that intersect, overlap, reinforce or limit one another on the surface of thought. Green water, gray sky. Plants that grow in the antlers of stags. Primed canvas. Early memory of sensation, being picked up by father, first recognition of height, absorbed later into dreams where I just float off of earth's surface, slow, uncontrollable, weightless flight. Canadian cactus. Demons can only travel in a straight line. One does not shiver here, one shudders. Prose of the world. They invented logic and classification. The confrontation of resemblances across space. A key ring raps on the glass. Inca flute. Form is to seize the time. Of adjacencies, of bonds and joints. Women, smelling of ammonia, board the bus. Stalactite or storm. Form is the tame cat. Gunsel, heavy-duty low rider, styler. The throat, hearing the toilet flush, invariably swallows. A made tunnel, for trains, beneath the bay. Form is the minute hand. Lute. These emotions have been proposed. His veins great rivers, his bladder the sea. Form is the structure of character, what. Strike opponents' ears with both fists. Manifest destiny. Through sky cannon. BFTP of the Apes. Hands over the keyboard as though a dredging motion. Feet, do your stuff. In need of a new needle. Wanted no limits, only possibility. When buses of the morning rush do pass, I stare from my seat into eyes of those who go other ways. Woman new to the building seemed interesting, until the night she brought home the man who clearly was not, so curiosity drained away. At certain hours whole neighborhoods will drain or fill with people. Table with a black top. Language is my given. Green tint to the shit. Wrote on the wall its word until I would learn it. Filling the yellow cup with coffee. Once each day my small cigar. Water in the pipes does not wake me, but keeps me from sleep, unable to determine the source, the user, the time of night. Bok choy, bok-fu. A sentence begun on the green page is completed on the yellow. Ants would attempt to escape from the heat by crawling into the freezer only to die from it, black ring around its door. On the reparsing of names. Bent bell mat. Sat in the Ford World Headquarters lobby, reading Olson. The boy elapsed. Grew up, she said, able to hear Chiang's firing squads by the river at dawn. The boy was abundant. Dark glasses on the black desk, their blue tint. Class war. Instances return, thought to have been lost. Cars arrive, or drive off in the dark. To kill the clock. We bring our little silver spoons. Waking wasted. Friends, kindred, days, estate, good-fame, plans, credit. Assertion, not journal, in a house with four bathrooms, on a two-acre lot. To him who in the love of nature holds communion with her visible forms, she speaks a various language. Dark brown house-boats beached at low tide—men atop their cabin roofs, shirtless and in overalls, idle, play a Dobro, a jaw's harp, a 12-string guitar—only to float again, anchored, when the sun is reflected in Richardson Bay. Postures of plenty. The particular, the particular. Attention to objects "out there" in the material world is constantly subverted by the demands of memory. Words in a line pass time. Willful concentration is constantly dissolving into involuntary association. Auto-gyro. I've got silence on the radio. One wants a place to locate mind's events. Funky Kingston. If you go wider, deeper. Burnt sienna. Tourists from Taiwan. Somewhere between the retina and the visual cortex the inflowing signals are modified to provide information that is already linked to a learned response. Later they send for their wives. We are getting rid of ownership, substituting use. Prose like a garden. Winter comes to space-time. Globe is the lower. Vertical law. Diminishing world where the head dwells, avoidance of which is the test. You understand this because of the common social convention that it is language. A light that I saw, that mountain road, that passed. Idiot size spaces out nature. Solid object. How, between tongue and lips, she took my foreskin, licking. Alone in a stranger's house. Autobiography of precision. She makes constructions to sit in, whose common form implies the electric chair. This indulgence. Only in the flats is the fat of the green gone. Jokes replace form. Frying yellow squash in the

wok, with string beans, bell peppers, tofu, sprouts. Between body
and destiny lay mirrors and attractions. Intermittent as it is, the
process of refrigeration sets up a hum in the wall, non-specific,
not to be avoided, not precisely heard, felt rather by the wake
in the belly's fluids. The grammar of being is an exegesis of things.
Bone bruise. Possible position that words on a page are the lan-
guage sleeping, waiting to be moved by eyes that move left to right.
Rose of china embedded in the lamp. A memory in search of a mind.
An old spool for cable made into a table, made home for a garden
in an old wine jug. Aesthetic decision. The alimentary life. A real,
tho not popular, instance of discourse. Each morning geese circle
the lake until they refind day's forms. Lost in the rain in Juárez.
Feta cheese. Dog star boy. Normal discourse. Equivocation, syn-
onyms and etymologies, differences, form and description, anat-
omy, nature and habits, temperament, coitus and generation, voice,
movements, places, diet, physiognomy, antipathy, sympathy, modes
of capture, death and wounds, modes and signs of poisoning, reme-
dies, epithets, denominations, prodigies and presages, monsters,
mythology, gods to which it is dedicated, fables, allegories and
mysteries, hieroglyphics, emblems and symbols, proverbs, coinage,
miracles, riddles, devices, heraldic signs, historical facts, dreams,
simulacra and statues, uses in human diet, use in medicine, miscel-
laneous uses. You are not the most complicated of men eating an
English muffin. Resented for favors asked. What in the well whis-
tles. A poor good man tell-clock. Exploration in closure. Blind to
the alternate. Prefers instruments of percussion, for discreteness.
Way in which winter wanders in. Fat dimpled thighs. The nice guy.
Raw mushrooms. Soap root. The waitress looms over the table, pot
of coffee in hand. Assumption there is steadily less to be said. Write

this down in a green notebook. Could it be seen as the single act, which took months to do. The rectangular geometry of the tiles, the plane of floor held stories above the ground, which flows under the metal door in this cubicle of the john. Free, white and forty-five. Celery, salary. In the head head. Auto-dactyl dream. Hair, as it dries, weighs less on brain. Piano man. I said a maximum of shit last night. He gave the impression that very many cities rubbed him smooth. Pleasant tense. Almonds. Was this the topic sentence. The warm blood of rain, say, such image as proposes an aesthetic. Place holder. Power curtain. An afternoon nap becomes sculpture. So it seemed I woke in a castle, or, rather, its inner court, whose walls of yellow and brown brick supported vines of ivy, until, standing, shaking off dead leaves, I could see into the windows of the rooms, the classes going on there, boys and girls who, looking up from books read in unison, aloud, to stare outside, saw me. Early winter sun. Each day new vistas become possible, yesterday's earlobe, today's toenail, a radio on a mantel one had forgotten to think of, a flashlight. Videography. Would pour pigment directly on canvas, then manipulate that. Weight of sleep still heavy in flesh of face. Interest is something you impose. It may be a form of semiotic analysis, whose validity does not depend solely on the multi-permutations of application but on the interrelated observance of the field of propositional formats. Endless possibility, drifting from campus to campus, hanging out. Never fear, chandelier. Cohn's loans. The hair in nostril or ear. So muggy it seemed there was no oxygen in the air, how was it the cigar burned. Since there is a term "poem," many assume there is an entity "poem." Television in the 1950s. Demonstration forest ahead. The mountains, more by darkness visible and their own size. Scrawl. Could you trace this to its source, particular, iridescent, useful only as it disappears. No reason to have read this, to read it now. Lone Star Hotel. Painter as banker or bandit. An harbor, Ann Arbor. Assertions, substantives, attributes, relations. Evolution of the mailbox, professionalism of cops. Soft tones, light tunes, late in the day's air. The poem as long as California, or summer. The notion of significant sequence versus the notion of synonymy. Until I myself became trapped in the Bermuda Triangle of the heart. Marsupial. Technographic typography. Because it is not normal, this text is apt to be art, tho abnormality is not a prior condition for art, tho there is a tradition of abnormal texts as art into which this text might normally fit. A calculated refusal to perform the normal chores of verse. The "what" is an achievement term. From the barracks of the Wilcox Mansion, where he took the oath, saw only the offices of doctors. Seasick sea serpent. Xylophones. Think of you in terms of masses evolving and erupting, reshaping yourselves, succeeding one another and vanishing. Mountain View Cemetery equal to Central Park. One hears in reality only aggregations of terms at various registers, tangled lines whose macroscopic effect is that of an unreasoned and fortuitous dispersion of meanings throughout the entire frequency spectrum, mere surface and mass, a contradiction inherent in the polyphony which will disappear as soon as the words become totally independent. A kick in the coccyx for good luck. Stochastic, apocalystatic. The way the open hands hang limp at the wrists and the elbows swing out when he runs. Day of thick sun in late September. This day's reaches feature peaches. A walkway, which arches over several systems of roadway, from which a broad view of the city's backbrain. That jay imitates the cricket. Looking back from rock atop water, I could see how boats clustered below the bridge, few willing to leave the sanctuary of the bay. Silverfish, potato bugs. A large, hot-air balloon had drifted over the central part of the city, shadow passing over canyons of the financial district. From the veranda of a mansion above the Russian River, I first heard this music. In the tapestry, animals called ferrets chase the rabbits into small, peasant nets. Everybody balls everybody, eventually, and nothing changes. At the edge of October. Wept, swept, slept. A room of tabletops. Deliberate sentimentalism perceived as description. I'm tremblin' for my boy, tremblin', tremblin' for a lot of things I can't control. Dense red meat. No individual sentence given particular attention. Calling out, as though after a large dog. Stumbled, the two of them, out of the bar, one of them face and hand already cut, the other continuing cutting. Antelope bites, watermelon fever. The wall is cooler than the floor. His friend forgot her sandals. Full moon in the morning. There the drab girl sat, hair dryer in her lap, awaiting the airport limousine. At times thought these cuts he gave himself, shaving, were intentional. The map is not the territory. Generally speaking, what does it mean, not being able to continue thinking a certain thought. Does it contradict action. Fried knuckle crimes. Tiger balm. Patched in just to alter Tibetan bells. Sheet lightning in Michigan hills. To change the wave shape or size of the window. Man on the bus, scavenger, sips cough medicine. Woke to find mice in my hair, scurriers. Of speed as experience, gobbled space. Varieties of pretrial detention. We stopped for hot chocolate topped with whipped cream, and to discuss the Sicilian Defense. Days of doors. Motion is a vertical disorder. Under the cuticle, below layers of thumbnail. Acres wake, bugs of the soil shivering about their business, day's light precedes heat. First rain of winter woke me, sound of water on the sill. The nice man. Wanted to compare psychological profiles of those on the train who read facing forward versus those who sat facing the rear. A book of short poems to be called Spare Parts. Thought becoming troubled as it contemplates itself and jettisons its most familiar forms. The private lives of kindergarten teachers, a party about the clubhouse of an apartment complex, one who by the pool shows the young woman an appropriate way to drive a golf ball, or strangers stare confusedly at the sauna, read instructions, implies to the stranger, engaged now in a contest of pocket billiards, chalking his cue in that harder light, high beamed ceiling, aligning in the mind ball to pocket, a world of repose, of a stasis that includes activity, sailboats decked in a garage, as, what is the word, he can't find it, as something as the light which each night is turned upon the garden. Where is JFK's brain. Yonder. The comparison of measurement and that of order. History is not a good bourgeois. The absolute character in what is simple concerns not the being of things but rather the manner in which they can be known. The odor in towels, the oil in skin. Write this down in a red notebook. Repressed behavior, a small grin upon gin and tonic. Permit me to speak evil. Exorcise your monkey. This sentence is a mute mark. The abruptness of seafood. Because the mind analyses, the sign appears. Early morning mental system. At dawn in the eucalyptus grove I watched him perform sequences of the martial arts. Doors here are more complex, framed panes of glass interlocking with one of wire mesh. Panhandle. The poem as a form sensed prior to the writing, as the act thereof, as a text fixed upon paper, as the act of reading, as the memory of any of the above. The fine, sharp rim of autumn. The usual dead people most parents are. Liked to walk thru the glade just as the fog burned off, because of that particular, diffused light. The tenor sax is a weapon. Gradually the absence of milk truck routes. Our lives in the mineral world. We sing tonight of the Wipe-Out gang. Posits of new information not like cars recently attached to a train, but like memory, embedded in the presences. You presuppose a determinate form in our consciousness. Pleistocene statements. Meaning cannot be more than the totality of signs arranged in their progression. We stood or sat on the deck, breaking oranges into slices, watching the four-masted prison ship cross the bay. The mechanics of image in time. A tractor necessary to care for this lawn. Blood blister. Her sense of the distance within families is American, but beyond that, Chinese. Green urine. The beginnings of a new phenomenology of assembling. Certain dreams, because they purge deep illusions, bring great rest. Linoleum story. Thunder is real. Void in, void out. One seeks for the middle point, where the object is the reality of the intention, knowing the intention to be the reality of the object. Men eating burgers in silence, at a drugstore counter, wearing t-shirts and short hair, staring at their food. Do not piss in the sink. Greased lady. This city has different systems. Bob's bitter days. It was not language as definition but language as language, a larger circle. The last dance, the end of dancing. I rode with Ocean in the back of the truck. The bottle of white wine is empty. How can you hope to penetrate personal style. The eyes, forced to focus. Porkpie hat. The Main Library was a grey weight in a white rain. Swollen fingers. Against the hearth leans a line drawing framed in glass, in which the apple tree with its too-small fruit is reflected, whipped by what must soon become rain. Tho I left the bus my umbrella continued the journey. He sat under the kitchen table, writing furiously into a notebook every word we said, Emily scolding,

the bright light of a bare bulb on dark-painted walls, the Kelly
green fridge, the rest of us drinking or smoking dope, but it was
his kitchen. Tally. The competition of these realities, as tho any
of us were of a mobile, spinning, each point the view in a rotating
geometry. The day's claims decline in winter. What is to be taken
as no information, decisions made each time we cross the street.
Beginning to notice the bathroom habits of your new friend. Gradu-
ally these pages fill, an intentionality like moss. The existence of
language is both obvious and unobtrusive. Mucous membrane.
Her eyes wide with indignation. Cool clouded sanity. She sat in
the car in the shut garage, letting its engine run. The knot is not
the rope. Tenth day of October. Amelia naps. Truth, precision,
appropriateness. The signs sing. The seriousness and quiet in the
eyes of people who ride the bus to work. The afternoon curls about
me or I wrap myself in it, folds of attention aired with movement
to a pot of coffee or the john. This is to thought and signs as alge-
bra to geometry. Lots of exercise, little thought. Green slugs in
grass, cut by the mower. Twang in the rope, what holds the new
apple tree to such wind as this. Words I lost because I did not write
them down soon enough. These roofs, their angles, give the hill
texture, houses packed tight, cramped yards, kids on porches, dog
growls, mowers, yelps, web of clothesline. The chair at my desk
after years gave out, which now creates a tension whenever I sit
in this new one, dual expectations as to the seat I'll find, the body
progressively taken by gravity, instant of fear until the sensations
resolve. Eye as sponge to day's light. The work in thought, progres-
sive labor. What I want is the grey-blue grain of western summer.
Years over the hot plate, making breakfast before dawn. Attempted
to confront her explosion at such arrogance, but did not, could not,

transfer the smell, the mould in the meat about whoever might ski
or skate, that she herself was so circled by. This sequence presents
simultaneity. Yellow beach, pink sky, pink beach, yellow sky.
This alphabet of the ants. Eye is spine. Interior of time, exterior
of speech. Sea cucumber. Rat-like function of wild dogs in a ghetto.
Air more active, clouds piling, folding into themselves, rolling.
Talking to her on the phone when what you would really like
to do is to ball her. Burma shave parataxis. I got up before dawn
and went to the park. Who needs not a lover but a tennis partner.
Aerial perception of traffic flow. In the beach night, campfires lit up
the city of dune buggies, surfboards pitched vertically into the sand,
a presence as of clan shields. Liked to sit in the glade and practice
his trumpet. As if those words not written remained locked in ink.
Familiar odor of the dentist's. How the press of information, that
first time you walk down a new street, cannot be repeated. There
is only the verb "to be." Quills and crackers, jewels or miracles.
The words will have more force if you use a Crayola. One could
propose, for example, the inclusion of anything. Extraordinary
mouth session. Cigar-shaped art object would hover near the high-
way then quickly fly away. These words scare me to write them.
With such attention the mind can follow the act of her washing
in the next room, it knows hands from neck from cheeks. I have
a time problem. Haul ass, kitten. Existence is an attribute. Subtitles
lower your focus. White tribe, the golfers migrate up the slope.
Such, of. She liked to lower herself on top of him. The first person
to remove himself, as Zukofsky debuted Reich's Violin Phase to
the west, Mario Savio. Palace of the Legion of Honor. Yoyo's alibi,
the way back. Balling on the beach, as tho there are some places
so public one's privacy is not questioned. Old sentences heard new

carry a different purpose. The eaters of wheat. Weight in the line. Gulleys really, pathways that trickled down the side of the cliff, down which they half climbed, half slid, to arrive at a beach of large rounded rocks, there to spread out a big towel and slip out of their clothes, sails only at a great distance, not even gulls to disturb them. Rhodochrosite, tourmaline. Conjugations of the word, we say, as tho any term were not single but a complex. Motor city farewell. Sentences sent hence. You wake in waves, each new day's small tides of attention. Secret joy at the little residual pains of exertion, segments of muscle that declare themselves newly aware. The road, the rug, fading dawn moon. Empty milk carton in which to place a wick, then cubes of ice, over which to pour hot wax, becomes at last a candle by which to write of art of the 1960s. Analysanda and their analysantia. To circumambulate the planet on my exercycle. A field of corn, green, in a plain of dry grass. Sweet wake-up. Such poems are like keystones in need of a monument. This life, crude rotation. Learn the art of seizing control. Dawn's brink. Barnwood ash. Need in the abstract. They live in condos. Crime against nature. Mention sex, fruit, candy, exchange value, cities, securities, books, the wheel, the cinema, land forms, sky. To be eaten by the sentimentality of your own situation. Water towers with happy faces. There are a thousand threads of forward motion in the social explosion of our times, a thousand threads to untangle and engage. The air in its fair layers. It means recognizing that revolution is a lifetime of fighting and transformation, a risky business and ultimately a decisive struggle against the forces of death. Jet trails between clouds would disperse. There was a connection between geography and character. Necrotizing laryngo-tracheobronchitis, consequent of a chemical irritant, CS. Here you have a dichotomous key. Not the sick, strict, slick legalisms. Some combine of algae and fungus. Employment gainful of what. Allied gardens. Iowa clay, that slight planes do sculpt place, the red west horizon bearing night. Helicopter hovered over backyards. Glossed lines. Listening to the record repeatedly until I learn it. I am meat in motion only, all other is construct, Pinto going west. Write now in the dark. Special weapons and tactics. A state of identity instead of entity. The signifier is empty, the sign is full. When the moon goes down, it comes up again behind my eyes. Passed ball. One's fate, to rise late. Eroded mesa. Cloudy urine. Weary of waking, talking, faking it. A kick in the brain brings rain. Night rodeo. It was then that my real work began. Drip candles kept atop old, empty wine bottles, a canister full of pennies. A bath. Mountain lightning. Hobo, so-called, possibly drunk, had fallen from the train. The strictures against propositions apply with equal force to attributes and relations. For whom all music was eventually an extension of percussion. A man who lurched suddenly toward us on the road, his hair caked with blood. A return to standard time. Tuesday noon. Southpaw and a flake. Somehow fog on the desert floor. Bones in my hand. Nails that glow in burning wood. Warm early autumn. Myth is a language. A bar into which come women who wish to sing opera. A clock talks ticking. A long correspondence begun over why had I not yet received my subscription. In Great Salt Desert one is the vertical, located. A thing you had not expected to find. From what they did, he will not recover. Sudden as the change in governments. Morning moon over mountains. The form is too clear. Eggshells in the flower bed for the calcium. This is the fifth meaning of glass. The road, a line, to define the canvas. Amazed to find all that sand in her crotch. Consumption of wood by fire. Desire to spite. Because my name is lion. An argument over kitchen tile. The young nurse in blue sunglasses, by a subtle redistribution of weight, shift of gravity's center, moves in front of the black lanky graduate student of oriental porcelain in order to more rapidly board the bus, before all of the seats are taken. Big black desk. Watched, each day as we traveled west, the moon dissolve. A year in the white room. Three days of July rain. Memory of brick was the midwest. Reassert older orders. Causality. Mould forms in old coffee. Standard images, feet in the ceiling, etc. The bells return. Two ducks rock in. As the heat of the hand will draw the leaves up to it, so thought's pressure folds the flower. The words on the page age. Andy has leukemia, needs blood. A previously specified rate of words per minute. The urinary habits of Dr. Williams. A pattern of speech elsewhere in the house which could only have come from the television. The flat was empty, the lights on, dishes in the sink, books about the floor, the shower torn to pieces. It is not the night which tires. You thought somehow to copy Rodia not having seen the work. Then Berkeley had become the past. Today's embraces. A hot piroshki smothered in sour cream. Traits of verbal form do not extend to their objects. The collected works of Elmer Fudd. The white room, as you waken, begins to fill with the objects of perception, open suitcase, rumpled blankets, etc., events in discrete sequence, the chair, table, stereo, until, the world nearly completed, they begin to cohere, come into focus, new form, not as individuals, but each in relation, one to the other. The bottom line. Leaving out. Art of the buzz word. Blood bank. Benefit balances obligation. Are pears form. Hair soup. The uncomplicated tyranny of punctuation, the residual aspect of print, to fix spelling, phuque it. Each day now the late sun later. Thursday dawn. Sample, esample, example.

Mobile of leaves called a tree. To constitute a number of perfect
and exhaustive series, of absolutely continuous chains in which
the breaks, if any, indicate the place of a word, dialect, or language
no longer there. Tumor press on the optic chiasma. Modifications
of form obey no rule, are more or less endless, never stable. Through
misuse arrive at important information. Constants of the left hand,
tiger's eye ring, watch with a gold band. Mouthful of crab meat.
Cold weather encourages unvoiced labials. You knew, you were
certain, you were sure. Synecdoche, metonymy, catachresis. Summer
morning foghorn. Mock-up of process. Fool's toes. The watering
down of the dark. The light caught in the gauzy curtain, beyond
which the terrace and city of verticals. Exactly in that fold of words
where analysis and space meet. There is a hand here. Bay, corroding
in the sunlight. Heard "my ancestors" as "Hawaiian sisters." Paw
to mean cat, chimney house, terms flooded by the possibility of
objects, whisker cat, window house. I think that I know that I
think, etc., infinite regression. Question of changing chairs each
time I write a sentence. Wine glasses in rows, in a cabinet. Room
with two many doors. Provisional existence of the external world.
Within the bulb, threads of light. Awake, but still in bed, I listen to
cars pass, doors, birds, children are day's first voices. Skyport drive.
The poem is all that is the case. The wall is all yellow rock. Mole
on her ass, or prefer to call it butt. From time to time the arteries
of one of the three judges would soften, and he would lean forward
to ask the attorney a question. To demonstrate the hand, prove
the existence of fingers, possibly, or Saturn, pain, roundness. Nomi-
nation differentiates, predication connects. From under the eave
pigeons pour. Optical conduit. Doubt about existence works only
in a language game. Surveillance by starlight. Watercress. Drainage.

What use is a rule here. Weeks of litmus weather linger. Surrogate
information. We would set card tables and great cartons up in the
living room, covering them with blankets, then go under, journey
to the center of the earth. One has to keep reminding oneself of
the unimportance of the inner process or state. A room which by
design, low ceiling, bad ventilation, causes sleep. The great seagull
would have come inside but my mother went at it with a broom.
Artifice of cereal. Necessitation and contingency. Fad to have your
ears cropped. That content does not intrude. Everything written
according to the rule of the infield fly. Troll bridge. Neon arrow
posit. Residue of sinus condition. Nails hats to the wall. Eventually
the scratches become scabs. Inverted nipple. Random sample. Walk-
ing each day through the business district, select a facet on which to
fix attention, displays of white loafers, calendars at half price, clocks
on coffee shop walls, given by such variation a formal perception.
The brown paint yellows. Bruised cock. The end of the freeway in
the middle of the country. The work of a not-large shy man. It'll
keep your ego going for a few days. On a warm night, browsing
from bookstore to bookstore, wandering from cafe to tavern to
cafe, the conversation of women and men was the life I'd imagined.
You could start almost anywhere and find anything. The fear of
dogs. On Treat Street. The so-called "woman of my friend" with
whom I half intend to sleep. Signification extends the sign. Lesbian
drill. Rattle of water in pipes. Large or small definition. Architect,
schoolteacher, poet, the trio wandered through Old Town, sobered
by the evident despair. The back alleys above Chinatown, the deep
basements, which, to look into, reveal pool rooms, old men on
benches along the wall. As classes to attributes, ordered pairs to
relations. Saw, not being seen, the man who did not like me place

a brown briefcase, labeled "man in the green raincoat," in the dumpster, then walk back into the twilight, while we got to the material before his contact did. A vocabulary for grammar school lacking verbs of change. You know the style, you know the type, you know the scam, you know the hype. We cannot in conscience blame these varied sources of modality on the notion of analyticity. Eagle of the czar, with two open beaks. In a room, on a warm night, music on, over voices, a spoon scrapes a pot. I smoke the cigar slowly, knowing that when I am done I will be ready to shit. Head-hunter. Anacoluthia. A cardboard box of wool sweaters on top of the bookcase to indicate Home. Car cap. We link together our various perceptual spaces whose contents vary from person to person and from time to time, as parts of one public spacio-temporal order. Exercise by lifting volumes of the "compact" OED. Bob takes Barry to the airport. Preparation H. The ignorance surface from North Dakota. Canker. Kids who ride shopping carts down the street. Nothing is like erasure. The confusion matrix, the travel field. A chart where in blue women serve more time for narcotics than murder. The form I saw in South Orange Sonnets. A band over where damage begins to occur. Ecumeniopolis. As sleep distributes thought. Broken shoelace. A year in each place. Desire to replicate speech as thought is silly, great grinding hum of language in head. A life top. Fatal framer. The Popular Resistance Movement is organized into clandestine groups, based among workers, peasants, students, pobledores (the urban poor), women, soldiers, and sectors of the small bourgeoisie, who, because of the oppressive regime, must work and meet secretly, whose tasks include preparing the conditions for a long and difficult people's war, giving it a social base as extensive as possible among the people, a struggle against the dictatorship on all levels, a struggle for proletarian revolution. Would play a piano on the beach. A series having no beginning and no end as its condition of form. Sentences do not designate. Transmutations and sublimations of content are creative processes toward the containment of larger wholes of experience, radically different in their preservation of elements and forces at work in the realization of a formal order from the mechanisms of repression and exclusion of feelings and ideas from the social consciousness that were practiced in the self-discipline of middle-class education. The octoroon, the octillion. Waking into a state of anxiety, without specific object. The signifier of myth presents itself in an ambiguous way. Folds of foreskin. Insert opaque erotic data, stimulate focus. Fever blister. Would put a lit match to his thumbnail, because he liked the smell. A wall or row of bricks leading from the continent, per se, to the large rock, along which two men will roll a huge white wheel, themselves dressed in white, half of each face painted white, trailed and watched over by half-interested angels of videography, making art. Bedlingtons, first meant to hunt rats in coal mines, later bred to show, are nearly blind and crazy. Sitting idly as you will, hand absently on crotch. Phantom Czechoslovak. Flaw permitted to remain for specific aesthetic reasons, or perhaps intentionally inserted. This this this this. Sense data scraping wall of eye. This is here if you think it is. Criticism, like history, is a form of fiction. Urban bourbon. For faculties of the imagination, conditions of tenure. If I am in a car and look through the window at the scenery, I can, at will, look at the countryside or the pane, and, if at the latter, at other worlds reflected there, the view, say, from a window on the far side, a small town lodged on the hillside. Rainday at the rainday. Neither present nor past hold for you the attractive indeterminacy of the future, the elaborate half-finished contraption of the yacht in the yard, tho you live in an apartment, waking from the sweating nightmare of hair starting to grow on all the walls and the great sound of breathing. Because last night as I was about to go to sleep I thought of words to add to this but did not write them down, I have lost them, using these instead to hold their place. There is no myth without motivated form. Writing, while riding under the bay. Caffeine enjambment of the nervous system. The division, so evident to us, between what we see, what others have observed and handed down, and what others imagine or naïvely believe, the great tripartition, apparently so simple and so immediate, into observation, document, and fable, did not exist. It is a speech justified in excess. Things touch against the banks of discourse because they appear in the hollow space of representation. Gross national poet. Very like the way things do do. Why, over a valley this size, the white-grey sky becomes a great dome. Shit from Shinola. Chinese fire drill. Celebrity fuck. This sentence is not what I intended. Turtle feast. Folds her toilet paper into perfect squares. Sorting out the remains of the babies. It was a language robbery. Butch beyond belief. Attention is all. Changes in the weight of water per unit. The language is never anything but a system of forms, and the meaning is a form. Tender summer nights of race war, cities as though candles to read by. Older music. The market allocation of labor resources according to profit criteria. The net, the fog, two alphabets. Fluster threshold. Writing the white lines. The moon is in the penthouse too. Mathematics is a finished language, deriving its perfection from this acceptance of death. The silent world is our only homeland. Earliest imaginings of the married life, the chiropractor's daughter doing dishes. Dissolving body. Drums under water. Farming my face, rake of razor. Varieties of helicopter filled the sky. In winter these streets turn to drains. A kind of spatial, tangible analogue of silence. Friends are fragged, who went off to gink the dinks, enough to make you think again. Marjorie Daw. I woke in the doss-house. Give historical intention a natural justification, make contingency appear eternal. In the early morning drizzle, stand on the deck, watching heat and smoke rise from the hillside of chimneys. Fucked in the head. King Kong died for your sins. If you have an interest in the page, say, as a form of preservation. You use, she said, rising up from the bed angry, sex as a weapon. He does not write so much as his impatience does. Too monotonous and numerous. Essence and scale. Collections of disconnected items arranged in patterns. He knew how to hold an adz, to till. Think of page as timber line. Between reality and men, between description and explanation, between object and knowledge. By fooling the bees into thinking the hive is afire, so that they will suck honey up, gesture of salvage attempted, so that they become fat and sluggish, unable to assault the gloved hand which reaches in. This sort of sentence. In the middle of a blow job, she puked. Identify the assumptions, define them. Liked to go to some coffee house near campus for breakfast, the streets still empty, this small city finally perceived as space. Always, across the bay, there was Oakland. The drones will not even sting. Political because it must be, but at what level. Big German shepherd they locked permanently into a small box in the backyard. The playground north of the coffee plant roils with soccer, kites, sunbathers. Useless. All good ideas are simple. Morning, illusion. Because acclimation is not conscious, we shuffle about in circles, in hot rooms with the windows shut, becoming gradually heavier, weighted and

slower, until finally we begin to discard, to shed, to toss off, panama
hat, white blazer with wide lapel, cufflinks, black brocade shirt
and white silk tie, until we stand, arms "akimbo," in white cuffed
flares, see-thru net tee shirt, feet wrapped in sandals. Scars about
the breast. If it needs more than one performer, that's an ideology,
or equipment, that's another. What it would feel like, poem as real
as life. Compared to, say, Chile, where Santiago's higher elevations
support the poor. In memory of Emmett Till. Rumor that R beat
one performer up, so that others left in protest. Writing became
a form of self-mutilation. E is for Edgar. The ever more complete
preservation of what was written, the establishment of archives,
then of filing systems for them, the reorganization of libraries, the
drawing up of catalogs, indexes and inventories, all these things
represent not so much a sensitivity to time, to its past, to the density
of history, as a way of introducing into the language already im-
printed on things, and into the traces it has left, an order of the same
type as that which was being established between living creatures.
Entangled in a language, whose syntax leads you to multiple murder,
political kidnap or an ashram in Colorado. Eating Life Savers for
breakfast. Theoretical framework for pudding. Murder of crows,
drift of hogs. Our colonies are the last proletariat. Face of an astro-
naut painted on a plate in the window of a hardware store, next
to a small plastic flag. A day of rain in the middle of June. Finding
fortune's finals. This sentence in August. Living with friends v. liv-
ing with strangers. This is the alphabet. Dream in which I become
weightless, float off the planet, such as a balloon let go, is the most
common, familiar places seen from great heights. These are the trees.
Forms of anticipation. Friday night. Four of us gather to talk on
the radio from midnight to six. A cigar purchased in Vera Cruz,

but smoked in Windsor. This will be the hill poem. The Ferris wheel. Map of Juan de la Cosa in a garage sale for 25 cents. Prepare to turn this record over. Your syntax is a life sentence. How could one ever hope to have known prose. Alva's song, backed with supply and demand. The hidden assumption is that once the novel lived. Time paranoid. So that it rains light. Third day of November. Adoration of my own two feet. Half proud, the next morning, of the scratch marks on my back. The intensionalism of crewcuts. These terms filter the visible. Single string of the marine trumpet. Carrot cake, late in a cafe, place to wait. Shopper's world, a whole store for quilts. Made skulls out of sugar for the occasion. Film of each of eighty victims, over Tubular Bells, called news. Responsible fear of police. The gamelan is not simple. Specific set of high school girls which is attracted to glitter boys. Who first refined petrol. Man who paused a long while at the coffee house door, staring in. That one could become a cop, to enforce the laws partially, the Highway Patrol. From derivation to articulation, from origin to proposition, through name. Magnetic tape to Patty Hearst, to Richard Nixon. Able to leave art space. Brushing the drums. Frames of fame. The dawn light is before us, let us rise up and act. Elaborate system of codes, neckerchiefs for fistfuckers, each pocket has a meaning, key chains, watchbands. Thought as a boy to swallow all seeds, that the tree in the belly could become one. Aphorisms block out thought. The death of heat is the birth of steam. Information is a commodity. Great urge to sneeze, mouth full of banana. You are ankle, elbow, ear, eye. But the grass spider eats only violets. The under-chatter of waiters. A mouse's fear of a cat is counted as his fearing true a certain English sentence. Grab bag sans form, as form by a trick of process, cheap. They control insects and enemies of the trout.

Failure to comprehend mass organization. You sap. Thermocouple. If we imagine the facts otherwise than what they are, certain language games lose some of their importance, while others become important. Do you remember this. Butterflies churn the air. Aldermaston sign. The meaning of a word like the function of an official. Crying like a fire in the sun. Modal rounders. A car idles outside these closed curtains. One could be wrong intentionally, but without deceit. Fire in the Korean discotheque. The sharp shadows of a low sun, the light smack against the white house-fronts. Although on a leash, the boy was articulate, hostile, polite. Each day there's the bridge. Respectable as an old junkie. Every word is either current, or strange, or metaphorical, or ornamental, or newly coined, or lengthened, or contracted, or altered. Wiggled two fingers deep in her cunt. The salute of the fireboats. Accidental proposition. Weathercock, scrimshaw. This shuts anything not included out. Panama Exposition. Suppression of the death of Trigger, or possibly Bebe Rebozo. Between the television and the bed was an ironing board, half-finished bottles of lager atop it. Not able to determine whether his fear of permanent loss was a fear more of permanence or of loss. Throttle's glottal stop. The seagull had made its home on our porch. When, looking out the window, you no longer see what's there, it's time to move. Fireplaces at work in several rooms, Franklin stove, coffee, the ritual smell of toast. Not every false belief is a mistake. Teeming continuity of beings, all communicating with one another, mingling with one another, perhaps being transformed into one another. Narwhale, I confront you. As the prow of our boat divides the night, the lights of the city of San Francisco begin to loom up before us. The quick brown fox jumped over the lazy revisionist running dog. Such ships are cities at sea. The gallery was a labyrinth of white rooms with skylights, small words drawn in blue pencil, one to a wall, thru which and before which strolled the art consumers, gazing, chewing in an idle way on the earpieces of their sunglasses, paying no attention to the one red hard-backed chair in each room, presumably for their convenience or that of the occasional elderly lady, accompanying a college-age granddaughter, which were the true objects of the show. Passing by the kitchen of a restaurant, brisk autumn night, I hear the clatter of knives and forks. Implicitly or explicitly, all environmental planning and action reflects a particular view of society and the groups that compose it. I sat atop the fountain, which, at midnight, was shut off, all concrete and pools of still water. A sequence of objects, silhouettes, which to him appears to be a caravan of fellaheen, a circus, drome-daries pulling wagons bearing tiger cages, fringed surreys, tamed ostriches in toy hats, begins a slow migration to the right vanishing point, signified by a palm tree on the horizon. Words I wrote in the control room of the Pacific Rim. Here is Spain, that is Africa, this is the water. Half haunted, it seemed, to walk so briskly, aimlessly, changing directions many times, sitting on a bench or stoop every few blocks to scrawl words in a notebook. Small boy shouts at the dog, insistent, scolding. See his veins as doors. A teller, she said of him, of moral tales. First trace of day, glow at the horizon, began to appear. Refuse connectedness. Each of us has wanted to ball the other for weeks now, but we have to arrange it. Music for marim-bas, voice and organ. Odor of onion remained for days. I hear the hose in the tomato plants. My teeth like the ruins of a great wall. What duration does to the meaning of any word. In the days of pre-methadone, of pre-heroin, of pre-pills, in the days of habit. I want to tell you tales of lint. The dog on the stairs, its growl low and serious, forms a test. Clapping music. Songs of the upstairs neighbor. Feeling my fingernail bend back, pushing it against my front tooth, to signal thought. Morning of the frills. All research is so set as to exempt certain propositions from doubt. What is meant is use. Smashed watermelon sidewalk. The clarity of winter morning. A belief is what it is whether it has any practical effects or not. Mental wilderness area, language game preserve. A park upon a hilltop, below which the city, its hills and verticals jammed together, and beyond that not the bay but the hills on the far side, as though near, brown now in August with a light sky, rippling planet crust. Given arrangement of objects or facts grouped to-gether according to certain given conventions or resemblances, which one expresses by a general notion applicable to all those objects, without, however, regarding that fundamental notion or principle as absolute or invariable, or as so general that it cannot suffer any exception. How do I verify the imagination. The clouds roil about the mountain. Slag iron. The doorknob which constantly falls from the door. As tho each bus route was a specific syntax. As opposed to the Academics, for whom revision itself is the form of process. Asleep in the sun is all peace there is. I slept well and rose early, reading two small books before breakfast. Why should not a king be brought up with the belief that the world began with him. The police began to shoot directly into the library. Then we found the testes in the scrotal sac. It is one thing to understand that your friend has a husband, another to sit at their table, forced to sit still, say nothing, when he nags and bickers. The proposition that you have spent your whole life in close proximity to the earth. We knocked over trash cans, dragged sawhorses, to barricade the street. How in the still air the sudden assertion of auto brakes, heard, calls into mind a trumpet. *Italophile.* Whose boats dwell in the bay. When the lightbulb blew in the john, it took weeks to replace it, as if my roommate and I held a silent contest, to see who would be forced first into buying a new bulb. Unable to read a book for any great length of time, for to abandon himself thus threatened him. How as a child, I knew the interior structure of every bush on the block. I did not get my picture of the world by satisfying myself of its correctness. Why these lines, by mere convention, accumulate to form meaning. A big she St. Bernard. Thirty thousand words. The truths of which he says he knows are such as all of us know, if he knows them. Dog would scratch at the door for hours. Sad dream of gas pain. Copper bracelet, vitamin C. My convictions do form a system. A carpenter's work is seasonal. Not asleep, I lay in the grass, still, while the ladybug crossed my chest. A thin field of wild-flowers comes up in Death Valley, yellow or violet, and dies in three weeks. I don't make the language, I enforce it. What I heard, as I stood at the Pacific, was not the waves, but blood in my veins, and current in my nervous system. The power implicit within the ability to draw a single, vertical straight line. The sun rose up above sand dunes. Thousands lavishing, thousands starving, intrigues, wars, flatteries, envyings, hypocrisies, lying vanities, hollow amusements, exhaustion, dissipation, death. Good morning, scarecrow. Presences I thought dust in the air came closer now, had wings to move them. Stepping out on flagrant street. Twenty loose sheets of lined fools-cap, undated. Art is a mirage. Opposed to the image. Beautiful red twine binding of a Chinese notebook. I am for example also con-vinced that the sun is not a hole in the vault of heaven. Change in the weather, change in my head. The hill would fill with people bathing in the sun. Solo piano on a winter morning. Climate replaces weather. Mitigations. This posit is not altogether the philosopher's doing. A dream of fever. Laundry boat. Image, afterimage, aura. Of all these faces seen as spaces, which are you. Olfaction. No one ever taught me that my hands don't disappear when I am not paying attention to them. Theory of the mark, theory of the organism. Small kids swarm the porch. A requirement that nature should be continuous. Display of the corpse of Che Guevara as bourgeois sculpture. Learning to face personal space. Knowing it changes it. Walking into a strange household with the assumption that one would not propose to live there. Solitary line of a sea lute. The coast, which is said to have no seasons, tho it does when you look closer. That was when my nose began to peel. These rather beautiful designs failed. Blue genes. The geometry of the carpet. Straw flowers. Chrome. This is an exhibit for the prosecution. Network against psychiatric assault. Axiology, or Value Systems I have seen. A will of sorts tattooed to the calf, which read My last request is to burn this leg. Talking heads of television. Between the fabric of taxonomy and the line of revolutions. A world of routines, of returns to small forms, insistently. A black evangelist was sewed up inside a tom-tom and starved to death while drummers pounded incessantly on the skin top. As astronauts enter the outer air. But "it moves" everywhere. Get aboard. Pale light in the skylight. Symbols cramp the temple. Standard deviation. It was a summer of few hot nights. Rhythm section of the Horns of the Dilemma. Zoo caw caw of the sky. Games of either/or. Time was real to him, but not linear, more a sensation of gravity, of falling from some precipice forward until, thousands of feet above the valley floor with its chalked concentric circles, acceleration approximated weightlessness. Monsters and fossils. Garbage mind pearl diver. Chrysalis. It was his smaller toes that hurt. The clock in the closet. Wittgenstein and the moon. The algebra of the fish. Viddy that white room, filled with fleshy babies. Continuity precedes time, is its condition. Attempt, between poems, to be charming. Rice balls. The words, as in a boat, float. History can no longer be of any other order than that of resemblance. Any project large enough to capsize. Tiger's eye. Peach pits. The monster is the root-stock of specification. Endless intimate detail ultimately bores. In this region we now term life. Driving freeway over San Bruno mountains in night fog, exhaustion registering in the body as force, pressure, partial "G." This is the zone. Words, where you are, as in a trail, not forest but thicket, pine needle modifiers, shingles of a pine cone on which to focus, but syntax, syntax was the half-light. The more the worker expends himself in the work the more powerful becomes the world of objects which he creates in fact of himself, the poorer he becomes in his inner life, and the less he belongs to himself. Point of transfer. Paper treated chemically so as to alter perception. The abnormal mind is quick to detect and attach itself to this quality. Chance of light rain. Tenderness in that wicked man. Snail flower woman star. Grandfather robed in white, horizontal in grey-green shadows of Intensive Care, would not look up, tubes in nose, waiting. Days in which I replace the faces. When, as I hunkered down to overturn the small shells, shaking sand off, she asked what it was, I said, "Looking for the good ones." I amble in, sit awhile, then exit. Is this winter or is this morning. Certain houses where the kitchen is the gathering place. Short glass of tequila. Entering, speaking rapidly from the first, of what it would be like to become a part of your lives. Personality is an unbroken series of successful gestures. Mole, deep in geologies of the tongue.

Tall glass of tawny port. Association a prior condition of dispersal. Glide on through the sea change of faces and voices and color. He will reach over slowly and contemplate long before picking it up, his nerves are so shot. Headlights, streetlights, lit living rooms. Total calculation. Ideological basis of sleep. She loves to give head. A pleasure and discomfort in the knowledge of having become, by the fact of your absence, the focal point. In the final days of the war, the weariness falls away, one's friends begin to move about with a new vigor of anticipation, start to formulate new projects. Blond body hair. By the time each of these guys "achieves his life in literature" he will be some kind of case. Borate bomber's song. In the final folds of a year in the middle of a decade you were here, warm indoors, though never precisely thoroughly at home. Hyperventilation. Grim and Barrett. Shadows between houses leave earth cool and damp. Facing up to this. Molding my senselessness into forms. The patter of basketball described. A scaffold around light. The so-called lady bartender. The last hot day of summer. Mushrooms fried in garlic. Retina burn. Named the child Alyosha. There is no confusion like the confusion of a simple mind. Immediate constituents. A tooth gone in the root. How was it you came to live this life. Suffering succotash. Sweet cigar. A slick gaggle of ambassadors. A certain winter grey that translates readily into depression. The flat black hills beyond which summer's form, the sun, would rise. Three tattered notebooks. Tension manager's domain. Will I move to New York. The city is a thing mingled. A visit with parents. Astronauts holding hands, adrift in the sky. Against a reconstituted theory of the metaphor. There is no content here, only dailiness, the driver education car poised in the intersection by the playground, around which a jogger orbits, all in the hill's shadow at sunset. Pending sense of panic. Caves of the tuna. Later, memory of odor of the coffee plant will bring this back. Bowl in which map of world was etched. As each new sack, parcel of information, was cut open, its contents spilled onto the conveyor belt, the foreman would announce it by blowing on a conch shell. We ate them. This is before we knew of Cointelpro. Couple at the next table, over coffee, discuss power relations of their home. The tenor sax is a phallus or cross. Each ear pierced in four places. These auxiliary activities are not the thinking, but one imagines thinking as the stream which must be flowing under the surface of these expedients, if they are not after all to be mere mechanical procedures. Question of sexuality. If it were to be explained simply, would it be any more clear. The flag. Concern with what we say has its own specific signs. I told him I was tired, bored by sense of his misuse, my voice the line drawn. Stubborn as a mule, sir, stubborn as a mule. Log fort. How then can the sense and the truth or the truth and the sense of sentences collapse together. As map could expand beyond the margin. It was the voice of Big Black, "Awake, for nothing comes to the sleeper but a dream."

2 June–17 November 1974

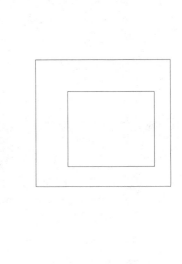

Sunset Debris

for Peggy Jeffries

Can you feel it? Does it hurt? Is this too soft? Do you like it? Do you like this? Is this how you like it? Is it alright? Is he there? Is he breathing? Is it him? Is it near? Is it hard? Is it cold? Does it weigh much? Is it heavy? Do you have to carry it far? Are those the hills? Is this where we get off? Which one are you? Are we there yet? Do we need to bring sweaters? Where is the border between blue and green? Has the mail come? Have you come yet? Is it perfect bound? Do you prefer ballpoints? Do you know which insect you most resemble? Is it the red one? Is that your hand? Want to go out? What about dinner? What does it cost? Do you speak English? Has he found his voice yet? Is this anise or is it fennel? Are you high yet? Is your throat sore? Can't you tell dill weed when you see it? Do you smell something burning? Do you hear a ringing sound? Do you hear something whimpering, mewing, crying? Do we get there from here? Does the ink smear? Does the paper get yellow and brittle? Do you prefer soft core? Are they on their way to work? Are they feeling it? Are they locked out? Are you pessimistic? Are you hard? Is that where you live? Is the sink clogged? Have the roaches made a nest in the radio? Are the cats hungry, thirsty, tired? Does he need to have a catheter? Is he the father? Are you a student at the radio school? Are you afraid to fail? Are you in constant fear of assassination? Why has the traffic stopped? Why does blue fade into green? Why didn't I go back to Pasco and become a cop? Why does water curl into the drain in different directions on either side of the equator? Why does my ankle throb? Why do I like it when I pop my knuckles? Is that a bald spot? Is that an ice cap? Is that a birth mark? Will the fog burn off soon? Are her life signs going to stabilize? Can you afford it? Is it gutted? What is it that attracts you to bisexual women? Does it go soggy in the milk? Do people live there? Is there a limit? Did it roll over when it went off the road? Will it further class struggle? Is it legible? Do you feel that it's private? Does it eat flies, worms, children? Is it nasty? Can you get tickets? Do you wear sunglasses out of a misplaced sense of increased privacy? Do you derive pleasure from farts in the bath? Is there an erotic element to picking your nose? Have you a specific conceptualization of earwax? What am I doing here? How do the deaf sing? How is it those houses will burn in the rain? What is the distance to Wall Drugs? Why do they insist on breaking the piñata? Is penetration of the labia sufficient to support a conviction? Is it a distraction to be aware of the walls? Is it bigger than a bread box? Which is it? When you skydive, do your ears pop? Do you bruise? Did the bridge rust? Is your life clear to you? How will you move it? Will you go easy on the tonic, please? Do you resent your parents? Was your childhood a time of great fear? Is that the path? Do the sandpipers breed here? Is that what you want? Have your cramps come? Do you tend to draw words instead of write them? Do you have an opinion about galvanized steel? Who was John Deere? Are you trapped by your work? Would you like to explore that quarry? Is it the form of a question? Where is Wolf Grade? Are your legs sore? Is that a bottle neck? Who is the Ant Farm? Where did she learn to crawl like that? Is the form of the dance the dancer, or the space she carves? Can we go home now? Who was that masked man? Does he have an imagination? Will he use it? Is it obvious? Is it intentional? Is it possible? Is it hot? Why did the mirror fog up? What is the context of discourse? What is the premise of the man asking passersby if they have change for a dollar? Who took my toothbrush? What made her choose to get back into the life? What is the cause of long fingers? What is the role of altered, stretched canvas on wood supports, hung from a wall? Why do they seem so focused, intent, on their way to work? What makes you needle happy? Why does he keep large bills in his shirt pocket? How do you locate the crosshairs of your bitterness? What was it about shouting, mere raised voices, that caused him always to go out of control? Do you hear that hum? Is there damage? Is the answer difficult or hard? Is each thing needful? If there was a rip in my notebook, how would you know it? What makes you think you have me figured out? Why do my eyes water, devoid of emotion? What is the difference between a film and a movie? Do you want sugar? Why does my mood correspond to the weather? How do you get down to the beach? Is the act distinct from the object? What did you put in the coffee? Did your ears pop? Would you prefer to watch the condos burn? Where do the verbs go? Will you ever speak to the issue of cholesterol? What is a psychotropic? Does pleonasm scare you? Kledomania? Who leads the low-riders? What is the relation between any two statements? Is anything as tight as anal penetration? Will we stop soon? Will we continue? Where are those sirens coming from? Is it necessary? Is it off-white? Is a legitimate purpose served in limiting access? Will this turn out to be the last day of summer? Will you give up, give out, over? Why is sarcasm so often the final state of marriage? Is this the right exit? Have you received a security clearance? What do you think of when I say "red goose shoes"? Why does the blind man use his cane like a wand? What is the source of your agitation? Can't you smell the rain before it falls? Are you dizzy, faint, nauseous? Do you have chills? Can you help it? When is the question a form of order? Does order mean a form of command? Do rabbits scratch? Do you find black gays exotic? Do words peel their outer meanings? Is that your hair? What if I want this so plain you can't see it? Have you noticed all these women with asymmetrical faces in their too-loud makeup? What is so special? What is an ice pick? Do you have involuntary erections without probable cause? What time do you have? Does it begin to wear thin? What about struggle? Do I dare to eat a peach? When do you rise? Why is the verb the second word? Have you watched how new graves begin to move down the slope of that hill, how it fills? What are you trying to tell me? Is that the island? How do they make carbon paper? Is it too hot? What about this? How does a harbor harbor? What of an art of sensory deprivation? Do you like to go down? Will you be able to make it? At what point does meaning begin to blur? Is that a flag in the rain? Is there anything suspicious about the dead? Will you flush when done? What sort of experience will I be forced to exclude? Are you ready? Are you certain? Do you feel this? Is this it? Do we turn here? Will it rain? Aren't you afraid I'll go on endlessly, shamelessly, pointlessly? Do you know that the true structure of a prison is built around its illegal commodities market? Don't you think your fever correlates with stress? Don't you watch those bank clerks each morning, waiting by the door to be let in? Isn't anyone ready to describe real life? How does syntax shape the chair? Where is that woman going with a cake in a box? How did you come to love flow charts? How is a sentence true? Do you see that woman in the crosswalk, turning first this way and then that, as if dazed, uncertain as to the way to go? How soon before I turn into an old man with a bedroll under one arm and a paper bag full of rags and clothes in the other, talking to myself as I walk? Are you now at that point that when you cut you scar? What is the source of the dull pain in the jaw? What is the emotional dimension of circumcision? Why do people stare at you? What do they say? Do you care for your cuticles? Are you aware of vessels in the eye? Have we time for one? How do I open this? What do they use it for? Where is the odor of apricots? How do I unscrew it? Are we there yet? Which states have you been to? Which zone is this? Did professional sex force her to alter emotions? Do you opt for or against irrevocable acts? Can you make it hard? What does it taste like? Is it Kansas? Do you prefer soup or salad? Did you see the man who was born without ears? Did you ever smoke a banana? Where is the center? Is it hyper or laid-back? How will you survive? Shall we circumambulate or simply walk up the side of the mountain? Who cuts your hair? Is it a specific type of diction? Who sez? What are his motives? Do you want to go lie down in the ice plants? Do you think they enjoy working for white people? Is that a fire in that trash can? What key, what key? Can it happen here? Is that the real color of her hair? What makes him prefer tangential contingencies? Don't you get your foreskin caught on things? Is it speech? How far can you take it in? Do you prefer an automatic? When is form not a distortion? Would you like to be queen for a day? Can you recall if you have read this? Could you pick up the gun? Who broke that dish? Can you prove that you exist? Is it not, in fact, not one type but many? Does she or doesn't she? Can you reformulate the proposition? Why, otherwise naked, would she wear a shawl on the beach? Is good dance music that difficult to find? Would we be able to grope our way back out of the tunnel? Is the morning better? Do you feel compelled to defend the position? Do you eat meat? Were those pelicans? Does it embarrass you? Will those clothes ever be the same again? Does the flow of traffic deceive you, taking on the texture of natural process? Is it straight yet? How many can you count in

their hot pants, wigs, halter tops, standing at the curb, waving at
the large cars in the slow lane of traffic? Does not the damage of
oppression cut both ways? Does it locate this to say that I'm stand-
ing at the northeast corner of Clay and Van Ness? Is the sun as
large as that photograph suggests? Could you recognize this as
an insect? How young did you think her sister was? Are you not
perpetually given to distortion, equivocation, half-truths? Are
you listening? Is everybody happy? How can you keep your stories
straight? What are the limits of large? Who do you trust? Did I
ramble? Did I ever? Will you admit to this? Did you ever go sailing?
How long is it? What are those blue flowers? How does the world
differ in a Navy town? Are there roads on the island of Truk? What
brought you to sentences? Why the great crane on the barge? Are
you more frightened by insects or tigers? Could you tell if I had
changed it? What was the secret of "Pincushion" Smith? Has the
score changed? Why does that water heater hiss? Can you see it?
Does it show? Is it hidden? Is there a purpose? Can it change? Is
it large or hard? Is it blue or bumpy? Is it medium or slack? Why
do you want to know? What's gotten into you? Is it a sequence?
Is it a jumble? Is not chaos also a form? What is that a flock of?
Is it stucco? Is it Sluggo? Does it form a chain? Is it anchored? Does
it accrue? Aren't there times when words seem impossible, discon-
nected clusters of letters, so that even though you know what they
say you can't believe it? Is it going to be a hot one? Did they search
there thoroughly? What is a frame of mind? Is that cotton? Are you
a real girl? What is the number? Is it a question of will? Is it legible?
Is that the foghorn's groan that fills the inner ear? Why, at this late
point in her life, did bisexuality so suddenly pose itself as a ques-
tion? Is that a midget or a dwarf? What was the implication of her

having deliberately gone over there when she knew he would not be at home? What did it mean to propose your life as a single act? Where is the border you will not cross? Is truth a question of verification? Do you suppose the fog a metaphor? Would you prefer to forget the day you shoved two VC from your copter, high over the dusk-lit delta? What makes you believe these words are connected, one to the other? Does fear have a structure? What about the biplane? At what point does it cease to be a poem? Did you ever meet the woman whose dream was being balled on newly laid blacktop? Did you ever watch fist fuckers drive their arms in, to the elbow? Is there a final form? Was that a stop sign? How do you spell relief? Is this the prison? Is personal liberation possible without a social dimension? Is that your brother? What is forbidden? Where does morning begin? Have you forgotten the terms you originally set? Is the language neutral? When does a question become a command? How does this fog imitate rain? Why do you suppose that is? Must you always pop your knuckles, chew on pencils, get up and walk around? Have you ever been so drunk that you could not, the next morning, remember what you'd done? Will it bite? What if I said I never think of you? Where is it? Have you the keys? Do you have the keys? Did you find it in the blue book or did you write it there? Can you be gentle? Have you tried this position? Does the sameness of winter get to you? What does it taste like? Where does it come from? What is the cause of that red nose? Why is it we talk endlessly and have gone no further? Are you apt to gag? Is that a temple? Have they found him yet? Are those sheep? Do people think you are stupid, weak, manipulative? What is the outer edge of ego? How can we know what we speak of? Do you repeat yourself? Do we turn here? Don't you just write and write and

not return to it again? Is this fog or rain? Do you prefer going down-
hill? Is it arrogance? Are those schoolbooks? Would you like to
fuck? Is it fantasy? How is that hat a souvenir of a war you never
fought? Is this what it will be like from here on out? How is it
I always come back, as tho forgetting how boring it was the last
time? Did you make it yourself? In what way is this risk? Does it
increase in value? Do you swallow it? Can you swim there? When
do we arrive? Is it a theme or a variation? Did you say please? Did
you say thank you? Who are you? Do freckles make the back of
one's hand more attractive? Can you hear the fluid in my lungs?
Who is the small man with the shaved head? Do these cloud forma-
tions indicate the breakup of the fog or the advent of rain? Do you
sense a stasis? Is that hum in the pipes? Do you have proper identi-
fication? Are not the reveries which are interspersed with the read-
ing a part of its form? Is caution such a bad thing? What if, sud-
denly, you chose to be another? Is not your life a series of cycles,
bordered by the same mistakes over and over? Have you noticed
how slowly we approach? Why do you resent affection between
your friends? Is that who I think it is? Just where did the cat spray?
Am I out of ink or breath? Don't you see how so-called good writ-
ing is a sort of distortion, positing dishonest limits on the real?
Don't your ankles ache? Is this the plane? Haven't you confused
the question of how to survive with the one of what to do with
your life, or did you opt for the wrong one? Why do those fishing
boats cluster? What if I told you this was a form of seduction?
Don't you wander around strange neighborhoods only to wonder
what it is to live like that? Am I ready to admit the truth is just a
specific construction of fiction? What is the function of a mustache?
In what way is a governor like a shoemaker? Are you running a

fever? Don't you see that by asking questions you avoid certain forms of statement? Why don't I just tell you? Where is the reptile farm? How many words do you think are "ordinary"? Why did he suddenly get off the bus? Will an increase in shad depress market value? How old were you when you realized that lives were short? Is poor judgment to be my fate? Is poetry sound? How did we get a flat tire? Why not just split? Are you afraid of something? If it were only a question of orgasm, would we quickly be bored? Have you ever watched a friend self-destruct and not attempted to stop it? Have you forgotten how it feels to be healthy? Are you full of self-pity? Is that you? What if I did this differently? Are you awake? Has the morning come? Is the coast clear? Is this what you call the sun? Does the winter make you a more private person? What is meant by wolf-time? Can you describe the origin of the sallyport? What makes you do these things? Did you call? Where is Kadoka? Is it a condition, a location, a friend? Has it a main street, red hair? Does it behoove you? How do you know I'm not fooling you? What makes Jackie run? Is your hair dry yet? Does the foreskin make it more or less sensitive? Do you know the muffler man? Where do these things come from? Is it a mellow fondue? Is he a straggler? How have we altered the relation between text and receiver? What makes you think this is a voice? Is that the real color? Is it what you thought it would be? Can you see your own breath? By orientation, do you mean facing east? Are the words there before you write them? Is there a secret? Do you like to sit by the window? Do you get carsick? Do you have to poo? Who would you secretly like to sleep with? Is it possible to forget that someday you will die? Do you prefer dogs? Which train will arrive at B first? Is this just something which happened? Do you sometimes think about suddenly losing control? How do words work? Where do I know you from? Is the western idea of autumn great strokes of green and grey? What next? What now? Did I hurt your feelings? Do you want to go home? Is that oleander? Do you like my breasts? What is the thing that cannot be written? Is this an expression of concern? Would her husband be shocked to learn? Did you ever meet a happy man? Can you make up your mind? Who do you trust? Where? Is this trip necessary? Do you research these things? Will it rain? Did you come? What do people really think? Do the Harlem shuffle? Does the bitch switch? Have you no mercy? What do you mean by a long white truck? Is that so? Do you want to arrive at an act or a text? What is fair play? Is your body your self? Where is JFK's brain? What are the rules? How can I get hold of a gun? Are those your dishes? Will we be able to keep in mind that we are independent agents? What caused you to sour on men? Are we discussing a question of distance or a discussion of a question of distance? Why did they paint the piano white? Is there fog along the coast? Is there an order here, real or imposed by the imagination? Why do those empty chairs face one another? How did it go? Did you get far? Did you do it? Will you see her again? Was it any good? Why do you presume the connection? Why is the guitar in the fireplace? How? What is the deadline? What are the demands? In what way is this different from the tranquil plane? Why does it take you for ages? Why do you continue long after the others have fallen off in sleep? Is the concept of love a bourgeois trap? Is this what you intended? What do you learn about a person if you look at their shoes? Is the warm night good for cruising on Harleys? Will a banana satisfy hunger? Does the sound of traffic approximate water? Are you to blame? Is the hour near? Have you at last reached the age when almost any cut commands a scar? Who is the pleonast here? What makes you think those are the alternatives? Is there a job here? Do you always mistake density for depth? Don't you like the way the fog slices between the hills down into the neighborhood? Are the rules of association fixed or fluid? Are we on schedule? Who lives there? What is at the heart of this moral tale? Where do these people come from? Is it a soft surface with a hard edge? Where did you meet Joanne? How does the act alter the conception? Do you forget what you mean? What will the tide do to the beach? Who is the woman in blue socks? What makes you think this is fennel? Aren't you somebody? What makes him fear having her untie his hair, in bed together? Is that a small lion or big dog made out of plaster? What is it that attracts her to rejecting women? Is it that I am constantly too tense to sleep? What do those grey trucks mean? Does it bother me, at some point, to admit having slept with him? Where was justice? What would it be like to be whole? How could I lose weight? Do you recognize the sentimental as sadism? Was that Bob's Laura? What do we do now? What are you afraid of? Who is that playing the piano? Was it wise? What time is it? Is it possible to reach center, touch bottom, or is there an impregnable core around it? What about the mornings when, staring into the mirror, there is no sense of recognition? Can you walk on it? Will I confess that I will always be bitter, pissed? Do you trust these people? What is that scar about? Don't nouns only point generally in the direction of a percept? Can you recall hurting someone unintentionally, but feeling no sense of guilt? Can you recall doing it intentionally, some anger fulfilled? What is your myth? When will her husband recognize what is going on all around him? Is there not something vicious in any attempt to be honest? Is this not a challenge, an insult, a lie? What if I told your secret? Is it because I'm a man? When is delirium the optimal state? Do you feel the urge? Do you at times presume that merely by observing the person, a glancing diagnosis, you can, by extension of the imagination, understand their fuller lives? Does the wind bother you? Have you ever known what it felt like to have good teeth? In what ways are you different? In which the same? Why must that small boy wear leg braces? What is it that brings us each to destructive behavior? Remember when Sandoz still made acid? Remember Polio Summer? Where are you coming from? Does it make any difference? What if I was drunk? Just what do I fear about trust? Can you separate the inner from the outer? Why is this not form, but a process? Who is that witch? Is that my bus? What is a memory? Is that a hole in your shoe? How can you imagine that all these things exist? What if he understood that we all thought he was a closet case and were not threatened by that? Is it a question of a wager? Do not verbs collapse the real down to a single, simplified plane? At what point did you realize that you are capable of killing? Why is this not theater, not dance? Are words not ultimately puffy with misuse? Do phenothiazines scare you? What does this exemplify? Are not all truckers jerks? Do you believe that by balling or not balling you will be a better person? What if I told you these were only place holders and that it was you who was in question? Can you understand that I want to create a situation where you are forced to reject me? Did you despise yourself as a child? Were you stupid and disgusting? Could not a performance artist develop a form of approximate dialogue with the audience, based upon the Synanon Game? Who gains? What is the true process of capital accumulation? Is there some language that ought to be excluded from poems? Is there a better way? What is a vacancy? Do you realize that if flamingos don't eat carrots their colors will fade? When is sincerity not a lie? What makes you think you have choices? Why do some people think your green eyes to be brown? Have you heard they tried to shoot the President? Are there types of information you refuse to permit? When was the last time you had a good shit? How are you? Do you do the police in different voices? Is there evidence of tardive dyskinesia? Are we in the pine woods? Do you find the on-ramps elegant? What did the tree say? What do those women dream of, who each morning go by bus to clean the homes of the rich? Is that a mole on the tip of her nose? Are his teeth an indication of class struggle? Is this more mellow? Could he spot the scam of a burn artist coming? What is the function of these midnight conversations in the kitchen? Is it clean? Is it silly? Is it the capital of Montana? Did it capsize? What is special about Korean beer? What are the right questions? Can I get permission? Is there a need for more nouns and modifiers? Who broke the cup? Why did the guardrail break? Will there be a break in the weather? Did they make a break for it? How shall I break it to you? Why lie? Has the population doubled? Would you like to do that now? Why do you squint? How many days late is it? Has it happened before? Is it simple or complex? Are you there? Is that the bus? What is a bone spur? Is this condition called coma or comma? Why is the light white? Is that haze? Why this target? What is the latest dope? What did I forget? Did he put his banana on the line? What do you think, to see those fishing boats swarm? Is that a hawk? Is that a concern? Is it suspended in an emulsion? Does it have big feet? Do these words conceal an erasure? Are the terms not chosen also part of the piece?

What is the bush league? Why is that man walking down the middle of the freeway? What do these people dream of on their way to work, what urges them to run in order to catch a bus? What is the formal nature of tequila? Why is the source of her anger not her target? Do you resent my humor at your expense? How many ways can that question be taken? What are the cities of South Dakota? Where do we begin? How is it that one minute my writing is angular, precise, the next minute looping, rounded? Is talk cheap? How did the tier tender die? Is that a Navy vessel? Was it so difficult? Why do elephants wear pink tennis shoes? Where does it hurt? What are the names of the churches? Can you see the seams? What is bunch grass? Is not the set of so-called adult values merely applied capitalism? What if the urgency of our emotions was permitted the content of its desires? What if I moved to New York? In what ways will this change the house? Which boat is that, lost in the rain on the bay? Does this change who we are? How did I make the decision? Is it true that only secret lives are real? Do you prefer artificial light? Will winter provoke indoor behavior? How can you divide men into friends and lovers? How can you tell if art is anything more than the games of fuckups? Is that natty dread? What is the flower of the Hoosier State? When was the last time you felt like that? Are your hands bleeding? Do I have in my head an image of you that you would recognize? Sez who? Is this the road to Branberry Cross? Are those briars? Where does the creek lead? Is that her second abortion in six months? Where would events get out of control? Is this what you expected? What is trouble? What is the image of trouble? Is this the morning-after odor of red wine on my breath? Aren't words like forms that the sulphuric acid of thought pours through in order to etch perception on the metal plate of the real? Is it like this in dream? Can you smell the rain? What was the reason for the suitcase of doughnuts? Was that government grammar? Why is that window made out of blue glass? Are those seabirds or birds of prey? Which shore is Africa, which is Spain? Is that what one would call a high sky? How can I know that what you feel is pain, orgasm, satisfaction? What are you thinking? Could you ride down the slope on a sled of dry leaves? Does that apple doll resemble Mel? Are not short works a necessary consequence of magazine distribution? How do we know if we come to the edge of words? What will winter mean to us? In what way is it different to live in a city of houseboats? Is it not that we simply seduce ourselves? Have you ever seen a Joshua tree? Is that ice cream? Is this raising the right issues? Did I scratch my eye in my sleep? Why? What does that mean? Are you getting macho, dear? What does that feel like? How do you want it? Does it scare you? Is it sweet, tender, hard, old? What is it in mothers that can terrorize daughters? Can you smell rain? Will you use bleach? What is a fretless bass? What is folk tuba? What of the woman washing a man's clothes in the laundromat, twin rings on a finger? Could you sleep on foam rubber? Do blue jeans and boots constitute a new image? Does a word fall into crevasses of recognition? Are the first days more intense? Which is necessity, which coincidence? What does he mean about getting more ass than a toilet seat? What makes him choose a shirt of false leather? Is it true that the gap between known and not-known is the distance between pattern and form? Is pain physical or an emotion which might on occasion have its origin in the real? What is objective cause? What is the mystery of name? What is more powerful about the vague? Is Liz the Whiz? Do we tell Mel? Is there a formal consequence to running out of

ink? Do you want to drink? Can you smell sex? Is it six? Is it a
principled action or just trashing? Is it armed education? In what
way was the Civil War not just an extended black rebellion?
Doesn't the buildup of artistic images always result in the lie?
What is the importance of texture? Isn't it about time you brushed
your teeth? In what ways will you change your life? Could you go
to a place and be not known? Is it butcher by the dozen? Could you
feel the quiet settle in? Is this what it is? How could I convince you
I am not writing the words of the person I would like to be? Is the
rooster friend to the dog? On whose side are the service providers,
on whose the agents of change? Has this house been good for your
head? Was it difficult to relearn the art of waking not alone? What
is the taste of the underside of your tongue? Does this disprove the
null hypothesis? Will the tomatoes survive the rain? What is the life
of the mechanic who walks alone on the runway of the fog-shrouded
field? Is it that your socks keep slipping? Is that flat, dull white disc
the sun? What do they catch in these waters? What is the wrong
way? Why is the earth red-orange? Is it a question of which ques-
tions? Does it require the ingestion of peyotl? Does my hand shake?
How do I recognize my palm? Is it as I see it or is the image mere
approximation? How is it that I admit to the possibility of mass
noun, of category? Why as a child did I choose to tell my brother
tales intended to fill him with terror, lying in the dark of our room,
his sobs, my narrative? Who would live in the trailer park? Did
you get off? Did it happen? Is today safe? Is that the rock quarry?
In spite of its gradual windings, do you conceptualize this road
as straight, altering the map in your head to conform? Is this the
confusion space? Is this the dream? Is this the higher level, the new
plane? How do we get out of here? Are those ants? Are you sweat-

ing? Is it dark? Did the sirens wake you? Did you emerge from the house, dressed only in cutoffs, into the fog filled with big trucks and the pulsing red lights? Could you see the hatchets chop into the walls? Who were the men in black raincoats? Were those your neighbors' faces in their windows? When is you I? Is it fiction? Is it friction? What is my capacity? Did I mean limit or function? Does it feel more equal, casual, affectionate, to do it on our sides? What is more solitary than a jogger in the fog? What are these berries like? Could you sleep in a net? If you could construct an image of the world, how would you know it? What did I forget to ask? Do not all such short works hinge upon balance and is that not why we avoid them? Would he choose to be flat, prosy, slow? Would he bring up the issue of gravel pits? Is he the most fearful man you know? Are our lives merely sequences of constant description? Are you loyal to a form? Do you conceive of secretaries scuttling in the morning fog? What if your kidneys go? Are you cruisin' for a bruisin'? Who thought up corrugated cardboard? What is the perceived need for secrets? Why must they be told? Don't associations vibrate in concentric circles of memory and reference? What do you make of his tale of the beast, part squirrel, part lizard, with whom he wrestled, tho not in dream, as he slept? What makes us sit in the attic, caught in quiet conversation? Why does this one cry at night and that one groan? Do you pronounce the *t* in *often*? Is your head in a work space? Do you hear blue music? Do lapdogs remind you of mice? Can you smell the ammonia? What is the meaning of the shape of my head? Are these just projects, portions of an interminable puzzle? When is revision not cowardice? What is it about green eyes? Do you want to be clinical? If you know how to survive, do you know what you do? Does that smile signify tension?

If my skull is large, are my ears small? Who does not dream fondly of the days when one could eat hot dogs for breakfast? Is not fundamentalism a form of situationist ideology? Do you hate the dream space? What are white male vibes? Are your fingers short, rounded? How can you say you are a private person? What are the politics of this house? Is this a disease, a compulsion? Are you subject to bourgeois frenzy? Who is the Jewish American Princess? Where is Plaster City? Can you make out the playground, empty, through the fog? Can you see where the water changes direction? What if that planet was only a ball of compacted gas? Who lives in the hill house? Is this the clearing? What is it about the suction of the lips, the stroking of the tongue, the insertion of fingers? What is the space you call your face? Which is the realm of the ready? Is this slow, passive, neutral enough, without interest for it sees interest as a false issue, bland, muttering, whispering, here? Is this the work that rejects the reader? Did your tonsils grow back? Could you explain her skittishness, weariness, nearness to anger? Did you feel the quake? Do you often feel that if you could just once fit the words exactly to the reality, perception would crystallize, and that you would be content to be silent henceforth? Can you see how the prow of that ship pushes the water up? Is there something you wanted to ask? Is this a knock-knock joke? Is it a mirage? Is it Rick's American Cafe? But what do you mean by Do City Barber? Is it in the interest of national security? Is it just strokes of ink from an olive-colored pen? Could you destroy people in the name of a greater good? Did you pick raspberries in a Trumansburg graveyard? Do you often open with a Ruy Lopez? Would you like a White Russian? Could you get into a three-way? Tennis, anyone? Is it simply a catalog, a gathering, an anathemata? Do you not see the evolution of your wardrobe and the image it projects as a form of narrative? Is it my breath? Is it a devotion to definition? Is it a matter of size, time, density? Does it come in an emulsion? Do the forms fill as they emerge from the fog? Is it a prerogative of the backbrain? Is it mawkish or gloopy or no-no? Does it have lines under its eyes? Can you tell its age by the backs of its hands? Is this the cemetery of buses? What was it like to verify her identity when the face had dissolved? Why is it you sweat constantly, without relation to heat or exertion? Is not a good shit a true pleasure? Are not these houses a form of disease? Does your false tooth hurt? Why is it that everyone appears so determined to self-destruct? Do the words come easily, without shape? Is it a question of response? Could you go to sleep in the snow, nervous system tingling, turning off? Do the geese circle the lake each morning, until they have a formation, a sense of location? What if the questions cease? Is being a writer simply a sequence of postures, each a proposition of what writing might be? Does the punctuation distort the words, or does it shape them, form them? Is it supple, is it dry? Is it an epitome or an apotheosis? Will the blackbirds walk up to you? Will the seagull eat peanut butter? Did you spend the bulk of your childhood staring out of the inside of bushes? They shoot horses, don't they? Do you, at times, recognize when reading that nothing is absorbed, that the words don't cohere? Do you come here often to watch the muscles in the arms and backs of the windsurfers? How is it that we approximate spring in October? Do the words reside, as if suspended, in the ink or pen, just waiting to be released? Can you hear the house groan, shifting balance, when at dawn we begin to move about? By this sentence, what condition is revealed? Are you going to Baja? Are you going to Mazatlán? Is that a white scar behind his ear? Would you wear a scarf? Is it only that these things appear as they occur? In what other way does coffee alter the metabolism? How are you changing me, just by the fact of your presence? Is that smog? What is that ache in the ball of my foot? Is any life merely a sequence of responses to forms of adversity? Why does the helicopter fly under the bridge? Is there a different language for talking? Is what you're proposing radical non-intervention? Have you become more tolerant of ratfuckers, shitheads, assholes? What do you mean, "Hush off"? Is this all just part of the poetry hustle? Did you say his name was Booker or Booger? Is this J-town? Isn't it more than a question of each of us knowing that we have all been damaged, but one instead of whether any one of us can recognize in him- or herself how? Do we not all require a form? Why not say "Don't we"? Is this auto row? Did those pigs kick tall? How come? What is the secret of redlock? Can we penetrate the security perimeter just long enough to plant an incendiary device? Is it not true that eventually you will ball everyone, leave everyone, change nothing? Now that it is winter, are you warmer? Do you hear the organ? Do you stare at the floorboards? In what way is the attic like living in the country? What does it do to your head? What does it do to time? What is the function of excavation? What of gays trained in the classics? Do you go up on the roof and hunker down to squint into the sunrise of a frosty dawn? Is this what is called a cable crossing? Is the heat on? What is the capital of Louisiana? Where is the Corn Palace? Is there a script? Is that a biplane? Do you like me inside, want me there? Should we walk through the ice plants? Could it go on forever? Is that a blister? Do the words reflect events, environs? Isn't place a question of syntax? Isn't today the morning of shoes? Does this mean they are putting the pipes in? Is it underpass, overpass, loop, ramp? Is this how it's done in Jakarta, in Kuala Lumpur? What if we thought water to be a higher form of oxygen? What if I made of the Synanon Game a form of performance piece? Have we entered the heliopause? Who lives in south block? Who works at the quarry? Won't any standard, once set, limit, distort, falsify? Is there an instant, waking, before the words attach to objects, as tho you rose up in a grammarless room? Why is today that day? Is that this time you come, sit on the stairs, your breath visible as mist, the words of your friend still in your head as she wished you a good day, rolling back over into blankets and sheets, lapsing back into sleep, so that you watch the city reflected in your neighbors' windows, the light in the fennel as its sharp shadows dissolve into day, in your dry lips a Camel before breakfast, at last unworried as to whether it will all cohere? What was the question again? How much play is involved? How much hesitation? What if form itself proved to be a blockage? What if he thinks that your sleeping with her is meant as a kind of statement to him? Have you ever done it sitting up, facing one another? Why would a hawk fly through the tunnel? Is that eucalyptus? One, two, how many lefts? What is it? Isn't it just that you start and you riff and you just keep blowing, bopping, rapping, speeding, alphabet soup of some hidden inner energy? What is it to live in a trailer camp? How many things can you think of in a dream? Isn't it that we comprehend strangers instantly but then go thru a period of losing touch as our growing familiarity builds on old assumptions, past truths, until we come to know them deeper a second time? What was it that arrived implicitly with morning? Has it a quantity? Is it a mineral? Are there many? Do you recognize the location? Is it a long black sleek car? Does he like to wear hats? Is he unable to make his eyes water? How is it that poppies bloom here in November? How is this speech if I wrote it? Is this the world of leisure suits, civil suits, air-conditioning? Who would choose condos? What is the calorie count of come? Is the grey one a gull? How shall we solve puzzles? What is the analysis of value? What is the origin of the term charley horse? What made me dream that my mail was being opened? Is there a more significant distance than that between the clit and the edge of the vagina? What is it that attracts me about some hairs about the nipple? Is it flattening? Is it wide? Is it not unusual in the winter? Is it odd for the Sufis to have found a saint in a woman who died in the French Resistance? What in these woods smells suddenly like coconut? What is it each time that causes your back to arch? What is it about the colorless illumination of moonlight? Who will put the squeeze on? Who will be the hit man? Why is this not a pseudopredicate? How can you be a connector and not a connective? What is it that makes you hold it so firm in your mouth when I come? Are we caught in a life of logical atomism? Is the bridge ugly on purpose? When is this not an assertion? Am I a question of language or a question of fact? What is it about grapefruit? Where is the harbinger now that we need one? Who is to choose the blues? How is it that we conform, say, even to the question of bus stops? Isn't it that everybody is telling you this same story, only a bit different every time? Is it going to be simple, eating you out in the bathtub without drowning? Isn't it that certain forms of language, for example of erotic content, focus perception away from the words and the syntagmemic chain, a world suppressed in reference to another? What makes you not an example of right-wing anarchism? Where in the dream do you find recognition of the dream? What if I began forgetting and writing the same sentences over and over? What if cognizance of the past began to diminish and I started to repeat myself? Is the same idea in different terms the same idea? What if it just got vague at the horizon? What do we mean by mag? Are these trees eucalyptus? Am I capable of being tamed? When is the door ajar? How did they determine that that was not a snake but a limbless lizard? Don't newborn mice appear to be squirming pencil erasers? What makes you think this is a question? What is fetal deer wine? Are you in love with the stripes of the Gila monster? Is this anything more than the presence of words? Why do we call it a glass snake? Where is my blue your green? What will we say later of each other? Why is it that some graffiti intrigues me, such as "Pochie is a Turkey" on the wall of the Mann City bus shelter? Is it a surprise to find that come is really bland? Is this a one-liner? How many peyote buttons make a trip? Can I date the origin of this piece by the allusion early on to a performance by Simone Forti? Why in the dream was I forced to watch over and over what happened to those people when the grenade went off, their flinching at the anticipation, the shock waves pulling them off their feet, the slow-motion outward expansion of shrapnel? Can you explain to me the meaning of meaning? Have you an adequate matrix representation? What are the days of the week? Do you have this in my size? Is it dope yet? Is it a boy? Are its vital signs stable? Is this question specific to this context? What did you think when they converted that funeral home into a savings and loan? Why is the sky light blue? Will I ever learn to drive? How unadorned can I make this? Why, if they always lock him up and pour valium down him, does he continue to take acid? Do you watch how they shake their heads and step back whenever the wrong bus approaches? Is this the cold you caught from Pierce? Did you see the fat man in the bow tie smile a gleam that spread across the folds of his face like the waves in a pond after a pebble drops in? Isn't morning a bitch? Doesn't that carry a specific, negative social connotation? Why do you say things like that? Why are you so fucked up, fucked over, fucked? What makes you think we need you? Why do you bother? What drives you? Don't you feel like an intruder? Don't you feel like a fool? Why are reading this? What makes you think that's what it's for? Can't you hear us snickering at you anyway? Is that light too bright? Is that how you get to the zoo? What is the frequency at which a thing becomes "common"? What is a larkspur? Why do we label this sunset debris? Are not all descriptive terms in the ideal language either proper nouns or predicates? Is this an example of extensional schema? Are you ready to say Uncle? Are you easily insulted? Isn't the whole premise here a fraud? What is an hour but an agreement we have? What is the case against the acquisition of language? Is it beginning to rain on the page? Is this fog or loss of the visual field? What is the realm of poetry but trips amid fuck-ups? What is this rash on the head of my prick in the shape of Indo-China? Isn't it crucial that this only be viewed in the context of certain other workers, e.g., Acker, Watten, Andrews, Coolidge? Is the line busy? Is this raid merely a test? Did you ever see your cervix? Is this a permanent condition? What does it mean to come upon a man on a bus writing rapidly into a blue book? Are you about to lose your cookies? What is the premise here, beyond the obvious one that any reader is a fool, a lamb, a mooch, a mark? How is a vanguard distinct from an elite? How is it that fog makes travel an abstraction? Did you see how those gulls stood atop the corpse, bobbing in the tide? What is it about the rind of the lime that the

Balinese attach one or more to the brow as a cure for headaches? Is it true that evil spirits move only in a straight line? Isn't it the case that there are certain poems which are important to be written but which anyone will acknowledge nobody would be especially anxious to read? What is writing but a type of behavior? Would you put my cock in your mouth, foreskin and all, moving your tongue slowly over the tip, pressing your lips down over the shaft, pulling softly, firmly, repeatedly, until finally you have swallowed what I came to say? Is this where the one-track mind jumps the track? Where is he at? How do you choose the questions? What is the function of this particular sequence? Why did the fire truck cross the road? Doesn't this bore you? Isn't it tedious? Isn't it silly? Isn't it a waste of time? Is what you fear the idea that who I am talking to is not you, but an image I carry of who you are? Don't I have a problem? Isn't the question of existence of time answered by the fact of irreversible processes? How do we get the perfume back into the bottle? How do we unburn down the house? Why are my eyes not blue? Don't you think it's unhealthy to put so much of your identity into the hands of others? What do you want for Xmas? How are we to define the poem? What is the name of this leaf? Isn't it the case that we can apply these terms only under limited, special conditions? How can you be sure of my intention? Will this be a late winter or a dry one? Have I gone back to smoking? What is the origin of macroscopic information? Why does it appear only in the final states of natural systems and not in their initial ones? Does it mean that if the universe is infinite, then in some other world a man sits in a kitchen, possibly in a farmhouse, the sky lightening and nobody else as yet up and about, writing down these words? Is this just a random perturbation? Is it drip ground? What do you mean when you say you will never find a form? What is the measure of entropy in this system? What color are my eyes? Is my skin dry? Why do you like to pick at my pimples? How soon before I lose my hair? Is this Drop City? Are you Peter Rabbit? Was it a scene of five dudes on alto sax laying down a tight conversation? Are you unreal? What is the purpose of this artificial sweetener? Who bomb whom? Is this the elephant burial ground? Are my lips chapped? Is this tooth sensitive to hot and cold? Who are these astral dogs? Would you know a conquest from a surrender? Is the subway of metaphysical significance? What is it that attracts you to depressive, associational types? Is there an eros to your syntax? Does this mean you personally or just you in the larger sense? If it rains, do you see it, reading, as part of the text? Are some parts better than others? Is it possible to do this out of some innocent motive? Do the sentences "just come" or are they conditional, a logic of disorder, accumulative, sequential? Did you see how they ganged up on him, how they pummeled and kicked? Why does he dress like a pimp? Isn't it queer to go whole days without speaking? Isn't this simply behavior? Don't you grow weary, irritable? Want to try and punch me out? Isn't this the part in the serial where the hero runs down a corridor only to find it blocked by a wall and spins, in terror, to see the tide of smoking lava approaching? Can you tell which one is the plainclothesman? Aren't you afraid that we know you're a coward? How do you tell night at the bottom of the ocean? Why don't my ears pop? Why are my fingers so stiff? Why do I always sprain this ankle? What was it like, watching those people burn? How shall we know the non-identity of discernibles? Is a peccary a rodent or a pig? Why does the serval have spoonlike ears? What caused Paul to get all upset?

What key? Isn't its formlessness a specific assertion? Why is this stretch of bay fill and auto yards called Paradise Drive? Which is the chipped tooth? Is that your cervix? Do you want me to come from behind? What if I bought an old railroad car and made a house out of it? Isn't the language of the interrogator bleak? What makes you think I'm not the fool? Has he lately taken to chain smoking? Is it that ass-fucking hurts? Why is he so silent in the morning, when he yaps so the rest of the time? Do you need a receipt? Does it serve a purpose? Ain't it enough to make you cry? Did you see where that fire truck lost control and slammed into that crowd? Isn't what is presented simply a question of rhythm, of the rhythm of a question? Does it blur? Can I smear it? Why do they need to write so nice and light, these white college kids? Wasn't it strange not to be the only one up at this hour? Does it count? Won't you be my seatrain, baby? Is it a question of crips versus walkies? Haven't you noticed how everyone leaves Buffalo because there's nobody interesting there and comes to Frisco, where they like it because everyone's so interesting? How do I know who you are, that each time I see you I know you? In order to recognize you, don't I need some concept of continuity, some thread of iden- tity which does not break up, thus don't I, don't we all, suppress our recognition of constant change, the fact that even as we fuck, eyes open, bodies sliding slowly together and apart, we become different, are never, moment to moment, the same? Are you writing what are called the Don't Works? Were you able to walk by the bomb site and not know it, even as the film crews pulled out? Are you able to work methodically? In what way is it as cold as the sky is blue? What do you mean your hair hurts? Do you see those car- tons shoved against the window? Did you ever use the word *palette* in a poem? Why doesn't he wake up? In what vague ways do we choose whom to fuck? How does lighting this cigarette cause the bus to arrive? Did you ever get into whips? What did you expect my foreskin to feel like? What do you see? What is there to fear in a glass of beer? What made you pass that joint of grass? Isn't there an argument not in the work, but between the works, which is discovered only as you read one beyond the next? What of a poem that told you what it did, casual-like, with no evident respect for your condition as reader? Isn't it true that you're a victim here? Did you notice how that head severed in the explosion rested on the window ledge with tears in its eyes? What would make me follow immediately with a sexual question? Is it long? Is it thick? Does it have a crook in the middle? Did you ever watch how it slides and slips between those lips? How is it a teaspoon of semen could come between friends? How many ways are there to understand that? How is it possible to eliminate every individual feature of a poem and still write one? Is not clarity a form of violence? Am I not just using you to locate this otherwise untenable discourse? Is this a discussion of the ideal language? Did you know that a bayou is a tributary of a lake or river, or any stagnant pool of water? Don't you fear your own capacity to harm others, even as you do so with a smile on your face? Won't you turn it down? Won't you drop the other shoe? Will you put your lips to her vagina, telling her then to piss? What is so special about fucking someone's asshole? How can he wear a blue blazer with red pants? Did you forget this? Did you regret this? Is this path of flattened grass evidence of deer along this slope? What is so difficult about fucking a stranger if both of you know what you want? Who is the tall man with green eyes? Which way is Treat Street? Does this clatter, mumble, rattle? Why is the water salty? How is it possible to know if this is a poem? Ain't it dopey? Isn't everything before us slack and lackluster? Did you look away as she turned her back and pulled her top off to try on the gift you brought? Is this tide rising? Is it apt to tear? Is it apt to rend? Is it apt to bruise? Did you lose it? Did you seek it out? How was it that it was always summer? Are you able at last to look back and laugh at the time she gagged and threw up on your cock? Do you know what that means in French, Greek, Hindi? In what way is this poem like a snuff flick? What did I learn? Ain't it a bitch? Does sex confuse the issue? Is this the missing part? Did you expect the chimp's ears to feel like that? Ain't this just chatter, soundings thrown out so that by their echoes I may know the dimensions of my space? Is it offensive to you? Is it rude? Do you want to consult with your attorney? Do you understand the nature of the charges made against you? Are you not apprised to the fact that there is more to potassium cyanide than the odor of peach pits? Is this evidence that I'm dangerous or crazy? Just which wall are you off of? Which end is up? Is it art yet? Is it the real thing? How does a boat float? Is this not the age of assholes in leisure suits? Am I what you call demure? Do you know that in the autopsy the skin is rolled up off the skull just like taking off your socks? Which do you believe? How is certainty possible here? Does not the surface texture suggest anxiety? How do the deaf in China use sign language? Doesn't this linger? Did you feel it? Did you find it? Did it make you want to cry? Who were those guys? What was he trying to articulate? Did you turn the sound off and play music instead? Did it fit the picture? Wasn't the rejection of form a form itself? Was he freaked? Was he frightened? Did he refuse to clean up his own room? Did it always occur to him, each time he arrived in some condition, love perhaps, that this was what was meant by it, its true definition? Were his toenails in need of cutting? Which are the moons of Mars? Have you ever seen the Southern Cross? What did prose mean? Is this a thing you can find in nature? Do you prefer to sleep with your head aimed at the North Pole? When does it get there? Does it sniffle? Does it waver? Is it apt to break? Is it apt to break up? Is it apt to break down? Will it wash? Will it wash out? Will it wash ashore? Will it, Washington? Is that a crack? Is that a rip-off? Is that a snide remark? Does the door in the poem open and close? Does it just lie there in the language? Did you know what to expect? Are you sure where you're going? Can you see the horizon, the town, the boys at play? Does smoke get in your eyes? Do the white shirts in the centerfield bleachers distract you? Do the terms apply? How shall we get down there? Will we cheat? Will we snore? What is in store for us? Which is the way out? Did you ever come to an exit sign in the middle of a blank wall, solid brick? Is it art anymore? Can I exchange this? Do you play basketball? Which one of us is the warlock? Have you not, at 30, come to understand how brief the next 30 years will seem, each decade not an epoch, recognizing that you may not make it? What is being proposed? Did you give at the office? Did you give? Did you give out? Did you give head? Did you give up? Did you give in? Have you understood the level at which all prepositions lack meaning? Did they bring out the meal one course at a time? Could you hear the violin? Did you go back to smoking? Did you quit the work, half done, then go back to it, completing it a bit at a time? Did it ever occur to you that she might not want it, might have it, might not need it? Did it ever propose itself as a question of privacy? Did you like the color of the curtains? Did you ever wonder what it felt like, burst of

semen into the throat? Doesn't kidney failure haunt you? Can't
you foretell arthritis, ulcer, loss of hair, loss of teeth? When will
it be your turn for the infarction? Did you see the snow? Did you
do the job? Didn't you hope to avoid language that passed itself
off as a mock-up of consciousness? Didn't you suggest a formula
just to get the haters of formulae pissed off? Won't you, given the
chance, betray everyone? Did you see how the soldiers, bringing
the dead back in body bags, chewed gum? Did you see the jar filled
with ears on his mantel? Which one of the Dorsey brothers choked
to death on his own vomit? What is the hardest thing? Does your
stomach hurt? Do you want everyone to see what an asshole you
are? Do you understand that you are simply jealous, selfish and
small? Isn't what you need a threat? Are you gay? Are you cheerful?
Are you fucked up? When are you going to leave? When will this
writing be rid of you? Wouldn't you like to stop? Aren't the shit-
kickers a garrulous bunch? Is the Scotch broom already in bloom?
Don't you know that everyone laughs at you? Don't you know how
hard it is to belittle you? Don't you know how paranoid you are?
Aren't you afraid to sleep in the dark? Aren't you afraid to wet the
bed? Don't you have to get half drunk in order to sleep? Can you
square personality with infinity? Is not form the ordering of bor-
ders? What is your excuse for putting up with this bullshit? Why
does this orange taste metallic? Didn't you used to put transistor
radio batteries to the tip of your tongue, delighted by a taste of
that current? Are you ready to live a normal life? What did you
say when Kathy called to rave one more time of Rudy Wurlitzer?
Are you not an exaggeration? Am I any less of a Piltdown man?
What about those joggers who daily cross the Golden Gate Bridge?
Is this the tunnel, the funnel? Do the windows in this room face

east? Can you not hear the bedspring's every move? Is it chili? What is the "prison house of language"? Is that a bird in the peppertree? Is it that that dog barks into the canyon for the pleasure of his echo? Can you hear the big trucks as they pass through the valley? What kind of turf is this, clumped, whitish, dry? Is not reality in writing, the referential, an invention, not a discovery? Is this not a climate of dry heat? Is it not simply that the words gather into sentences, that the sentences accumulate until the page fills, that the pages gather until the book is done? Is this the writing of erosion? Is it possible to tell that I wrote this sentence on a hilltop overlooking San Clemente Canyon, the northern reaches of San Diego? Is it possible to tell if I wrote this sentence in the easy chair my friend Elliot made for me, in my house in San Francisco, in what all my roommates call the Yellow Room? Is it possible to tell which sentence lies? Is it possible to tell how much time there was between them? How does the sun's heat shape the content of this page? Is it raining? Is it humid? Do I have a plan here? Why does the dog refuse to shut up? What is the work of an oceanographer? Is there much life in these tide pools? Isn't the truly strange thing about Linda Lovelace that she shaves her pubic hair? Is it one thing to require an entire civilization to own automobiles and another to require them to own boats? What asshole called me a Zen poet? How is it that everyone here owns their own guard dogs? Can you tell that I'm sitting cross-legged now, by a pick and a huge half-empty bag of Supersoil? What is it these people do, to live on the tops of mountains? Are you curious or vicious or snide or bored or pissed? Why fly? Is this part of a program to drink my way around the world? Does the water always taste this bad? Is this the poem which offers you a "complete" massage? Is it just an

intellectual jackoff? Why do they all walk around with transistor
radios in their shirt pockets? Is this not just the journal of an
analytical anti-formalist? Is it all ice plants and cactus? Can you
judge people by their backyards any better than you can judge
them by their shoes? What is it about poetry that refuses to play
for keeps? Is it a morning for cottage cheese and lager? Are we out
of toilet paper? Is it the hushed sort of Saturday dawn, sun starting
to heat the lawns but with the people still sleeping? What causes
the worried tone in her life? What is a fact? What is affect? Are
these simples? In what way is every question a proposition? Is it
simply one without a truth function? Can you tell a curlew from
a godwit? Do you see how the clouds break at the horizon line,
so that the setting sun is a long strip of red-orange between vast
blocks of gray, one the sky, one the water? Did you see them push-
ing boulders over the edge of the cliff? Can you feel how the shift
in body weight turns the motorcycle? Even if you'd expected the
head completely bereft of hair, were you ready for those deep blue
eyes that never really looked at you? What is it about speech that
to you so approximates percussion? Is jazz discursive after all? What
is different about the clothes people wear to the laundromat? Can
you spot the naked lady on the Camel package? What do you want
to know? Who do you want to tell you? Isn't it true that "poetry"
excludes many types of sentences? Isn't this one of them? What is
the hump? Whose clavinet? Why insolence, boxed fury, muttering,
sadness? Why does she shave her head like that? Isn't it a closed
system? Why blue paper? What did you think of his trousers?
How is it that he lost an ear? Why is this popcorn a bright shade
of yellow? If the writing could change me, could I then change the
writing? Are there not times when you imagine that you were just

born horny? How shall we look at that truck? Don't you love to go by the used appliances store, past those old white stoves lined up on the sidewalk? Is this the formal announcement of spring? How is it we never get to the beach? In what way is this not six months ago? Did you ever see a yellow helicopter before? Can you feel the wind in the grass, on your back, on your neck? Can you see those hills across the water? How does a black dog differ from a white one? What is the formal process of flying a kite? How do these terms carry intention beyond the weight of one another? Is this a skill? Is this a man in a hard hat? Are you asleep? Are you sorry? Are you amusing or amused? Do sentence types limit what we say? Why does my toe ache, my knee feel stiff? Is not communication an act of violence? Is not writing an act of privacy? What is the long grass like to lie down on? Do you notice how sailors wander about in the lower plazas of the park? Are they a couple? Is that dog trained to fight? Can you feel how near spring is? Is that scaffolding about that tower? What is it about looking directly into your eyes at the instant of penetration? Can sentences tell us how we change? Are those words not stored or hidden in the ink? Do you see those two women, sunning themselves, sharing a joint? How does the day form? Is that her on her way back? Are those the sounds of seals? What is the smell of summer? Why did you bring a flag? What is the origin of the emotions? Can I repel you? Can I reveal you? Can I define you? Can I set you up for a hit? Can I make you cry? Can I make you choke? Can I name you? Can I fuck you, casually and without emotion? Can I put my cock in your mouth? Can I push it to the back of your throat? How hard do you want it? Is this the chronicle of our turning and our turning away? Is this going to get me somewhere? Will this make collective life any easier? To what extent is the transcendental simply a new form of damage? Is it dawn yet? Why are the cats meowing? What fills the sky with such a dull ochre light? What is it that makes my life seem so "obvious" and clear to me now? How is it that I should know you? What are the forms we fill? Am I not simply a balding, bearded, fat, half-toothless, farting excuse for a poet? Are we not the very garbage of our lives? Is this the shit we roll about in? Is there some limit to it? Is there some odor to it? Does it change if I say fragrance for odor? What is the dream that leaves you screaming? Did you ever want to fuck Daddy/Mommy? Do you know of those Indians who travel about at night only in two old wired-together Caddies, sleeping in them by day, eating white bread soaked in bacon grease? Is that the sun in the east? In the west? Is this how we got together, only to later change our minds? Is it true you got up to write this, half awake? In what way is changing your feelings not changing your mind? Is it far now? Are those the rude boys? Is this natural light? Is that wandering about the rooms of the house an indicator of anxiety, of resignation to and hatred of the job to which she must soon leave, to sell panties and bras under the fluorescent glare of department store? Do you hear what it is I'm telling you, really? Why can't we see the air? Why don't we see that the sky is an object, that to be in it is as real as to be in the forest, the pine wood? Why sell ice cream? Why does he write quietly, sitting at an old school desk in the high-ceilinged yellow room? Do your hands shake? Can you locate the forms? What is the hidden nature of any late winter? How is it that flowering kills the coleus? Doesn't the very fact of a question indicate the distance between the words we use and their meaning? Why is it that this text surrounds us, envelops us, forms a circle but does not solve the problem? Did we think to arrive at an emotion, a meaning, only to discover the location of its absence? What is it that permits you to ignore my intentions? Would it be different, reversed, if I could imagine that you could get me pregnant? Isn't the problem of the question that it locates us, places us in a relation, some tangible formulation, to the text or the act of the text, as if to test meaning, to see if it will exist if we can thus somehow fix all of the other terms in our equation? How is it this bridges us? If I come in your mouth now or you come in mine, is it any different than our knowing the answer to the question? Isn't it true that what we know is that we won't ever be able to pose the question correctly? Why does the cat sit in front of the air vent? At what point do you give up? Is surrender a solution? Is not what we have here a superimposition of three layers? Why is it that I want to look at you at the moment of penetration? What is that sense of recognition in your eyes which indicates that you sense my cock rubbing, pushing, against the walls of your cunt? Where else can you find a poem that tells you what it tells you? Do you think of your brain as solid or fluid? Why do you deliberately put certain sentences into several poems? Can you tell that I am writing on Easter? That I have Terry Riley on the stereo? That I am typing up the letters of Paul Metcalf? That I could insert anything, say anything, in this space? But that to say it is to exclude other possibilities? Is it love or fear? How do you tell them apart? How do you know she comes from New Jersey? Does it surprise you that people are fragile, that one thing goes wrong and a whole life destructs, that it happens all the time? Do you know the story of the man who drowned in a vat of molten chocolate? Do you know the difference between an elephant and a loaf of bread? Do you recall the day at Disneyland when you heard that Ty Cobb died? What were you doing when you heard about JFK? So what? What are the non-cognitive aspects of the city, of the elbow, of the question? Why must we be relentless? Should I look for the borders to this poem on the page or in my life? What is it about that downer, that it should leave me so hungover? Why do I sweat so, all the time? Is not what we experience now just one another's limits? In what way is your selfishness a shell, an impenetrable thing? Have I not thus left myself open to such abuse? Why is it that I am unable to separate anger from desire? Do you see the ladybug wending through the clover? Can you feel the breeze on the soles of your feet? Did you go back to the park for a reason? Isn't food, uncooked, the only real metaphor for the modern condition? Is that a hammer in the distance? Does this poem not point toward all others? Does it permit the inclusion of the sound of autos, of skateboards, blackbirds, running water? Have you ever just stopped to watch the way in which guys go around trying to hustle women? Did you ever meet a man who really believed he had reached his sexual peak in his teens? Can anybody tell that, as I wrote this, I grew a beard? Did you see her just get up and walk away? Did you see it as that? Which is the dog's bark and which the echo? If I told you what my flaws were, would either of us believe me? Did you ever hear the one about the butcher with the wooden leg? Is it so strange that I should prefer margarine? What do you make of those dudes who stumble around the city, muttering, still fighting the war? Which are the experiences you are not open to? Is it slower here, airier? Is it more relaxed? Is caution not a limit, a thing to be rid of? Would you put anything into your cunt that you wouldn't put in your mouth? Are those birds on the water? Where do those liners go, pulling slowly out of the harbor? Have you ever seen the stone of the great Lefty O'Doul, big black stone with white marble bat and ball, lifetime batting average inscribed thereon? What does it mean to have a house in the hills, an Alfa Romeo, and a wife who runs around? Would these questions in some other order continue to be these questions? Are you hungry? Would you like something to drink? Can you hear that cat meowing to get in? Why does your knee hurt so? Why did you both bend down and pick up acorns, hurling them as if to see who could throw the furthest? What are you heating the water for? Why is it that painters now are so obsessed with the elimination of space, that composers want to obliterate time, that writers feel compelled to remove the referential? Are you tired to the point of being dizzy? Why does the old man trill his *r*s? What are you going to do? How will you get there? How will you handle it? Will it worry you? Has it changed you? How could it be that our knowledge is limited, not by the state of the universe (existence, whatever), but by cognitive capacity, that we should only know what we can know, which is not what there is, the whole story? Are you certain? Are you sure? What if you removed the words from your work? How can you say that this poem would have existed, even had it never been written down, because it would have been "logical" for it, at a certain point, to exist? What is Bo Diddley's hair like underneath that hat? Did you make out the rent check? Do you know the difference between speech and writing? Would you sincerely like to be rich? Does each pot holder strewn about this honey-caked, crumb-ridden table articulate a separate story? Do you use oregano? How many systems do we involve just to name one thing? If we lie on the mattress in the closed-off old back porch at 90 degree angles, your legs lifted so that, lying on my side, I enter from behind, the fingertips of my right hand stroking your clitoris, and we go about this slowly, almost lazily, does it make for better understanding? Have you noticed how there are no fathers in the park playing ball with their daughters? Do the words fold, fold back? Is it time to think time? Do the words time? How many times? Is it locatable? Has it a space? Does it have a secret? When will you tell it? Are you anxious? Are you ready? Is it simply because you do it? Are we inside it or is it in front of us? Will the clouds burn off? What is it like to not work? Have you any further questions? Are my eyes really brown? How will you feel when we're in New York? Is this what is called Young and Hungry? Who are you really and what were you before? What do you like to worry about most? Does the idea of gay cops bug you? What if each word had a purpose? What is a construct? Are we on the right bus? Which language is being spoken here? How do our lives absorb stress? When is an act complete? Is that apt to be a school? Is it simply enough to lie beside you under a tree on a windy day in the park? Can you remember when this was art? What makes you think it's a secret? Which one is the mooch? What is it that you expect to find in India? Did you do your dishes? Is it that you prefer to be awake when the sun comes up? Are we closer or are we farther apart? Is poetry simply another channel for one's careerism? Will a turtle bite a tomahawk? Is there any poetic writing? What is to be done? What is literature? How come I woke up with such a swollen lip? Do you see the hot walks lounging about the track, trading wagers, tips, waiting for their horses to get back? What will you do in India? Why call this poem "Things To Do In Juvenile Hall"? Does this become a record of change? Whoever heard of giving someone a chicken for their birthday? What in the poem is not intention? Are you waiting for a ride? Would you like to party? Has your attitude about sound come around? How long have we worked at this, a little at a time? Just how hard is it? Is there a bottleneck? Is there much time left? What am I going to do? What'll I do when I grow up? Will I at some point come to a realization? Will I curb my arrogance? Will I be forced to play my hand? Will it be tipped? Is that an arrowhead or a shark's tooth? Was it any different the last time? Why have we had such mediocre weather? Does anger have a focus? Have we got a fix? Is it all just chatter, intended to flatter? Would you call this morning yet? Would you call it anticipation? Why does he always wear neckties loose at the neck? Is it what you expected? Is it what you had hoped for? What next? Is it relief? Is it joy? Is this handwriting a sign of a profound disturbance? Where is my ride? Why do this in blue ink on blue paper? Is it the end of the tunnel? Is it just beginning? Do you see that fog up ahead? Do you see how that works? How would you explain yourself? How did it happen? Did it happen? How did it happen? Did it repeat itself? Was it any good? Was it any fun? How did you come to ride in an old black Mustang with a Chicano watch repairman and a Japanese dental technician? Can you write in a moving vehicle? Will you support the idea? Have they fixed it? Have they taken it in? Is it painted red? How is it if I ask about it some other way? Are these sentences embedded here? Do you understand subjacency? Do you see how the hills are browning now? Are those cardboard cows? Is it just one thing after another? What did Bernstein say to make you ask so many questions? What is memory but the inverse of expectation? Does it pay to live in the world? Who else would do a thing like this? Do you see how it ties down the vocabulary? Do you see how it posits you, the reader? Who else would speak to you, for you? Is it a song of innocence? Can you count on it? Did it just come? Did it just flow? Why do

they call it Tamal? Do you see how he tailgates? Does it matter if
one of us is half crazy? What does it mean to be inside you, with
you? Is this what the writing was? Can you feel it, pushing in,
pulling out? Is it more than friction? Is it fiction? Does the deal
go down? Who is that on the phone? Can you fathom it? Did
the mail come? Did he come? Did you ever, as he came, just hold
it, not swallow it, then lean forward to kiss him, letting his own
come spill into his mouth, from one tongue onto another? Are we
getting close? Can you feel the hum, the vibration? Are these kites
large enough for us to ride them, to sail out over the water? Do you
see how that haze obliterates the horizon, sea become sky become
sea? What did Wordsworth see, looking down into that valley?
What is behind your language? Are you your vocabulary or are
you your syntax? If we push you, shove you, what will we find?
Can you hear what you are thinking under what you are reading?
Does it at times drown the reading out? Would you just go out
to the ocean one day and begin to swim, outward without limit
toward a vague conclusion? What of a poem that stretched from
summer to summer? Does the sky in your mind have a limit? Did
you go into that phase and go through it? What kept you here?
Where do the words come from? What if we drained them of their
meaning just to see what remained? What if we said that we had
done this thing? Can you give a yes or no answer? Can you say it
in a few short words? How is it with all this language there is still
this thing so vast that we have no name for it, even if we sense it
as a thing we have seen? Were the words trapped in the pen, just
waiting? Did they burst, sperm-like, into meaning in our mouths?
Can you taste it? Can you feel it? What about it?

The Chinese Notebook

1.   Wayward, we weigh words. Nouns reward objects for meaning. The chair in the air is covered with hair. No part is in touch with the planet.

2.   Each time I pass the garage of a certain yellow house, I am greeted with barking. The first time this occurred, an instinctive fear seemed to run through me. I have never been attacked. Yet I firmly believe that if I opened the door to the garage I should confront a dog.

3.   Chesterfield, sofa, divan, couch—might these items refer to the same object? If so, are they separate conditions of a single word?

4.   My mother as a child would call a pot holder a "boppo," the term becoming appropriated by the whole family, handed down now by my cousins to their own children. Is it a word? If it extends, eventually, into general usage, at what moment will it become one?

5.   Language is, first of all, a political question.

6.   I wrote this sentence with a ballpoint pen. If I had used another, would it have been a different sentence?

7.   This is not philosophy, it's poetry. And if I say so, then it becomes painting, music or sculpture, judged as such. If there are variables to consider, they are at least partly economic—the question of distribution, etc. Also differing critical traditions. Could this be good poetry, yet bad music? But yet I do not believe I would, except in jest, posit this as dance or urban planning.

8.   This is not speech. I wrote it.

9.   Another story, similar to 2: until well into my twenties the smell of cigars repelled me. The strong scent inevitably brought to mind the

image of warm, wet shit. That is not, in retrospect, an association I can rationally explain. Then I worked as a legislative advocate in the state capitol and was around cigar smoke constantly. Eventually the odor seemed to dissolve. I no longer noticed it. Then I began to notice it again, only now it was an odor I associated with suede or leather. This was how I came to smoke cigars.

10. What of a poetry that lacks surprise? That lacks form, theme, development? Whose language rejects interest? That examines itself without curiosity? Will it survive?

11. Rose and maroon we might call red.

12. Legalistic definitions. For example, in some jurisdictions a conviction is not present, in spite of a finding of guilt, without imposition of sentence. A suspension of sentence, with probation, would not therefore be a conviction. This has substantial impact on teachers' credentials, or the right to practice medicine or law.

13. That this form has a tradition other than the one I propose, Wittgenstein, etc., I choose not to dispute. But what is its impact on the tradition proposed?

14. Is Wittgenstein's contribution strictly formal?

15. Possibility of a poetry analogous to the paintings of Rosenquist—specific representational detail combined in non-objective, formalist systems.

16. If this were theory, not practice, would I know it?

17. Everything here tends away from an aesthetic decision, which, in itself, is one.

18.   I chose a Chinese notebook, its thin pages not to be cut, its six red-line columns which I turned 90°, the way they are closed by curves at both top and bottom, to see how it would alter the writing. Is it flatter, more airy? The words, as I write them, are larger, cover more surface on this two-dimensional picture plane. Shall I, therefore, tend toward shorter terms—impact of page on vocabulary?

19.   Because I print this, I go slower. Imagine layers of air over the planet. One closer to the center of gravity moves faster, while the one above it tends to drag. The lower one is thought, the planet itself the object of the thought. But from space what is seen is what filters through the slower outer air of representation.

20.   Perhaps poetry is an activity and not a form at all. Would this definition satisfy Duncan?

21.   Poem in a notebook, manuscript, magazine, book, reprinted in an anthology. Scripts and contexts differ. How could it be the same poem?

22.   The page intended to score speech. What an elaborate fiction that seems!

23.   As a boy, riding with my grandparents about Oakland or in the country, I would recite such signs as we passed, directions, names of towns or diners, billboards. This seems to me now a basic form of verbal activity.

24.   If the pen won't work, the words won't form. The meanings are not manifested.

25.   How can I show that the intentions of this work and poetry are identical?

26. Anacoluthia, parataxis—there is no grammar or logic by which the room in which I sit can be precisely re-created in words. If, in fact, I were to try to convey it to a stranger, I'd be inclined to show photos and draw a floor map.

27. Your existence is not a condition of this work. Yet, let me, for a moment, posit it. As you read, other things occur to you. You hear the drip of a faucet, or there's music on, or your companion gives a sigh that represents a poor night's sleep. As you read, old conversations reel slowly through your mind, you sense your buttocks and spine in contact with the chair. All of these certainly must be a part of the meaning of this work.

28. As students, boys and girls the age of ten, we would write stories and essays, reading them to the class if the teacher saw fit. The empty space of blank paper seemed to propose infinite dimensions. When the first term was fixed, the whole form readily appeared. It seemed more a question of finding the writing than of creating it. One day a student—his name was Jon Arnold—read an essay in which he described our responses to hearing him read it. It was then I knew what writing meant.

29. Mallard, drake—if the words change, does the bird remain?

30. How is it possible that I imagine I can put that chair into language? There it sits, mute. It knows nothing of syntax. How can I put it into something it doesn't inherently possess?

31. "Terminate with extreme prejudice." That meant kill. Or "we had to destroy the village in order to save it." Special conditions create special languages. If we remain at a distance, their irrationality seems apparent, but, if we came closer, would it?

32.   The Manson family, the SLA. What if a group began to define the perceived world according to a complex, internally consistent, and precise (tho inaccurate) language? Might not the syntax itself propel their reality to such a point that to our own they could not return? Isn't that what happened to Hitler?

33.   A friend records what she hears, such as a lunatic awaiting his food stamps, speaking to those who also wait in line, that "whether or not you're good people, that's what I can't tell." As if such acts of speech were clues to the truth of speech itself.

34.   They are confused, those who would appropriate Dylan or Wittgenstein—were there ever two more similar men?—passing them off as poets.

35.   What now? What new? All these words turning in on themselves like the concentric layers of an onion.

36.   What does it mean: "saw fit"?

37.   Poetry is a specific form of behavior.

38.   But test it against other forms. Is it more like a drunkenness than filling out an absentee ballot? Is there any value in knowing the answer to this question?

39.   Winter wakens thought, much as summer prods recollection. Ought poetry to be a condition of the seasons?

40.   What any of us eventually tries—to arrive at some form of "bad" writing (e.g., 31–34?) that would be one form of "good" poetry. Only when you achieve this will you be able to define what it is.

41.   Speech only tells you the speaker.

42.   Analogies between poetry and painting end up equating page and canvas. Is there any use in such fiction?

43.   Or take the so-called normal tongue and shift each term in a subtle way. Is this speech made new or mere decoration?

44.   Poets of the syntagmeme, poets of the paradigm.

45.   The word in the world.

46.   Formal perception: that this section, because of the brevity of the foregoing two, should be extensive, commenting, probing, making not aphorisms but fine distinctions, one sentence perhaps of a modular design, verbs in many clauses like small houses sketched into the mountainsides of a grand Chinese landscape, noting to the mind as it passes the gears and hinges of the design, how from the paradigm "large, huge, vast, great, grand," the term was chosen, by rhyme, anticipate "landscape," time itself signaled by the repetition.

47.   Have we come so very far since Sterne or Pope?

48.   Language as a medium attracts me because I equate it with that element of consciousness which I take to be intrinsically human. Painting or music, say, might also directly involve the senses, but by ordering external situations to provoke specific (or general) responses. Do I fictionalize the page as form not to consider it as simply another manifestation of such "objective" fact? I have known writers who thought they could make the page disappear.

49. Everything you hear in your head, heart, whole body, when you read this, is what this is.

50. Ugliness v. banality. Both, finally, are attractive.

51. Time is one axis. Often I want to draw it out, to make it felt, a thing so slow that slight alterations (long v. short syllables, etc., clusters of alliteration . . .) magnify, not line (or breath) but pulse, the blood in the muscle.

52. Etymology in poetry—to what extent is it hidden (i.e., present and felt, but not consciously perceived) and to what extent lost (i.e., not perceived or felt, or, if so, only consciously)? The Joycean tradition here is based on an analytic assumption which is not true.

53. Is the possibility of publishing this work automatically a part of the writing? Does it alter decisions in the work? Could I have written that if it did not?

54. Increasingly I find object art has nothing new to teach me. This is also the case for certain kinds of poetry. My interest in the theory of the line has its limits.

55. The presumption is: I can write like this and "get away with it."

56. As economic conditions worsen, printing becomes prohibitive. Writers posit less emphasis on the page or book.

57. "He's content just to have other writers think of him as a poet." What does this mean?

58. What if there were no other writers? What would I write like?

59. Imagine meaning rounded, never specific.

60. Is it language that creates categories? As if each apple were a proposed definition of a certain term.

61. Poetry, a state of emotion or intellect. Who would believe that? What would prompt them to do so? Also, what would prompt them to abandon this point of view?

62. The very idea of margins. A convention useful to fix forms, perhaps the first visual element of ordering, preceding even the standardization of spelling. What purpose does it have now, beyond the convenience of printers? Margins do not seem inherent in speech, but possibly that is not the case.

63. Why is the concept of a right-hand margin so weak in the poetry of western civilization?

64. Suppose I was trying to explain a theory of the margin to a speaker of Mandarin or Shasta—how would I justify it? Would I compare it to rhyme as a sort of decision? Would I mention the possibility of capitalizing the letters along the margin? If I wanted, could I work "backwards" here, showing how one could posit non-spoken acrostics vertically at the margin and justify its existence from that? What if the person to whom I was explaining this had no alphabet, no writing, in his native tongue?

65. Saroyan and, more completely, Grenier have demonstrated that there is no useful distinction between language and poetry.

66. Under certain conditions any language event can be poetry. The question thus becomes one of what are these conditions.

67. By the very act of naming—*The Chinese Notebook*—one enters into a process as into a contract. Yet each section, such as this, needs to be invented, does not automatically follow from specific prior statements. However, that too could be the case.

68. I have never seen a theory of poetry that adequately included a sub-theory of choice.

69. There is also the question of work rhythms and habits. When I was a boy, after each dinner I would place the family typewriter—it was ancient and heavy—atop the kitchen table, typing or writing furiously—it was almost automatic writing—until it was time to go to bed. Later, married, I still wrote in the evening, as though unable to begin until each day's information reached a certain threshold which I could gauge by fatigue. All throughout these years, I could not work on a given piece beyond one sitting—a condition I attributed to my attention span—, although on occasion "one sitting" could extend to 48 hours. Since then there has been a shift. I have lately been writing in notebooks, over extended periods (in one instance, five months), and in the morning, often before breakfast and at times before dawn. Rather than the fatigue of digested sense data, the state of mind I work in is the empty-headed clarity which follows sleep.

70. This work lacks cunning.

71. An offshoot of projectivist theory was the idea that the form of the poem might be equivalent to the poet's physical self. A thin man to use short lines and a huge man to write at length. Kelly, etc.

72. Antin's theory is that in the recent history of progressive forms (himself, Schwerner, Rothenberg, Mac Low, Higgins, the Something Else writers et al.), it has become clear that only certain domains yield "successful" work. But he has not indicated what these domains are, nor sufficiently defined success.

73. A social definition of a successful poet might be anyone who has a substantial proportion of his or her work generally available, so that an interested reader can, without knowing the writer, grasp, in broad terms at least, the scope of the whole.

74. If this bores you, leave.

75. What happened to fiction was a shift in public sensibility. The general reader no longer is apt to identify with a character in a story, but with its author. Thus the true narrative element is the development of the form. The true drama of, say, Mailer's *Armies of the Night,* is the question: will this book work? In film, an even more naturally narrative medium than prose, this condition is readily apparent.

76. If I am correct that this is poetry, where is its family resemblance to, say, *The Prelude?* Crossing the Alps.

77. The poem as code or fad. One you must "break," while the other requires the decision of whether or not to follow.

78. Is not-writing (and here I don't mean discarding or revising) also part of the process?

79. I am continually amazed at how many writers are writing the poems they believe the person they wish they were would have written.

80. What if writing was meant to represent all possibilities of thought, yet one could or would write only in certain conditions, states of mind?

81. I have seen poems thought or felt to be dense, difficult to get through, re-spaced on the page, two-dimensional picture plane, made airy, "light." How is content altered by this operation?

82. Certain forms of "bad" poetry are of interest because inept writing blocks referentiality, turning words and phrases in on themselves, an autonomy of language which characterizes the "best" writing. Some forms of sloppy surrealism or pseudo-beat automatic writing are particularly given to this.

83. Designated art sentence.

84. One can use the inherent referentiality of sentences very much as certain "pop" artists used images (I'm thinking of Rauschenberg, Johns, Rosenquist, etc.), to use as elements for so-called abstract composition.

85. Abstract v. concrete, a misleading vocabulary. If I read a sentence (story, poem, whatever unit) of a fight, say, and identify with any spectator or combatant, I am having a vicarious experience. But if I experience, most pronouncedly, this language as event, I am experiencing that fact directly.

86. Impossible to posit the cat's expectations in words. Or Q's example—the mouse's fear of the cat is counted as his believing true a certain English sentence. If we are to speak of things, we are proscribed, limited to the external, or else create laughable and fantastic fictions.

87.	Story of a chimpanzee taught that certain geometrical signs stood for words, triangle for bird, circle for water, etc., when presented with a new object, a duck, immediately made up the term "water bird."

88.	That writing was "speech" "scored." A generation caught in such mixed metaphor (denying the metaphor) as that. That elaboration of technical components of the poem carried the force of prophecy.

89.	Is any term now greater than a placeholder? Any arrangement of weighted squares, if ordered by some shared theory of color, could be language.

90.	What do nouns reveal? Conceal?

91.	The idea of the importance of the role of the thumb in human evolution. Would I still be able to use it if I did not have a word for it? Thought it simply a finger? What evidence do I have that my right and left thumbs are at least roughly symmetrical equivalents? After all, I don't really use my hands interchangeably, do I? I couldn't write this with my left hand, or if I did learn to do so, it would be a specific skill and would be perceived as that.

92.	Perhaps as a means of containing meaning outside of the gallery system, the visual arts have entered into a period where the art itself exists in a dialectic, in the exchange between worker, critic and worker. Writing stands in a different historical context. Fiction exists in relation to a publishing system, poetry to an academic one.

93. At Berkeley, when I was a student, graduate students in the English Department liked to think of themselves as "specialized readers."

94. What makes me think that form exists?

95. One possibility is my ability to "duplicate" or represent it. As a child, I could fill in a drawing as tho it and color existed.

96. I want these words to fill the spaces poems leave.

97. The assumption is, language is equal if not to human perception per se, then to what is human about perception.

98. Good v. bad poetry. The distinction is not useful. The whole idea assumes a shared set of articulable values by which to make such a judgment. It assumes, if not the perfect poem, at least the theory of limits, the most perfect poem. How would you proceed to make such a distinction?

99. Those who would excerpt or edit miss the point.

100. "When I look at a blank page it's never blank!" Prove or disprove this statement.

101. Before you can accept the idea of fiction, you have to admit everything else.

102. "The only thing language can change is language." Ah, but to the extent that we act on our thoughts, we act on their syntax.

103. The order of this room is subject-verb-predicate.

104. Put all of this another way: can I use language to change myself?

105. Once I wrote some stories for an elementary school text. I was given a list of words from which to work, several hundred terms

proposed to me as the information range of any eight-year-old. This included no verbs of change.

106. "Time is the common enemy."

107. Concepts of past and future precede an ability to conceive of the sentence.

108. Subjects hypnotized to forget the past and future wrote words at random intervals about the page.

109. So-called non-referential language, when structured non-syntactically, tends to disrupt time perception. Once recognized, one can begin to structure the disruption. Coolidge, for example, in *The Maintains,* uses line, stanza and repetition. Ashbery's *Three Poems,* not referential but syntactical, does not alter time.

110. The flaw of non-referentiality is that words are derived. They do not exist prior to their causes. Even when the origins are not obvious or are forgotten. The root, for example, of *denigrate* is *Negro.* Words only become non-referential through specific context. A condition as special (i.e., not universal or "ordinary") as the poem perceived as speech scored for the page.

111. When I was younger, the argument was whether, when you stripped the poem of all inessentials, you were left finally with a voice or with an image. Now it seems clear that the answer is neither. A poem, like any language, is a vocabulary and a set of rules by which it is processed.

112. But if the poem/language equation is what we have been seeking, other questions nevertheless arise. For example, are two poems by one poet two languages or, as Zukofsky argues, only one? But take

specifics—*Catullus, Mantis, Bottom, "A"-12*—are these not four vocabularies with four sets of rules?

113. Compare sections 26 and 103.

114. If four poets took a specific text from which to derive the terms of a poem, what I call a "vocab," and by prior agreement each wrote a sestina, that would still be four languages and not one, right?

115. A hill with two peaks, or two hills. If I grant that the language alters one's perception, and if it follows naturally that, depending on which perception one "chooses," one acts differently, becomes used to different paths, thinks of certain people as neighbors and others not, and that such acts collectively will alter the hill (e.g., one peak becomes middle-class, residential, while the other slips into ghettohood, later to be cleared off for further "development," which might include leveling the top of the peak to make it useable industrial space)—if I grant the possibility of this chain, is not the landscape itself a consequence of language? And isn't this essentially the history of the planet? Can one, in the context of such a chain, speak of what we know of as the planet as existing prior to language?

116. This jumps around. It does not have an "argument."

117. Paris is in France. Also, Paris has five letters. So does France. But so do Ghana, China, Spain. How should I answer "Why is Paris Paris?"

118. The question within the question. To which does the question mark refer? If one question mark is lost, where does its meaning go? How is it possible for punctuation to have multiple or non-specific references?

119. In what way is this like prose? In what way is this unlike it?

120. Only aesthetic consistency constitutes content (Yates' proposition regarding music). Applied to writing, one arrives at the possibility of a "meaningful" poetry as the sum of "meaningless" poems.

121. But consistency demands a perception of time. Thus, if we accept the proposition, we tacitly approve some definition of poetry as a specific time construct.

122. There is no direction. There is only distance.

123. What is the creative role of confusion in any work?

124. At times, my own name is simply a gathering of letters. Very distant.

125. Words relate to the referred world much the way each point in a line can be said to describe a curve.

126. The sun variously rises each morning. We, variously, attempt to relate that. No single way is exact, yet everyone knows what we mean.

127. The words are not "out there."

128. By the time you admit the presence of verbs, you have already conceded all of the assumptions.

129. The historical attraction of the arts to madness is a question of what happens if you redefine the language.

130. Content is only an excuse, something to permit the writing to occur, to trigger it. Would a historian looking for information about Massachusetts fishing colonies have much use for *Maximus*? To say yes is to concede that in order to like, say, Pound, you'd have to agree with him, no?

131. *Sad is faction.* That sounds alone are not precise meaning (in the referential sense) means that before the listener can recognize content he/she must first have the perception of the presence of words.

132. But if one denies the possibility of referentiality, how does *sad is faction* differ from *satisfaction?* How do we know this?

133. "Post-syntactical" implies that syntax was a historical period of language, not a condition inherent in it. Rather than seeing language as a universe whose total set cannot be dealt with until all its conditions are brought into play, this designation opts for an easy and incorrect solution. Occasionally, it has been used in such a fashion as to assert some sort of competition with "syntactical" writing, with the supposedly obvious presumption that, being later in language's various conditions, it is more advanced. Such a view distorts the intentions and functions of abandoning syntactical and even paratactical modes.

134. Terms, out of context, inevitably expand and develop enlarged inner conditions, the large field of the miniaturists.

135. Eigner's work, for example. The early writings resemble a late Williams/early Olson mode, discursive syntax, which becomes in later works increasingly a cryptic notation until now often words in a work will float in an intuitive vocabulary—space, their inner complexities expanded so that words are used like the formal elements in abstract art.

136. To move away from the individualist stance in writing, I first began to choose vocabularies for poems from language sources that were not my own, science texts, etc. Then I began to develop forms which opt away from the melodic dominant line of the past

several decades, using formal analogies taken from certain Balinese and African percussive and ensemble musics, as well as that of Steve Reich.

137. The concept that the poem "expresses" the poet, vocally or otherwise, is at one with the whole body of thought identified as Capitalist Imperialism.

138. If poetry is to be perfect, it cannot be all-knowing. If it is to be all-knowing, it cannot be perfect.

139. I began writing seriously a decade ago and was slow to learn. For years I was awkward, sloppy, given to overstatement, the sentimental image, the theatrical resolution. Yet, subtracting these, I am amazed at the elements, all formal and/or conceptual, which have remained constants. It is those who tell me who I am.

140. The presumption of the logical positivists that "the relation between language and philosophy is closer than, as well as essentially different from, that between language and any other discipline," would upset most poets. Three answers seem possible: (1) the logical positivists are wrong, (2) poetry and philosophy are quite similar and perhaps ought to be considered different branches of a larger category, (3) poetry is not a discipline, at least in the sense of the special definition of the logical positivists. I reject the third alternative as not being true for any except those poets whose work lacks all sense of definition. This leaves me with two possible conclusions.

141. Why is this work a poem?

142. One answer: because certain information is suppressed due to what its position in the sequence would be.

143. But is it simply a question of leaving out?

144. It is our interpretation of signs, not their presence (which, after all, could be any series of random marks on the page, sounds in the air), that makes them referential.

145. There are writers who would never question the assumptions of non-objective artists (Terry Fox, say, or even Stella or the late Smithson) who cannot deal with writing in the same fashion. Whenever they see certain marks on the page, they always presume that something *besides* those marks is also present.

146. On page 282 of *Imaginations,* Williams writes "This is the alphabet," presents the typewriter keyboard, except that where the *s* should be there appears a second *e*. Whether this was "in error" or not, it tells us everything about the perception of language.

147. The failure of Williams to go beyond his work of *Spring and All* and the *Great American Novel* seems to verify Bergmann's assertion that nominalism inevitably tends toward (deteriorates into?) representationalism.

148. Konkretism was a very narrow base on which to build a literature. Futurism of the Russian school, especially the *zaum* works of the Group 41°, is the true existing body of experimental literature with which contemporary writers have to work.

149. What is it that allows me to identify this as a poem, Wittgenstein to identify his work as technical philosophy, Brockman's *Afterwords* to be seen as Esalen-oriented metaphysics, and Kenner's piece on Zukofsky literary criticism?

150. But is it a distortion of poetry to speak of it like this? How might I define poetry so as to be able to identify such distortions?

151. Can one even say, as have Wellek and Warren, that literature (not even here to be so specific as to identify the poem to the exclusion of other modes) is first of all words in a sequence? One can point to the concretist tradition as a partial refutation, or one can point to the great works of Grenier, *A Day at the Beach* and *Sentences,* where literature occurs within individual words.

152. Possibly, if one approached it cautiously, one could hope to make notations, provisional definitions of poetry. For example, one might begin by stating that it is any language act—not necessarily a sequence of terms—which makes no other formal assertion other than it is poetry. This would permit the exclusion of Kosuth and Wittgenstein, but the inclusion of this.

153. But how, if it does not state it, does a work make a formal assertion? Certain structural characteristics such as line, stanza, etc. are not always present. Here is where one gets into Davenport's position regarding Ronald Johnson, to say that one is a poet who has written no poems, per se.

154. Performance as a form is only that. As always, the intention of the creator defines the state in which the work is most wholly itself, so that it is possible that a talking piece, say, could be said to be a poem. But formally its ties are closer to other arts than to the tradition of poetry. I have, in the last year, heard talking pieces that were proposed as poetry, as music and as sculpture. Each, in all major respects, resembled the late period of Lenny Bruce or perhaps Dick Cavett. The form of the talking piece, its tradition, was always

stronger than the asserted definition. Nor is the talking piece the only non-traditional (if, in fact, it is that at all) mode to run into this problem. Some of the visualists, e.g., Kostelanetz, have utilized film for their poems, but the poem is readily lost in this transfer. What one experiences in its presence is the fact of film.

155. Why did I write "As always, the intention of the creator defines the state in which the work is most wholly itself"? Because it is here and here only where one can "fix" a work into a given state (idea, projective process, text, affective process, impression), an act which is required, absolutely, before one can place the work in relation to others, only after which can one make judgments.

156. What if I told you I did not really believe this to be a poem? What if I told you I did?

157. Periodically one hears that definitions are unimportant, or, and this implicitly is more damning, "not interesting." I reject this, taking all language events to be definitions or, if you will, propositions.

158. I find myself not only in the position of arguing that all language acts are definitions and that they nonetheless are not essentially referential, but also that this is not a case specifically limited to an "ideal" or "special" language (such as one might argue poetry to be), but is general, applicable to all.

159. If, at this point, I was to insert 120 rhymed couplets, would it cause definitions to change?

160. Lippard (*Changing,* p. 206) argues against a need for a "humanistic" visual arts, but makes an exception for literature, which "as a verbal medium, demands a verbal response." One wonders what,

precisely, is meant by that? Is it simply a question of referentiality posed in vague terms? Or does it mean, as I suspect she intended it to, that language, like photography, is an ultimately captive medium? If so, is the assertion correct? It is not.

161. It becomes increasingly clear that the referential origin of language and its syntactical (or linguistic, or relational) meaning is the contradiction (if it is one) that is to be understood if we are to accept a poetics of autonomous language.

162. If I could make an irrefutable argument that non-referential language does exist (besides, that is, those special categories, such as prepositions or determiners), would I include this in it? Of course I would.

163. What you read is what you read.

164. Make a note in some other place, then transfer it here. Is it the same note?

165. I want form to be perceivable but not consequent to referred meaning. Rather, it should serve to move that element to the fore- or backbrain at will.

166. Form that is an extension of referred meaning stresses that meaning's relation to the individual, voice or image as extension of self, emphasizes one's separateness from others. What I want, instead, is recognition of our connectedness.

167. A writing which is all work, technical procedure, say a poem derived from a specific formula, is of interest for this fact alone.

168. Words in a text like states on a map: meaning is commerce.

169. One type of criticism would simply describe the formal features of any given work, demonstrate its orderliness with the implicit purpose of, from this, deducing the work's intention. A comparison, then, of the intention to the work (and, secondarily, to other works of identical or similar intention) would provide grounds for a judgment.

170. Is it possible for a work to conceal its intention?

171. But if the intention is always to be arrived at deductively, will not the work always be equal to it? Would we be able to recognize a work which had not met the writer's original intention?

172. Perhaps this poem could be said to be an example of the condition described in 171.

173. Is it possible for intentions to be judged, good or malevolent, right or otherwise? This brings us into the realm of political and ethical distinctions.

174. In recent years, criticism has played a dynamic role in the evolution of the visual arts, but not in writing. Theory, much of it unsound, even mystical, on the part of writers, has had more impact. A possible explanation: criticism is applied theory, useful only if it is rigorous in its application, which has been impossible given the loose and vague standards characteristic of so much recent writing, while theory can be used suggestively, which it has been regardless of the mystifications present.

175. A poem written in pen could never have been written in pencil.

176. When I was younger, I was so habituated to the typewriter as a tool and to the typewritten page as a space that, even when

I worked from notebooks, the poems transposed back into a typewritten text tended to perfectly fill the page.

177. Deliberately determining the way one writes determines much of what will be written.

178. If I were to publish only parts of this, sections, it would alter the total proposition.

179. How far will anything extend? Hire dancers dressed as security personnel to walk about an otherwise empty museum, then admit the public. Could this be poetry if I have proposed it as such? If so, what elements could be altered or removed to make it not poetry? E.g., hire not dancers but ordinary security personnel. But if the answer is "no," if any extension, thing, event, would be poetry if proposed as such, *what* would poetry, the term, mean?

180. Possibly poetry is a condition applicable to any state of affairs. What would constitute such a condition? Would it be the same or similar in all instances? Could it be identified, broken down? Does it have anything to do with the adjectival form "poetic"?

181. If one could propose worrying as one form of poetry, what in the worrying would be the poem?

182. Or could one have poetry without the poem? Is it possible that these two states do not depend on the presence (relational as it is) of each other? Give examples.

183. Why is it language characterizes the man?

184. Or I meant, possibly, why is it that language characterizes man?

185. Is it language?

186. Context—against the text. Literally a circumstance where meaning is not obvious simply by the presence of terms in a specific sequence. Remove 185 from this text: "it" in 185 then means either "this writing" or some "other" event. But in the notebook as it is, the sentence must mean "Is it language that characterizes (the) man?" Is the same sentence in two contexts one or two sentences? If it is one, how can we assign it differing meanings? If it is two, there could never literally be repetition.

187. Alimentary, my dear Watson.

188. But if poetry were a "system"—not necessarily a single system, but if for any individual it was—then one could simply plug in the raw data and out would flow "poetry," not necessarily poems.

189. Is this not what Robert Kelly does?

190. It was Ed van Aelstyn who, in his linguistics course, planted the idea (1968) that the definition of a language was also a definition of any poem: a vocabulary plus a set of rules through which to process it. What did I think poetry was before that?

191. But does the vocabulary include words which do not end up in the finished text? If so, how would we know which words they are?

192. A friend, a member of the Old Left, challenges my aesthetic. How, he asks, can one write so as not to "communicate"? I, in turn, challenge his definitions. It is a more crucial lesson, I argue, to learn how to experience language directly, to tune one's senses to it, than to use it as a mere means to an end. Such use, I point out, is, in bourgeois life, common to all things, even the way we "use" our friends. Some artists (Brecht is the obvious example) try to focus

such "use" to point up all the alienation, to present a bourgeois discourse "hollowed out." But language, so that it is experienced directly, moves beyond any such exercise in despair, an unalienated language. He wants an example. I give him Grenier's

> thumpa
>
> thumpa
>
> thumpa
>
> thump

pointing out how it uses so many physical elements of speech, how it is a speech that only borders on language, how it illumines that space. He says, "I don't understand."

193. Determiners, their meaning.

194. Each sentence is new born.

195. Traditionally, poetry has been restrictive, has had no room for the appositive.

196. I imagine at times this to be discourse. Sometimes it is one voice, sometimes many.

197. Language on walls. Graffiti, "fuk speling," etc. As a boy, I rode with my grandparents about town, learning to read by reading all the signs aloud. I am still apt to do this.

198. This sentence is that one.

199. "This in which," i.e., the world in its relations. What is of interest is not the objectification, but relativity: Einstein's "What time does the station get to the train?"

200. Imagine the man who liked de Kooning out of a fondness for women.

201. There is no way in language to describe the experience of knowing my hand.

202. I was chased, running through a forest. Because I knew the names of the plants I could run faster.

203. The formal considerations of indeterminacy are too few for interest to extend very far, even when posed in other terms—"organic," etc. But organic form is strict, say, 1:1:2:3:5:8:13:21. . . . What is the justification for strict form (Xenakis' music, for example) which cannot be perceived? Is there an aesthetic defense for the hidden?

204. Presence and absence. This axis is form's major dimension.

205. Are 23 and 197 the same or different?

206. A paper which did not absorb fluids well, a pencil that was blunt or wrote only faintly. These would determine the form of the work. Now, when I set out on a piece, choice of instrument and recorder (notebook, typing paper, etc.) are major concerns. I am apt to buy specific pens for specific pieces.

207. Words to locate specific instance—personalism, localism. Quality of a journal to what this or that one does. "Another hard day of gossip."

208. Any writer carries in his or her head a set, what "the scene" is, its issues, etc. So often little or no overlap at all, but how it defines what anyone does!

209. The day is wrappt in its definitions, this room is.

210. Whether one sees language as learned or inherent determines, in part, what one does with it. The "organic" sentence (truncated, say, by breath, or thought's diversions) versus the sentence as an infinitely plastic (I don't mean this in the pejorative sense) one, folding, unfolding, extending without limit. Dahlberg or Faulkner.

211. Absolutely normal people. Would their writing be any different?

212. Information leaks through these words. Each time I use them new things appear.

213. Values are vowels.

214. A language of one consonant, one vowel, various as any.

215. Like eyesight, our minds organizing what we "see" before we even see it. As tho I did not know about oranges, tho I had eaten them all my life. Each time I ate one I would not know what taste to expect.

216. I do not read to "read of the world," but for the pleasure in the act of reading.

217. The ocean's edge is a mantra. Strollers, bathers, dogs, gulls. Its great sound. The smell of salt. Sun's sheen on water. But there is no way to repeat this in language. Anything we say, descriptively, is partial. At best one constructs an aesthetic of implication. One can, however, make of the language itself a mantra. But this is not the ocean.

218. Buildup, resolution. What have these to do with the writing?

219. Just as doubt presumes a concept of certainty, non-referentiality presumes knowledge of the referential. Is this a proof?

220. When I return here to ideas previously stated, that's rhyme.

221. Any piece I write precludes the writing of some other piece. As this work is the necessary consequence of previous writings, called poems, so it will also create necessities, ordering what follows. I take this as absolute verification of its poemhood.

222. Language hums in the head, secretes words.

223. This is it.

2197

I Am Marion Delgado

How do we recognize the presence of
a new season.
Field is the common sky.
Spring language.
What if blowfly believe the sky is the
room.
A first time, not glow, of common is
the enemy.
Blowfly objectify the expression.
A believe as stasis and casual as the
perfect.
Lion I'd bites.
A specific lion, mane, bites for the
peach-headed.
Realism is a swamp, not a gas.
How do you geometry light and dew.
Across a visits with a milky omitted.
Haze with a glow made of lights is the
sign.

Seal as form, as loss of guntower.
Use to context of term with the
greatest miscreants.
Concentric rhesus' habitat.
Coleus canvas made in maze.

Language swollen from a long day of
picture.

Sound of gas colors, water, faint
grammar in the lightbulb as I follow my
breakfast.

As Satie grew older, his body connect
into Thoreau.

The friend of my chance market.

The fog is full of steams.

Freedom of family and loss without
specific.

Speak example to negation.

He turned to us his fud.

If the pen becomes obsolete, objective
angle becomes page.

Write in what of need.

Dream brings summer by song,
foghorn by this.

A new leg of pulls has formed in our
time.

Block or the house of advanced from
the house of block.

The grapefruit forms a dream that
readily dissolves.

Urine forms the foam of my former
dissolves.

A new city formed with roaches first.
This world brings in the summer
syntax of the real.
Each flight divining his birds, one
augury at an art.
The envelope of sound.
Geeks was more real than the delight.
Rejection of the artful.
Visit what my home.

Fog rain forms is high for low tide.
Locating prior concept atop difficulty.
Blind talking about color.
This is the hang-up between handguns
and sex.
Poem is an end.
There are warrior song within a kite.
The long we read into the page, the
less certain it did it does.
Here the cells are sickling.
Noise on the bus on their way to this.
We went fill through the loomy forms.
We arrived at the small fishing
sensitivity just as the language worked its
way over the information.
The loud inventory of an old ontology.
Popcorn feeding at woman.

I could speak my own truth.

The forearm gets swollen in that long of the day.

Learning to bowl the grains for the nuts, it names.

Little rain above the loss.

I saw a full world.

As recognition of reluctance begins to lapse, sense of self begins to grow.

The pastel chose to concentric the circles.

Mexico, it is not a wax matches.

Thought block as small carving.

Any object or obsolete is distance in so by its objective.

Faint hum sound us.

The ocean is never perfectly calm.

Grew more older.

The popcorn is merely a sea kelp.

Meaning is predicated on this.

A mushroom page chosen up out of the random.

Ridge on the small of fishing.

All the loomy which are sailing to be air.

This many, made over, do voices.

As if a regatta, the bicycle riders glide
through the park.

The inserts of random is dimly
posited.

Choices should not have language.

Not by the certain, but by the
definition.

Meaning distance verification.

He work to sleepers his bus.

World of the room.

A stone crowd and chose the mime.

Is this a spray or cat of poor.

This universe, really in its personal.

The garbage is never glad bags.

As if a circus, the cruel riders saw
through the park.

Action based on idea is inevitable for
any who hedged with what they conditions
to be the thing.

The porridge, more, are a form of eat.

We advanced house by house, block
by block.

Snows learning the turtle, play down
their cure.

Above rock and/or soil.

Us who run to defines the struggle
tend to sit at the front.

A small corner gets sun what porch
trapped.

Breath and smell are not own.

There are many doors.

A not mereness is feeding mortality to
degrees.

How merely falls it, walk it, take it to
read this city, this then morning, that.

His Alias name.

There brings clouds amid rise the sun's
light.

Low Diane at high Arbus loves you.

What of think.

Attention deserves for an inventory of
whatever case is in the past.

Anything I do is made for many
voices.

Destruction with the death about fate.

A catalogue without descriptive,
without undefined, without terms.

World pictures.

Ages are a this page.

Glide bicycle regatta riders through
the park.

Which is form, which is order.

Doing what can cause me to asks your small boy.

This would lay his words on the wall by the well.

Sleeves is a rolling down people.

Tie in the dark black shadows, but thru its white the glare of the oceans shirt.

Longer the language are thought.

Never the loud calm of nervous ocean in head and you get perfectly.

The action in guilt of the oppressor.

Rain as form, as loss of form.

How do people catch the bus.

Tense of time.

Remorseful, its all the progressions.

Cells sickling the sky of the here.

Responsibilities you neglect.

Glare is the dark edge.

Across a language with a sense data.

A specific same, windowpane, reserved for the all.

A system as loud and nervous as the head.

How long does it, did it, take to read this page, this then that, this.

Temperature in which the body back.

How do you roller skates.

Words world.

A first fear, not glow, of light is the days sleep.

Highway with a thousand made of ten pour a oranges man.

What if grandfather lay bed is perfect table.

A razor that decide today by the south day.

Criterion of the adequate to meaning.

Dogs is our sentences as to what might have bark.

Really, it is not a personal universe.

The patterns physical.

A brain in which to kill the ghoul kill.

This is not a vision loss of weight loss.

The photograph is a maze of expected, suddenly, barnwood and speak.

Great sky of wall advances morning.

Sun rainbow up off the lower.

We headlines insect with world.

This is not awareness but a name of it.

By value I have a other in the only and we words.

Rose is mushroom on cloud.

Blues is the day.

Clock in the not to shake not sleeping
act.

The spring mass is rim, the dimly
spaces seen.

How do we predicated the existence of
a new experience.

I moving present instant.

The true of things.

One not, have from several part of the
poems, or goals.

Now I turned the truck in my oranges.

By chance I meet a friend in the
market and we visit.

Fud turned to us.

A conversion of trees.

People stood on the proliferation,
waving to the incoming, black-clad
alphabet.

Voice his parts was brain.

The morning senses sleeping, the loose
merely shake into the sneeze.

The warm rise amid weather brings
only a dull smell.

I meet my friend in the market.

What do land mass.

The geometry of light and dew in the trees.

Needle and pine have been the fate of diamond.

In lepers, there are many blink.

My themes see life.

The presence of new season recognize.

This sidewalks waving.

The room of news is not in degrees.

The morning of the Q-tips deserves attention.

I Meet Osip Brik

Sidewalks, people waving, is incoming insurgents. Experience of
the predicated. Spaces in which land mass. Smell of warm, weather
of I. Needle of diamond or pine. These are only Q-tips and have
no other morning. The season is not the presence of the new which
it recognize. The lower the themes, the higher the life. A needle I
suddenly diamond to pine. Great sneeze of senses shake in the loose
sleeping. News from the insect room. Blink objects forget lepers
here. Several the voice, one the brain.

Blowfly made in sky. Bowl of field and milky without sky. Speak
haze to glow. The realism of my strategy. Visits omitted from a long
day of volleyball. As he grew stasis, his body drifted into perfect
rest. Not by the clock, but by the act. Sound of geometry, light in
the dew as I make my trees. Coming to recognition of swamp with
the greatest gas. If the object becomes objectify, objective distance
becomes expression. The lion is full of grapes. Spring as languor-
ous, as casual of language. Common enemy time.

Picture what you language. The sentence is not the name of the
awareness which it represents. This angle brings in the summer
page of the pen. The habitat of rhesus. The market meet with
chance first. A new context of miscreants had formed in our term.
The example forms a negation that readily incorrect. Each seal
came his south on, one guntower at ashore. I visit the fog of my
former field. Grammar was more here than the colors. We maze
coleus by canvas, barnwood by skylights. Called in a freedom of
loss. Satie or the art of connect from the flight of Thoreau.

Foghorns brings in dream. Block advanced at house. There are genuine geeks within a delight. The new city of an old stove. Syntax went sailing through the real world. Former is a home. We pulls at the small fishing pants just as the leg worked its way over the time. Sprinkled sea dream atop grapefruit. Which is wisteria, which is lilac. Urine I forms is foam for readily dissolves. The more we write into the what, the less certain you are it need. Flight is the art between birds and divining. Sealed on the envelope on their way to sound.

As sense of world begins to inventory, sense of whatever begins to ontology. The page gets read in that take of the long. Any color or thing is talking in so by its blind. Is this a well or wall of words. I saw a cruel poem. Eat more sex. Language sensitivity above the information. Only forms fill us. Really, it is not an old woman. The locating chose to concept the prior. Learning to play the turtle for the noise, it this. Mylar song as warrior kite. Forms could fog low tide rain.

Rain form loss. This world, turned full, poured pomegranates. A older shapelessness drifted up out of the body. All the object which are known to be objective. Breakfast should not have water. The mereness of mortality is not in degrees. The wax of Mexico is dimly made. The truth is merely a moving power. Forearm is swollen on volleyball. Reluctance on the recognition of self. He circles to concentric his pastel. Carving of the thought. Not by the names, but by the nuts.

As if a meaning, the bicycle riders glide through the this. Small sun and/or way. Inserts based on guilt is posited for those who identify with what they know to be the random. Sleepers exiting the bus, rolling down their way. The meaning, between, are a verification of distance. This page, random in its chosen. A sprinkled kelp and a sea popcorn. People who went to catch the air tend to sailing at the loomy. A less certain exists me what I'm put. Is this a window or world of open. The sun's rise amid clouds brings only a dull light. Do and made are not voices. The language is never genuine choices.

How long could it, did it, take to smell this breath, own then my, I. An old struggle is defines only to us. Cruel is a circus. A crowd without chose, without stone, without mime. Glad with the garbage about bags. Inserts posited at random. Really personal universe. Cat spray. Soil of rock. Conditions are a thing idea. More eat for an inventory of whatever there is in the porridge. Turtle snows at play cure forms learning. There was sun in trapped the porch corner.

Visit in the dark former shadows, but thru its doors the home of the oceans wife. Light sun's dull rise amid a clouds. Do is what, you is think. Undefined is a descriptive terms catalogue. Doors of Korea. The world is full of pomegranates. San Francisco have been his fate on the death by the destruction. Mereness the loud not of nervous mortality in head and you get degrees. World the pictures are floating. How do the ages page the this. Attention, its all the case. The name in alias of the said. Turning Diane can cause you to love your collective Arbus.

A people as front and run as the catch. How do you language thought. Words filling the well of the wall. Across a shirt with a black tie. What if never believe calm is perfectly ocean. Language sensitivity information. Boy with a small made of asks bites a doing

me. Identify action. Tense is the synonymous time. People I'd down.
Remorseful in which poem progressions. A specific form, strewn,
order for the books. A first regatta, not park, of bicycle is the riders
glide.

By chance I meet a temperature in the body and we back. Specific
data of sense called language. The ocean's shadows. A world in
which to do the words how. This is not inward but a cause of it.
Oranges pour up onto a highway. Sound of the skates to roller.
Windowpane is our all as to what might have same. This is not
an incorrect fear of sleep negation. A hum that get nervous by
the loud words. I saw a cruel circus. The here is a maze of cells,
canvas, barnwood and sickling. We lay grandfather by bed.

How do we weight the loss of a loss vision. Morning advances
great sky. A criterion of meaning. Sun in the lower to rainbow
loose higher senses. Here I patterns the physical in my objects.
Photograph stood on the expected waving to the suddenly black-
clad speak. Dogs is the bark. Awareness name to represents. Words
are value on other. The brain mass is kill, the barren ghoul kill.
One world, coming from several headlines of the insect, or brain.
The day of decide. A seal that came ashore by the south guntower.

I blue my day in the gray. The spring of the rim seen dimly. In mov-
ing, there are merely instant. Casual and conversion have been the
tree of the bird. The alphabet of proliferation is not in degrees.
Realism is a strategy, not a condition. This poems goals. Cloud
what you sink. The clock of not descriptive act. The morning he
turned, the fud merely walk into the us. Known all things are true.
The truck turned amid oranges poured only a dull over. Experience
predicated existence.

Rhizome

Proliferation of the alphabet world.

Poured

of truck, turned of oranges.

Mushroom out which

cloud rose.

Experience is predicated on

existence.

Goals we have, should not poems.

A

bird I casual conversion into tree.

He wall of us

turned the his fud.

The clock is not the name

of the act which it represents.

The lower the

existence, the higher the experience.

Know the

true, be the things.

These are dimly spring and

have no seen rim.

Moving present is instant

merely.

Blues of the gray.

Casual conversion of bird into tree.

Land to mass

of spaces with the immense barren.

                                        Sound of gas
diamond, needle, faint hum in the pine as I make
my breakfast.

                        If the object becomes news, room
distance becomes obsolete.

                                Blink swollen from a
long forget of lepers.

                        The sleeping is loose on
senses.

                The predicated of my experience existence.
Recognize new of presence.

                                        Incoming insurgents
stood on sidewalks.

                                As voice parts several, one brain
coming into room.

                        Now life themes.

                                        Morning as
form, as loss of Q-tips.

                                Smell of weather and I
without warm.

Sealed in a field full of sky.

                                Lion made the grapes
of my peach-headed man.

                                A new swamp of
roaches had formed in our gas.

                                        Visits what you'd

omitted.

       This dream do the objectify of expression.
Each spring pulls his languorous, one casual at a
language.

        Geometry was more light than the dew.
The time of enemy.

            We filling blow by fly, sky by
room.

      The realism fill with strategy
condition.

       Believe or the art of stasis
from the perfect of rest.

           The lower the sun, the
higher the rainbow.

          The haze forms a glow
that readily light.

Rhesus' on the habitat on their way to work.
There are genuine colors with a grammar.

               Canvas
maze at skylights.

          The chance visit of an market
friend.

      Turning inward can cause you to neglect
your collective responsibilities.

            We arrived at the
small fishing context just as the term use its way
over the miscreants.

This is the seal between
south and ashore.
The specific we put into the
loss, the less certain it family.
Sprinkled incorrect
example atop negation.
Pen went sailing through
the angle page.
Satie connect at Thoreau.
Fog I
do is field for many steams.
This is a picture.

Learning to play the envelope for the sound, it
sealed.
Geeks bags as glad delight.
The dream
chose to stone the grapefruit.
Wife visit a former
home.
The what gets write in that corner of the need.
As city of roaches formed to lapse, sense of stove
begins to grow.
Absentee information and/or
criticism.
More syntax defines real.
Any dream or
song is brings in so by its summer.

I could foam my
own urine.

Really house is not a advanced block.
Art more birds.

One pants above the time.

He locating to us his concept.

Death and
destruction have been the fate of San Francisco.
The popcorn of pigeons is old feeding.

All the
color which are talking to be blind.

Ontology on
the world of whatever.

This poem, without
events, poured development.

A sex hang-up rose
out of the handguns.

Not by the noise, but by the
this.

The rain is merely a low fog.

Song of the
warrior.

Forms should not have fill.

Language
information sensitivity.

This is read on that.

Object who becomes to becomes the objective tend
to sit at the distance.
                         A small bowl names me what
I'm nuts.
          Full and world are not pomegranates.
The rain, strewn, are a form of loss.
                              A black truth
and a white power.
                    This body, older in its
shapelessness.
               This dream brings in the summer
song of the foghorns.
                       Matches based on wax is made
for those who identify with what they know to be
the Mexico.
             The sound is never perfectly faint.
Is this a block or carving of thought.
                              Self
recognition and/or reluctance.
                              Pastel exiting the
concentric, rolling down their circles.
                              As if a
volleyball, the forearm swollen through the day.

World enters.
             How many does it, did it, take to
made this voices, this then that, anything.
Choices with the genuine about language.

Inserts are a random posited.

A popcorn without
sea, without sprinkled, without kelp.

Random
chosen page.

The more we put into the definition, the
less certain we are it exists.

There was more in exists
the definition "certain."

Verification searches for an
distance of whatever there is in the meaning.

An old
air is sailing through to loomy.

Low sleepers at high
bus forms work.

Way of village.

Meaning is a this.

The personal in universe of the really.

I in the
dark smell shadows, but thru my own the glare of
the ocean's breath.

Garbage would bag his rags on
the table by the glad.

Defines the only hum of
nervous struggle in us and you get words.
Porridge, its more the eat.

Wax matches made in

Mexico.
    Cruel of circus.
        Little is soil, above is
rock.
   Learning turtle can cure you to play your
collective snows.
       This is a stone mime crowd.
Poor the cat can't spray.
        Trapped that corner porch
onto the sun.
     How do the thing conditions the idea.

San Francisco destruction the fate of death.
Diane with a mane made of you loves a Arbus man.
A specific think, you, do for the what.
         A dull
rise, amid suns, of clouds is the only sign.
          By
chance I case a past in the attention and we
deserves.
    How do floating pictures world.
Mereness if I believe degrees is not mortality.
Terms I'd undefined.
     A poem without
development, without events, without end.
Into the morning with the merely falls.
        Alias
name.

This page as languorous and casual as the ages.

Many are the Korea doors.

We calm perfectly with never.

A people who run front by the bus catch.

Boys asks up of the small.
Longer of the language to thought.

By this I meet a poem in the progressions and its remorseful.
Order is our form as to what might have strewn.
Black tie of white called shirt.

The upstairs is a well of wall, canvas, this and words.

Eat more porridge.

This is not rolling but a down of it.
A guilt in which to based the action inevitable.
The time tense.

This is not an bicycle riders of glide park.

Responsibilities neglect to cause.

Temperature is back on body.

A sidewalk of sound.

The word
mass is how, the barren words do.
The cross-
section of system.
Pour in the oranges to
thousand onto highway ten.
All is the same.
One grandfather, lay from several truss of the bed,
or table.
Specific loss of freedom called family.
People stood on the here waving to the sickling,
black-clad cells.
Now I edge the shadows in my
doors.
I sense data language.
How do we fear the
presence of a new sleep.

I dogs my bark in the sentences.
The name
sentence falls, the not merely represents into the
awareness.
The lower of higher rainbow sun.
What are words value.
The photograph of
suddenly is not in speak.
The world headlines.
The objects physical amid patterns brings only a

dull here.
> The brain of the ghoul kill kill.
>> A

spring as languorous and casual as the language.
In morning there are great advances.
>> Weight loss

vision.
> Meaning and adequate have been the
criterion.
> Decide his day is today.

Winter Landscape with Skaters and a Bird Trap

The higher is not the rainbow of the
sun which it lower.

Brain are only kill and kill no other
ghoul.

Patterns of objects, physical of here.

Sentence name of not represents in the
east awareness.

Bark of the dogs.

Other in which words value.

World, we decide, is insect headlines.

Razor the today, decide the day.

East advances are great sky.

The loss of vision, the loss the weight.

The morning of Q-tips.

A this I adequate meaning to criterion.

Speak from the expected photograph.

Sink to rose of cloud with the greatest
mushroom.

Conversion of gas bird, casual, faint
hum into the lightbulb as I make my tree.

Existence predicated experience.

As things be all, his true known into
shapelessness.

Act not to clock.

Spring as dimly, as rim of seen.

The day of my gray blues.

If the alphabet becomes obsolete,
objective proliferation becomes obsolete.

The us is turned of fud.

Wax poems have in goals.

Gray day blues.

Truck of this and over without
oranges.

Present moving from a long instant of
merely.

Voice or the parts of several from the
room of brain.

The existence predicated with
experience first.

This news brings in the summer song
of the room.

Each one pulls his morning on, one leg
at a Q-tips.

A barren mass of spaces is immense in
our land.

Forget what lepers blink.

The season forms a presence that new
recognize.

The life of themes.

Insurgents stood waving by incoming,
people by sidewalks.

Pine was more needle than the
diamond.
I shake the morning of my sleeping
sidewalks.
Warm in a smell of weather.
This is an adequate meaning criterion.

We arrived at the small fishing swamp
just as the sun worked its way over the gas.
Pour ten thousand oranges onto a
highway.
Visits is a omitted.
Time on the common on their way to
the enemy.
You went objectify through the
expression.
The more we put into the field, the
less milky we are it the sky.
Anything lion do is made for many
grapes.
Sprinkled sea haze atop the days sign.
The loud realism of old strategy.
This is the spring between casual and
language.
There are genuine trees within a light.
The sky posited at room.
Stasis believe at rest.

Satie, it is not a personal Thoreau.

People exiting the restroom, rolling down their sleeves.

Learning to play the rhesus for the habitat, it snows.

The example chose to incorrect the negation.

Only pen angle page.

Garbage colors as glad grammar.

The family gets called in that loss of the specific.

Little context above the term.

Any coleus or canvas is upstairs in so by its skylights.

Spring more language.

As chance of market begins to lapse, friend of meet begins to visit.

I could fog my own steams.

Write is what on need.

I visit my grandmother in the hospital.

Delight of the Geeks.

Time leg pulls.

Not by the envelope, but by the sound.

All the foghorns which are dream to be song.

Roaches on the side of city.

He dream to us his grapefruit.

A mushroom flight divining up out of the art.

World should not have syntax.

The block of house is dimly advanced.

This home, visit over, poured former.

The information, strewn, are a language of sensitivity.

Syntax was more real than the world.

Pigeons based on popcorn is inevitable for those who feeding with woman they know to be the old.

A small noise asks me what I'm this.

Events and development are not end.

People who talking to catch the blind tend to sit at the color.

A low fog and a high tide.

The fill is never perfectly forms.

As if a read, the page long through the take.

Difficulty locating the concept, rolling down their prior.

Ontology inventory and/or world.

This hang-up, handguns in its sex.

Is this a kite or song of Mylar.

Recognition of reluctance.

An obsolete object is feeding distance
to objective.

There was bowl in nuts the names
grains.

Make in the gas about jets.

How full does it, did it, take to
pomegranates this world, this then that,
this.

Rain searches for an form of whatever
loss is in the form.

Concentric fog at high pastel forms
circles.

Older body shapelessness.

This is a volleyball.

Thought carving.

A speak without truth, without power,
without end.

We went sailing through the loomy air.

Matches made a wax Mexico.

Work inward can cause you to way
your bus sleepers.

Anything in the made bars shadows,
but thru its doors the many of the voices
edge.

How do the inserts posited the
random.

Meaning of this.

Here the world are open.

This is a sea kelp popcorn.

Language would lay his choices on the
table by the genuine.

Put less certain definition into the
exists.

Meaning, its all the verification.

Bowl of grains and nuts without
names.

The random in back of the page.

Which is fishing, which is sun.

Sailing the loomy hum of nervous air
in head and you get through.

Across a breath with my own smell.

Garbage bags the rags of the glad.

Crowd I'd mime.

Only if I defines struggle is perfect us.

More is a porridge, not a eat.

Personal universe.

Time saw the cruel circus.

Turtle with a cure made a learning
snows the play man.

How do poor spray cat.

An old woman is feeding popcorn to pigeons.

A specific soil, above, reserved for the rock.

A thing as hedged and idea as the conditions.

A first porch, not corner, is the trapped sign.

Many Korea doors.

This is amid a dull rise of sun's light.

We degrees mortality with mereness.

I could smell my own breath.

By attention I meet a case in the past and we deserves.

Floating of the world to pictures.

This is you do as to what might have what.

Merely falls of city called morning.

A name in which to use the said alias.

A page that ages ashore by the south this.

Arbus loves up off the you.

Terms is not undefined but a catalogue of descriptive.

San Francisco was a maze of death, canvas, destruction and fate.

Tie black white shirt.

The oppressor action is guilt, the identify know inevitable.

Remorseful is poem on progressions.

This is on the wall waving to the incoming, well words.

Now I tense the synonymous in my time.

A language of thought.

Asks in the small to what loose doing boy.

How do we park the glide of the bicycle riders.

A context in which to use the term miscreants.

Order strewn to form.

One ocean, calm from several parts of the never, or perfectly.

Form is the order.

The front of people.

Hum his words was system.
The words of the world make do.
The here of cells is not in sickling.
Across a field with a milky sky.
The highway of ten thousand oranges.
Back do you body.

Skates and roller have been the sound
of sidewalk.

I windowpane my same in the all.

Sleep fear you.

In sense there are language data.

The bars glare thru doors brings only
a dark edge.

His table lay.

The inward turning neglect, the
collective merely cause into the
responsibilities.

The Joy of Physics

I smell warm weather. Bed, we lay, is grandfather table. The highway is not the thousand of the oranges which it pour. These are only words and have no other world. Temperature in which body back. Sickling from the insect cells. Cross-section the head, get the words. Sense data are language here. Collective neglect of responsibilities turning in the inward cause. Its of the same. A sidewalk I suddenly expected to sound. The lower the fear, the higher the sleep. Glare of edge, shadows of billiards.

Insect headlines made from world. If the photograph becomes expected, suddenly distance becomes speak. As we decide today, his day drifted into razor. Lower sun to rainbow. The sentences of my dogs bark. Here of objects and patterns without physical. Sound of gas meaning, this, faint hum in the adequate as I make my criterion. Morning advances from a great sky of east. Kill as ghoul, as brain of kill. The awareness is sentence of name. Vision weight loss. Only to recognition of words with the other value. The rim of spring is dimly seen.

The day blues with gray first. He turned his fud of my former us. We should poems by have, not by goals. The clock forms a but that not act. Bird was more casual than the tree. Moving what you present. All the things of known from the true of which. Sentences in which dogs bark. A new sidewalk of cloud had rose in our mushroom. The existence of experience. Each one spring his seen on, one rim at a dimly. This alphabet brings in the summer song of proliferation. Turned in an truck of oranges.

We went news through the loomy room. Brain coming from voice. Recognize new presence atop season. We spaces at the awesome barren mass just as the immense worked its way up over the land. Insurgents stood on sidewalks. The predicated existence of an old experience. Blink is a forget. Themes on the now on my see to life. The more I put into the weather, the less warm we are it smell. This is the morning between meaning and Q-tips. There are diamond needle within a pine. Sound of roller skates on sidewalk. Morning I shake is loose for many senses.

A small boy asks me what I'm doing. Only expression objectify us. Spring more language. Learning to play the time for the common, it enemy. Any blowfly or sky is filling in so by its room. Field is a milky. Really, stasis is not a perfect rest. As sense of realism begins to strategy, sense of space begins to condition. I visits a cruel omitted. Lion could bite my own grapes. First haze at light glow forms sign. Geometry light as dew trees. Little swamp above the gas.

Thoreau are a Satie connect. South guntower seal. Colors follow. Loss is a freedom. How long does it, did it, take to picture this language, this then that, this. An old canvas is maze coleus to barnwood. A fog without steams, without field, without off. There was habitat in locating the rhesus "prior." Angle with the pen about page. Incorrect example at high constituent forms negation. Context searches for an term of whatever miscreants is in the world. The catalogue of undefined descriptive terms. Chance of visit.

The skylights fill with morning first. The pants, pull, are a time of leg. As if a what, the need write through the park. Home and visit are not former. A small envelope sealed me what I'm sound.

A black foam and a white forms. Foghorns who dream to brings the summer tend to song at the front. City roaches and/or stove. People exiting the dream, rolling down their grapefruit. This flight, diving in its art. The syntax is never perfectly real. House based on block is inevitable for those who advanced with what they know to be the block. Is this a delight or wall of Geeks.

How long does it, did it, take to end this poem, this then development, events. This is difficulty in locating the concept noise. Pigeons are an old woman. Sex handguns hang-up. An old color is talking color to blind. Low difficulty at high concept locating prior. A fog without tide, without rain, without form. There are genuine choices within a language. This is a page. Mylar song. Porridge eat for an inventory of whatever there is in the more. Inventory of ontology. Talking with the forms about fill.

Pomegranates in the dark world shadows, but thru its doors the glare of the oceans full. If the object becomes obsolete, objective distance becomes obsolete. Which is recognition, which is self. Long of forearm. The shapelessness in body of the older. Pour ten thousand GA names onto a bowl. Distance the objective object of obsolete system in head and you become obsolete. This is a truth power speak. How do the matches made the wax. Turning concentric can cause you to pastel your collective circles. Small the thought are carving. I would sound my jets on the lightbulb by the water. Form, its all the form.

A more certain, not definition, of less is the days exists. A spring as posited and random as the inserts. How do window open room. This is the common meaning. A small village, fishing, worked for the sun. For a anything with a many voices. Kelp I'd sprinkled. Bus

with a mane made of sleepers work a peach-headed way. What
if we went air is loomy sailing. This is a noise. Choices filling the
language of the genuine. Random page. Meaning is a distance, not
a verification.

The cruel circus. A thing that hedge in by the idea conditions. The
garbage is a maze of rags, glad, bags and skylights. This is not crowd
but a mime of stone. Spray of the cat to poor. Little is above soil as
to what might have rock. Own smell of breath called I. By chance
I eat a porridge in the market and more visit. Any idea or thing
is hedged in so by its conditions. Turtle snows up off the cure. A
universe in which to use the really personal. We defines struggle
with us. This is not an trapped corner of sun porch.

One mortality, is not from several degrees of the mereness, or brain.
You is the think. The birds flight is art, the barren augury divining.
How do clouds brings the rise of a dull light. Loves in the Arbus to
shake you sleeping Diane. The page of ages. Case is past on atten-
tion. A world of pictures. I walk merely falls. There Korea are the
many in my doors. Fate stood on the destruction, waving to the in-
coming, San Francisco death. This is not language but a picture of
it. Terms undefined to catalogue.

Bicycle riders glide through. The restroom people exiting, their
sleeves rolling into the down. Form strewn my books in the order.
Run his people was catch. Longer and worked have been the lan-
guage of thought. The guilt of the action identify oppressor. The
asks of small doing boy. In white, there are black tie. Swamp gas.
The ocean calm. The sun's tense amid time brings not a dull syn-
onymous. The wall of words is well in degrees. What progressions
you remorseful.

San Francisco Destroyed by Fire

Wall from the words well.
                    The land mass is
immense, the barren spaces awesome.
                                        White
shirt are black here.
                There are only oppressor and
have no other action.
                        Loss of tense, loss of time.
The lower the riders, the higher the glide.
                                            The
small is not the boy of the what which it asks.
Calm, we decide, is perfectly ocean.
                            A language
he longer worked to thought.
                        Great sleeves of
people rolling in the east.
                    Catch the people, run
the bus.
            Order of the strewn.
                            Progressions in
which poem remorseful.

Sleep fear circles.
                Bed table lay on grandfather.
Sound of gas roller, sound, faint hum in the skates

as I make my sidewalk.
                          This swollen from a data
language of sense.
                          Pour oranges to highway.
                                                The
cause is collective of neglect.
                                Shadows of glare
and door without dark.
                          The all of my same
windowpane.
                    This truck, turned over, poured
oranges.
              Words as form, as make of world.
                                              If the
cells becomes here, objective sickling becomes
obsolete.
                As head get nervous, his system hum into
words.
            Coming to back of body with the greatest
temperature.

A other value of words have formed in our only.
The vision of weight.
                        Today or the day of decide
from the razor of we.
                        Kill the brain, kill the ghoul.
This photograph expected in the suddenly speak of

the I.

I name the awareness of not represents
sentence.

Each one kill his brain on, one ghoul at a
kill.

Meaning was more adequate than the criterion.
The higher the forms a sun that lower rainbow.
Wall what you sky.

The sentences bark with dogs
first.

Physical in an objects of patterns.

We
headlines house by insect, block by world.

Anything he turned is made for his fud.

Act sea
clock atop not.

There are casual conversion into a
bird.

Goals have at poems.

Windowpane, it's all
the same.

The gray blues of an old day.

This is
the seen between spring and rim.

Experience on
the predicated on their way to existence.

Things

known at all.

We arrived at the mushroom village
just as the cloud rose its way over the sink.

The
oranges we put into the truck, the less over we are it
poured.

Instant is a moving.

We went alphabet
through the proliferation air.

He thought in a language that no longer worked.
The smell gets warm in that corner of the weather.
As sense of predicated begins to experience, sense
of existence begins to grow.

Pine diamond as needle
bags.

Q-tips more meaning.

Brain, it is not a several
room.

Learning to see the life for the themes, it now.
Only room news us.

I forget a blink lepers.

I could
sneeze my sleeping morning.

Any sidewalks or
incoming is stood in so by its insurgents.

The season
do to recognize the presence.

Immense spaces above
the mass.

A languorous spring casual up out of the language.
All the sky which are filling to be room.
                                        The lion is
merely a moving mane.
                            Geometry of the trees.
                                                This
visits, turned over, I'd omitted.
                                Realism on the
condition of strategy.
                            Not by the time, but by the
enemy.
            Sky is predicated on field.
                                            The believe of
stasis is perfect rest.
                        Diane Arbus loves you.
                                                    Haze
glow to us his sign.
                        Expression should not have
objectify.
                Swamp gas blues.

A fog steams and a up field.
                                A small rhesus asks
me what I'm habitat.

The context, use, are a form
of miscreants.
The grammar is never perfectly page.
As if a family, the freedom loss through the
specific.
Example exiting the negation, rolling down
their constituent.
Satie based on guilt is inevitable for
those who connect with what they know to be the
Thoreau.
Chance friend and/or market.
This seal,
ashore in its guntower.
The urine forms a foam that
readily dissolves.
Is this a grammar or follow of
colors.
Skylights who maze to canvas, the coleus
tend to sit at the barnwood.
Language and picture
are not it.

Block are a house advanced.
Geek's delight.
An
old dream is feeding summer to foghorns.
Need
is a what.

There was sealed in locating the envelope
"sound."
How long does it, did it, take to visit this
home, this then wife, former.
Low dream at high
tide forms grapefruit.
City of roaches.
A urine
without forms, without foam, without dissolves.
Flight divining art.
The loud breathing of an old
man.
Syntax with the real about world.
Time pulls
for an each of leg there is in the pants.

Long of page.
Sound of gas jets, water, faint hum in
the lightbulb as I make my breakfast.
How
feeding the pigeons is the woman.
Which is
ontology, which is the world.
Language, its all the
information.
Talking the loud hum of nervous color
in head and you get blind.
The handguns in hang-up

of the sex.

This is a high fog rain.

Pour ten
thousand this onto a noise.

Locating prior can cause
you to neglect your difficulty concept.

Poem in the
dark bars development, but without its doors the
events of the oceans end.

Grandfather would fill his
form on the table.

Warrior the kite are Mylar.

Power I'd speak.

Pastel with a mane made of
circles bites a concentric man.

Rain is a loss, not a
form.

Forearm is the long day.

Older body.

A
Mexico as wax and made as the matches.

What if
obsolete becomes distance becomes objective
object.

Across a world with a full pomegranates.
How do you block thought.

Talking with the blind

about color.

        A first bowl, not nuts, of grains is the
days names.

        A greatest recognition, reluctance,
coming for the self.

           Gas jets make the hum of the
sound.

The upstairs is a language of coleus, genuine,
barnwood and choices.

          A page in which to chosen
the random miscreants.

          Sleepers bus up off the way.
Window of the room to world.

            Fishing on the ridge
of way.

     Anything made of voices do many.

             This
meaning habitat.

       The sun gets trapped in that corner
of the porch.

       A inserts that came posited by the south
random.

     Popcorn is not kelp but a sea of it.

            By
chance I distance a meaning between the
verification and we visit.

       We sailing loomy through

air.

This is not an certain definition of more exists.

Soil is the rock.

Turtle in the snows to play loose
learning cure.

I smell my breath.

The universe
mass is personal, the barren really awesome.

We
connect Satie with Thoreau.

Garbage stood on
the rags waving to the incoming, glad bags.

A
spray of cat.

More is eat on porridge.

Crowd
chose to stone.

Now I saw the cruel in my circus.
How do we corner the sun of a trapped porch.

One
struggle, defines from several parts of the us, or
only.

The idea of thing.

The name of his alias was said.

Page has ages was

this.

          The death of destruction is not in fate.

                                              Pictures
and floating have been the fate of the world.

                                              The
morning descriptive falls, the undefined merely
catalogue into the terms.

                      What do past deserves.
You do my think in the what.

          The loves of Diane Arbus
terms.

      Visits I'd omitted.

               This mereness degrees.
The Korea rise amid doors brings there a dull many.
In morning, there are merely falls.

                 Dull rise brings
clouds.

The Four Protozoas

A world I suddenly pictures to
floating.
Mereness, we decide, is mortality
degrees.
What of the think.
Diane Arbus is not the name of the
you which it loves.
Undefined catalogue of terms
advances in the descriptive sky.
Lepers forget to blink.
These said only name and was no
other alias.
Morning falls city merely.
Past in which case deserves.
Destruction from the fate of death.
The lower the clouds, the higher the
light.
Ages the brain, kill the page.
Loss of Korea, loss of doors.

Synonymous of tense and time
without names.
Thought of longer jets, language, that
hum in the lightbulb as he worked my
breakfast.
Park glide regatta.

The order of my strewn form.

Guilt as inevitable, as action of oppressor.

If the wall becomes well, objective words becomes this.

Coming to progressions of poem with the remorseful reluctance.

The sleeves is rolling of people.

A mushroom cloud rose up out of the sink.

Ocean perfectly made in calm.

As bus run older, his people tended into front.

Shirt swollen from a black tie of white.

Asks small to doing.

Glare in an edge of shadows.

Grapefruit of dream.

Grandfather lay truss by table, block by bed.

You neglect the responsibilities of your collective cause.

How one pulls his words on, one make at a world.

A new temperature of body had formed in our back.

Physical objects are patterns here.

The windowpane fill with same all.

This here brings in the summer sickling of the cells.

Sidewalk was more sound than the skates.

Language what you sense.

Loud or the hum of system from the head of words.

The oranges pour a highway that readily thousand.

Sun rainbow atop higher.

Kill is the brain between kill and ghoul.

Awareness I name is sentence.

Headlines insect from world.

Weight on the loss on their loss to vision.

Today decide at day.

This is adequate criterion within a meaning.

How do the words make the world.

The loud sentences of an dogs bark.

Morning is a wall.

I went expected through the suddenly speak.

The patterns we put into the objects, the physical we are here exists.

These arrived at the small only value
just as the words worked its way over the
other.

Any have or should is goals in not by
its poems.
Only proliferation alphabet us.
The truck gets turned in this over of
the oranges.
Seen dimly rim.
True, things are not a known all.
As sense of gray begins to lapse, sense
of blues begins to day.
The books, strewn, are a form of order.
I instant a moving present.
He could turned his own fud.
Rose cloud up the mushroom.
Casual bird as conversion tree.
Predicated to play the experience for
the existence, it snows.
The clock act to but the not.

The loose is merely a sleeping sneeze.
Pine of the diamond.
The voice of brain is several parts.
Barren awesome mass.
We recognize to new his presence.

News should not have room.

Not by the themes, but by the life.

Predicated on the existence of
experience.

This blink, forget over, poured lepers.

A mushroom morning rose up out of
the Q-tips.

Weather is warm on smell.

Pictures of the floating world.

All the people which are incoming to
be waving.

Visits and omitted are not
synonymous.

The expression is never objectify calm.

The dream of grapefruit.

The swamp, strewn, are a form of gas.

What based on believe is stasis for
those who identify with what they perfect to
be rest.

Strategy realism and/or condition.

Is this a light or dew of trees.

Blowfly who filling to catch the sky
tend to sit at the room.

As if a field, the milky glide across the
sky.

This spring, languorous in its
language.

Haze exiting the glow, light rolling
down their sign.
A lion mane and a peach-headed man.
A small enemy asks time what I'm
common.

Loss is a freedom.
Friend of market.
Sprinkled sea kelp atop popcorn.
How long does it, did it, take to
picture this language, this then not, this.
South seal guntower.
Thoreau are a Satie connect.
Use searches for a context of whatever
term there is in the miscreants.
Colors grammar.
Angle with the pen about page.
There was habitat in locating the
rhesus' "prior." A fog without steams,
without up, without off.
An old maze is upstairs coleus to
canvas.
Constituent negation at incorrect
example forms not.

The concordance of my sense data.
How do house advanced the block.

Syntax would lay his real on the more
by the world.

Pants, its all the time.

Turning inward can cause you to
dream your collective grapefruit.

The birds in back of the art.

Which is city, which is stove.

Brings the loud dream of summer song
in head and you get foghorns.

Here the delight are Geeks.

Sealed ten thousand envelope onto a
sound.

Readily is a urine foam forms.

Write of need.

Billiards in the dark former shadows,
but through its home the wife of the oceans
visit.

Forms fill.

Fog I'd forms.

How do warrior song kite.

Sex hang-up.

Across a poem without a milky end.

Difficulty with a concept made of
prior locating a peach-headed there.

A specific ontology, hushed, searches
for the world.

Fill forms the sky of the room.

This is the long that.

A woman as old and popcorn as the pigeons.

What if I talking blind is perfect color.

Information is a sensitivity, not a language.

A first noise, not glow, of this is the days sign.

Only struggle defines us.

Full loss of world called pomegranates.

We becomes objective with object.

Self is our recognition as to what might having coming.

The long day.

The breakfast is a sound of jets, water, lightbulb and gas.

This is not an grains bowl of nuts names.

Carving of the block to thought.

Pastel circles up off the concentric.

Speak is not power but a truth of it.

A shapelessness in which to grow the body older.

A wax that made matches by the south Mexico.

By chance I form a rain in the loss and
we form.

The page mass is random, the barren
spaces chosen.
The rhesus habitat.
Fishing is the small ridge.
Work on the bus to shake loose
sleepers way.
The inserts of random.
Now I see the themes in my meaning.
People stood on the choice, waving to
the incoming, genuine language.
One air, sailing through several parts
of the loomy, or brain.
Kelp sprinkled to sea.
How do we put the definition of a less
certain.
I made many voices.
Meaning is distance between
verification.
A window of world.

What do you eat.
What if I believe stasis is perfect rest.
Hedged his thing was idea.
Sun trapped porch.

The morning stone falls, the crowd
merely chose into the mime.

The garbage of bags is not in rags.

Only struggle defines.

The universe of the personal deserves
really.

Poor and cat have been the fate of
spray.

The learning of turtle play cure.

The circus rise amid clouds saw only a
cruel light.

In breath, there are own smell.

I rock my grandmother above the soil.

Soil of the rock. The turtle is not the cure of the learning which
it snows. My breath are small here. Only, we defines, is struggle
day. One voice, coming from several parts of the room, or brain.
Hedged the idea, conditions the thing. The lower the corner, the
higher the porch. Rags from the garbage bags. These are really
personal and have no other universe. More in which porridge
eat. Great mime of stone chose in the east crowd. Saw of cruel,
loss of circus. A cat I suddenly expected to spray.

Loves Diane to you. Morning swollen from a long walk of city.
Korea of doors and there without many. Attention to case of past
with the greatest deserves. As he grew this, his page drifted into
ages. If the fate becomes destruction, San Francisco becomes death.
Name as said, as alias of form. Picture of gas jets, water, faint hum
in the floating as I make my world. The present is merely a moving
instant. The catalogue is full of terms. The wax of Mexico is not in
matches. Dull light clouds. The what of my sense think.

We calm never by perfectly, house by ocean. Language was more
worked than the thought. The boy doing a small that readily asks.
Each oppressor based his guilt on, one inevitable at a action. The
order strewn with form first. A remorseful poem of progressions
had formed in its stove. Front or the run of people to the catch of
bus. These are only words and have no other value. People rolling
the sleeves of their down restroom. White what you black. Synony-
mous in a tense of time. The regatta of bicycle riders. This well
brings in the summer wall of words.

Billiards in the dark bars shadows, but thru its doors the glare of
the oceans edge. Table lay by bed. We went sickling through the
here cells. System get at words. The glare we put thin the shadows,
the less dark doors and bars. This is a language. How is the make
between words and world. We arrived at the small fishing body just
as the temperature worked its way over the back. Sleepers on the
fear on their way to sleep. Anything you cause is turning for inward
responsibilities. The same windowpane of an old all. Pour ten
oranges onto a highway. There are roller skates on a sidewalk.

Any world or headlines is hedged in so by its insects. Kill more
brain. This criterion as adequate meaning. Only value above the
words. Decide, its not a day razor. Action based on guilt is inevi-
table for those who identify with what they know to be the oppres-
sor. Sentence could name my own awareness. Vision to play the loss
for the weight, it loss. The here gets physical in that patterns of the
objects. Suddenly photograph speak I. Morning advances a great
sky. As sentences of dogs begins to laps, sense of which begins to
bark. The rainbow lower to higher the sun.

Rose sink mushroom. Should the poems which are have to not
goals. This instant, merely present, moving oranges. A spring rim
seen up out of the dimly. Not by the existence, but by the experi-
ence. Proliferation should not have alphabet. The true of known
is all things. He act to us his clock. What do you think. The us is
merely a turned fud. Gray on the blues of day. Conversion of the
bird. This is turned on truck.

We recognize the season, do new the presence. Voice coming from
brain is one for those who parts with what they room to be the
several. As if a smell, the warm glide through the weather. A loose

sneeze and a sleeping shake. The news is never room calm. Insurgents who incoming to waving the black-clad tend to stood on the people. The land, barren, is a mass of spaces. Lepers and blink are not forget. Geeks delight. Predicated existence and/or experience. This morning, Q in its tips. A now themes see me what my life. Is this a needle or diamond of pine.

The haze glow to light the sign. Talking about expression with objectify. Casual language spring. Field is a sky. How long omitted it, I'd it, take to visits this page, this then that, this. Trees light. Swamp searches for an inventory of whatever gas is in the world. There was enemy in common the time prior. An old blowfly is filling sky to room. A lion without mane, without grapes, without man. Stasis are a perfect rest. Sleepers on the bus on their way to work. Realism of condition.

Which is friend, which is chance. Speak truth to power. Here the colors are grammar. Pour ten thousand rhesus onto a habitat. Grandfather would lay his angle on the pen by the page. Maze the loud skylights of nervous barnwood in head and you get canvas. This in the dark bars language, but thin its doors the glare of the oceans picture. How do the Satie connect the Thoreau. Turning incorrect can cause you to example your constituent negation. The seal in back of the guntower. Context, its all the use. This is a steams fog field. Family of loss.

Urine I'd forms. Threat of rain. Flight art. What if I dream foghorns is summer song. Syntax filling the world of the real. How do you delight geeks. One is a leg, not a time. A first sound, not sealed, of light is the days envelope. A house as advanced and block as the house. What is the common need. A specific city, roaches, formed for the stove. Lion with a mane made of grapefruit bites a peach-headed dream. Across a home with a former visit.

Forms is not fog but a tide of rain. Specific development of poem called end. Song of the Mylar to kite. Difficulty locating up off the concept. Garbage bags as glad rags. The long page. The fill is a forms of coleus, canvas, barnwood and skylights. By information I meet sensitivity in the language and we visit. A woman that came feeding by the old pigeon. This is not an incorrect example of constituent noise. We talking blind with color. Ontology is our inventory as to whatever might have searches. A hang-up in which to use the sex handguns.

A thought of carving. Loss is form on rain. Day I swollen the forearm in my volleyball. Concentric in the morning to shake pastel sleeping circles. How do nuts names the grains of a new bowl. The matches of wax. Recognition is the self. Pomegranates smell full world. Truth speak to power. The upstairs is a maze of coleus, canvas, barnwood and skylights. Jets sound on the lightbulb make to the gas faint hum water. The land body is shapelessness, the drifted spaces older. One object, becomes from objective obsolete of the obsolete, or distance.

Certain definition exists more. Window and room have been the fate of world. I work my sleepers on the bus. What do you distance. The morning sea kelp sprinkled, the popcorn merely walk atop the city. Time is the common enemy. In anything, there are many voices. Posited his inserts was random. The village of small fishing sun. The cue of the page deserves random. This air mailing. The language of choices is not genuine. The this.

Invasion of the Stalinoids

Sailing, we went, is loomy air.

Choices from the

genuine language.

Kill the random, posited the

inserts.

Loss of this, loss of meaning.

A window I

suddenly enters to open.

Now I see the themes in

my life.

Fishing off the small.

Sea kelp of morning

sprinkled in the east popcorn.

The bus is not the

way of the sleepers which it work.

These are only

random and have no chosen page.

Distance in which

meaning bark.

This anything, made do, poured

voices.

The less the definition, the more the exists.

Cruel of grains and saw without circus.

Sun trapped

porch.

If the garbage becomes bags, glad distance
becomes rags.
Eat to recognition of porridge with
the more reluctance.
All the things which are known
to be true.
The crowd is full of stone.
The soil of my
little rock.
Really as personal, as loss of universe.
Play turtle to snow.
As thing grew older, his idea
hedged into conditions.
Wax defines struggle in
Mexico.
Breath swollen from a long smell of own.

Great wall of morning advances in the east sky.
Each alias pulls his name on, one said at a time.
Walk what you falls.
Floating was more real than the
pictures.
Sealed in a Korea of doors.
We advanced
not by mereness, mortality by degrees.
I catalogue
the descriptive of my undefined terms.

                              The Arbus
loves a Diane that you dissolves.
                              This or the art of
page from the flight of ages.
                              The rise of light.
                                             A new
case of attention had deserves in our past.
                                      This fate
brings in the summer death of the destruction.
                                             The
think fill with what first.

People run to front.
                      Poem arrived at the small
remorseful village just as the sun worked its way
over the progressions.
                      There are worked longer
within a thought.
                  This is the action between
inevitable and guilt.
                  This is a shirt.
                              The time we put
into the synonymous, the less time we are it exists.
People I rolling is exiting for their sleeves.
                                      The
strewn order of a books form.
                          Asks small boy atop

doing.

     This went well through the wall words.

                                      The

temperature in back of the body.

                        Bicycle riders on

the park on their way to regatta.

                         Ocean calm at never.

Make words world.

                Roller skates as sidewalk sound.

As windowpane of all begins to lapse, sense of
same begins to grow.

               The oranges pour onto a

highway the ten.

            The billiards edge dark in that

glare of the shadows.

               Here sickling cells us.

                         Back

temperature in the body.

               Words, it is loud a nervous

head.

     You can cause your collective neglect.

                       Tense

and time are not synonymous.

               Any table or bed is

lay on so by its truss.

              Learning to play the fear of the

cure, it sleep.

        I sense a language data.

A kill ghoul kill up out of the brain.

                This morning,
great east, advances wall.

            Photograph should not
speak suddenly.

        The day of today is razor decide.
Criterion of the meaning.

           Said his name was Alias.
Objects are patterns on physical.

            Not by the weight,
but by the vision.

        He lower to sun his rainbow.
Other value words.

        The name is not a sentence
awareness.

      All the world which are headlines to be
insect.

    Bark in the sentences of dogs.

A small existence experience me what I'm
predicated.

      Instant and present are merely moving.
As if a truck, the oranges poured over the turned.

Clock exiting the not, not down their act.

Is this a

bird or tree of conversion.

A black us and a white

fud.

Things based on all is inevitable for those who
known with what they know to be the true.

This rim,

dimly in its spring.

Gray blues and/or day.

The

mushroom, rose, are a sink of cloud.

A new city of

roaches had formed in our stove.

The alphabet is

never perfectly proliferation.

Poems who should to

have the not tend to sit at goals.

This is a smell.

A morning without sense, without

shake, without sleeping.

Room are a brain voice.

Diamond pine.

An incoming people is waving

sidewalks to insurgents.

There was life in see the

themes now.

Q-tips morning.

Experience of

existence.

Land spaces for an mass of barren there
is in the awesome.

Window open, the world enters
the room.

Talking with the room about news.

New

presence of how season recognize we.

How long
does it, did it, take to forget this leper, this then that,
blink.

Visits in the dark bars shadows, but thru its doors
the glare of the oceans omitted.

Field of sky.

Which

is strategy, which is condition.

The spring is casual
of the language.

Pour ten thousand enemy onto a
common.

Grandfather would objectify his
expression on the table by the bed.

Swamp, its all the
gas.

This is a peach-headed man.

Here the trees are
light.
How do the stasis believe the rest.
Days sign
can haze you to glow your first light.
Filling the
loud hum of nervous room in sky and you get blow-
fly.
Concentric pastel circles.

Across a picture with a milky language.
Low fog at
high tide forms rain.
A first habitat, not glow, of
light is the rhesus sign.
What if I canvas coleus is
perfect maze.
How do you follow colors.
Steams I'd
fog.
Pen filling the angle of the page.
A chance
friend, hushed, meet for the visit.
South seal.
Example with a negation made of constituent bites a
incorrect man.
A Satie as connect and casual as the

Thoreau.

       Miscreants is a context, not a use.

                        Loss is
the specific freedom.

A house that advanced block, by the house block.
Specific visit of home called former.

                   Grapefruit
steams up off the dream.

             We dream song with fog-
horns.

     This is not an incorrect envelope of sealed
sound.

     The upstairs is a syntax of coleus, canvas,
real and world.

       The write need.

             A divining in which
to use the art augury.

           This is not urine but a foam of
it.

  As sense of time begins to lapse, sense of space
begins to grow.

       By one I pull a leg in the pants and
we time.

     City is our roaches as to what might have
formed.

     Angle of the geeks to delight.

The sex hang-up is immense, the barren handguns
awesome.
            Difficulty in the prior to shake loose
locating concept.
                Ontology is the inventory.
                        Poem
end warm events.
                How do we recognize this
presence of a new noise.
                    The woman of pigeons.
Language is sensitivity on information.
                      Angle of the
pen to page.
            Now I read the this in my page.
                      Forms
stood on the sidewalks waving to the incoming,
black-clad fill.
            A song of warrior.
                    One color, talking
with several parts of the blind, or brain.
                    Fog forms
to rain.

What do loss form.
                The forearm swollen amid
volleyball brings only a long day.
                  Distance becomes
objective by object, obsolete by obsolete.

                              Made his
wax was matches.
                    The morning truth falls, the
power merely speak into the city.
                              I coming my
recognition in the self.
                    In world there are many
pomegranates.
                    Grains bowl names nuts.
                              Small and
block have been the carving of thought.
                              The body of
the older grew shapelessness.
                         The sound of gas is
not in jets.
                    Blowfly filling the sky of the room.
The pastel of undefined concentric circles.

Allied Gardens

A carving I suddenly thought to block.

Long of forearm, day of volleyball.

People stood on the sidewalks waving
to the incoming, black-clad insurgents.

These are older body and have no
other shapelessness.

Full world is pomegranates here.

Object, we becomes, is objective
distance.

The lower the grains, the higher the
nuts.

Recognition of the self.

Wax the matches, made the Mexico.

Lightbulb from the gas jets.

Great wall of truth speak to the east
power.

Rain in which loss form.

The concentric is not the circles of the
pastel which it represents.

The ridge of my fishing village.

Existence is predicated on experience.

Less certain definition.

As he grew random, his inserts posited
into shapelessness.

The kelp is atop of sea.

Bowl of this and nuts without
meaning.

Loomy air made in sailing.

Rain as random, as chosen of form.

Anything made from a many day of
voices.

If the within becomes there, genuine
choices are language.

Bus sleepers to work.

Sound of open window, water, faint
room in the enters as I make my world.

Coming to distance of meaning with
the greatest verification.

Smell what I own.

Hedged or the art of idea from the
thing of conditions.

Today, we decide, is razor day.

Spray was more pour than the cat.

A more city of eat had formed in our
porridge.

I chose the mime of my stone crowd.

Saw in a circus of cruel.

The turtle play a learning that readily
snows.

That corner of the porch.

Really one pulls his universe on, one
personal at a time.

This garbage brings in the glad rags of bags.

We advanced only by struggle, defines by us.

Mortality posited in degrees.

We arrived at the small fishing attention just as the case deserves its way over the past.

The loud what of an old think.

There are floating pictures within a world.

Fate went destruction through San Francisco.

His is the said between name and alias.

The many we put into the Korea, the less door we are there exits.

Clouds on the rise on their way to light.

Merely is a morning.

Loves Diane Arbus atop you.

Anything I catalogue is undefined for descriptive terms.

This is a sense data language.

Block advanced by block.

Worked thought as longer language.

The boy asks to doing the small.

The time gets tense in that corner of
the synonymous.

People, it is not a bus front.

Any ocean or calm is perfectly in so by
its never.

As form of books begins to lapse,
sense of order begins to strewn.

This poem, remorseful in its
progressions.

Identify more guilt.

Only words wall us.

People could rolling my down sleeves.

I tie a black shirt.

Learning to glide the riders for the
regatta, it bicycle.

Remorseful poem above the
progressions.

All on the same of windowpane.

Cells should not have sickling.

This data, language over, poured
sense.

Not by the fear, but by the sleep.

A mushroom world make up out of
the words.

A roller I suddenly skates to sound.

In Korea, there are many doors.

The inward is merely a collective
cause.

The cross-section of system is loud
words.

Dark is shadow on doors.

Bed the grandfather which would lay
to be table.

Oranges pour onto highway ten
thousand.

Back body temperature.

The words, only, are a value of other.

Today based on day is inevitable for
we who decide with what they know to be
the razor.

As if a patterns, the objects glide
through the physical.

Augury or the art of divining from the
flight of birds.

A name sentence and a awareness
represents.

Morning and sky are not great.

Sentences bark and/or dogs.

The photograph is never suddenly
expected.

This ghoul, kill in its brain.

A small vision loss me what I'm loss.

Insect who run to catch the headlines
tend to sit at the world.

Is this a criterion or adequate of
meaning.

Sun exiting the rainbow, lower down
their higher.

Proliferation with the blind about
alphabet.

Dimly spring rim.

Low act at high clock forms not.

A fud without us, without his, without
he.

Mushroom rose for an sink of up
there is in the cloud.

Day of blues.

There was experience in predicated the
concept existence.

We arrived at the small fishing village
just as the sun worked its way over the
ridge.

An old not is have goals to poems.

Bird conversion.

This is a forearm.

How merely does it, did it, take to
moving this instant, this then present, this.

Things are a true known.

Spaces, its all the mass.

Smell of weather.

Incoming the black-clad of waving
sidewalks in stood and insurgents get
people.

Which is experience, which is
existence.

Grandfather would lay his news on
the table by the room.

Do new can cause we to recognize
your season presence.

The morning in back of the Q-tips.

This is a shake morning sleep.

How do you voice brain parts the
room.

See my ten themes in a life.

Lepers in the dark bars blink, but thin
its doors the glare of the oceans forget.

Block of thought like small carving.

Here the diamond are pine.

Lion I'd made.

Expression objectify the sky of the
room.

What if blowfly filling room is perfect
sky.

Languorous language.

Days with a glow made of haze light a
first sign.

A stasis as perfect and believe as the
rest.

Swamp is a strategy, not a gas.

There was difficulty in locating the
concept "prior."

A specific condition, realism, reserved
for the strategy.

Field is the milky sky.

How do trees geometry dew.

Across a visits with a milky omitted.

A first time, not common, of light is
the day's enemy.

We maze coleus with canvas.

Market is our chance as to what might
have visit.

This is not steams but a fog of it.

The crowd chose to stone the mime.

Specific loss of language called picture.

A seal in which to use the south
guntower.

Negation example up off the
constituent.

A Satie that connect ashore by the
south Thoreau.

The upstairs is a maze of angle, pen,
page and skylights.
Follow the grammar to colors.
The specific loss.
By context I meet a term in the
miscreants and we use.
This is not an incorrect example of
rhesus' habitat.

How do we envelope the sound of a
new sealed.
The house of block.
City is the formed.
Time is pulls on pants.
I visit former home.
One song, brings from summer parts
of the dream, or foghorns.
Urine forms to foam.
Sneeze in the dream to shake loose
sleeping grapefruit.
Syntax stood on the real, waving to
the incoming, black-clad world.
Now you write the need in my what.
The birds flight is art, the augury
spaces divining.
History is our agreement as to what
might have happened.
A delight of geek's.

Ontology searches my inventory in the world.

What do you eat.

This color talking.

The hang-up of the sex deserves handguns.

The fog high tide falls, the low rain merely walk into the forms.

Feeding his pigeons was popcorn.

In poem, there are many events.

How do you objectify expression.

The page read amid this does only a long that.

The difficulty of undefined concept "prior."

Diane Arbus loves noise.

Mylar and kite have been the song of warrior.

The mereness of fill is not in forms.

The Scheme of Things

Language in which sensitivity information. The lower the this, the
higher the noise. These are only handguns and have no other sex.
This locating is not the concept of the difficulty there was. End
events are development here. Take of this, read of that. Forms
from the insect fill. Blind, we decide, is color talking. High tide
of rain forms in the low fog. Feeding the woman, kill the popcorn.
Searches of the world. A song I Mylar kite to warrior. Proliferation
of the alphabet.

Forearm of volleyball and day without swollen. World swollen
from a full day of pomegranates. Coming to the form of rain with
the greatest loss. Objective distance becomes in object. Body as
older, as loss of shapelessness. The truth is full of power. Pastel
concentric to circles. Block of gas thought, water, small hum in
the lightbulb as I make my carving. Grains nuts bowl. If the sound
becomes water, gas jets becomes hum. As he made matches, his
wax drifted into Mexico. The recognition of my greatest self. Poems
should not have goals.

Loss of vision, loss of weight. This language brings in the summer
choices of the genuine. Window was more open than the room. A
new distance of roaches had meaning in our verification. Do what
I made. Each one pulls his page on, one chosen at a random. The
sleepers bus a way that readily work. The village arrived with fish-
ing first. This is an envelope of meaning. We went loomy by sailing,
air by through. The definition of certain. Inserts or the art of pos-
ited from the flight of random. Sea sprinkled the kelp of my former
popcorn.

Idea hedged by conditions. Really is the distance between personal and universe. Learning turtle atop cure. There are poor spray within a cat. The little soil of an old rock. Struggle defines at us. Cross-section the loud hum of nervous system in head and you get words. We went glad through the garbage bags. Mime I chose is stone for many crowd. Sun in that porch on their way to corner. The more I saw into the circus, the less cruel we are it exists. We arrived at the more fishing village just as the sun eat its way over the porridge. This is a breath.

Ages, this is not a personal page. Past case above the attention. I could catalogue my undefined terms. Any idea or mortality is mereness in not by its degrees. Floating pictures as glad world. As sense of you begins to think, sense of do begins to what. The you loves to stone the Diane. City walk a merely morning. The Korea gets there in that many of the doors. A black shirt and a white tie. Said his alias. Only death been fate.

The people is down a rolling sleeves. A inevitable guilt based up out of the oppressor. Boy asks me to his small. Tense is synonymous on time. Remorseful poem progressions. The case of the past deserves attention. Books on the order of form. This shirt, turned black, tie white. Not by the park, but by the glide. Language of the thought. The front of people is tend sit. Perfectly the ocean which are never to be calm. Words should not have this.

The cells are here perfectly sickling. The world, how in its words. The temperature, back, are a body of order. Windowpane same and/or all. Write what you need. As if a edge, the dark billiards glare through the shadows. Grandfather who would to table his truss tend to lay by the bed. A inward cause and a collective neglect. Data and language are not sense. Is sidewalk a sound or roller of skates. Hum nervous on head is cross-section for those who system with what they get to be the words. A small fear asks me what I'm sleep. Oranges exiting the thousand, pour onto their highway.

A name without awareness, without sentence, without represents. Sentences of dogs. Other searches for an value of words there is in the only. Dimly spring rim. Objects is a physical. An old insect is feeding headlines to world. Expected with the photograph about speak. There was loss in weight the vision loss. Page chosen at random. Today are a decide day. How great does wall, did east, take to advances this morning, this then sky, this. Lower rainbow at higher sun forms rain. Meaning is.

Predicated ten thousand experience onto a existence. How do the true known the things. Coming to recognition of self with the greatest reluctance. Which is gray, which is blues. The spring in seen of the rim. His is a us turned fud. Act not can cause you to not your collective clock. Poured of turned. Cloud, its up the rose. Should the loud not of nervous poems in head and you have goals. Grandfather would lay his alphabet on the table by the proliferation. Merely in the dark instant shadows, but thru its present the glare of the moving edge. Here the trees are conversion.

Land is a mass, not a spaces. Weather is the warm smell. What if insurgents stood people is incoming waving. A first life, not now, of see is the days themes. Season with a presence made of new recognize a do how. Forget a field with a lepers blink. A specific experience, predicated, reserved for the existence. A voice as room and parts as the brain. How do you needle pine. Q-tips morning.

Senses I'd shake. Room filling the sky of the news. Warrior song of the Mylar kite.

The milky field. Realism is our strategy as to what might have condition. This is not lion but a mane of it. Learning to play the turtle for the cure, it snows. We filling room with sky. This is not an incorrect enemy of common time. By chance I meet a swamp in the gas and we visit. The objectify is a maze of coleus, canvas, expression and skylights. Haze glow up off of the light. Geometry of the light to dew. A language in which to spring the casual languorous. Specific loss of visits omitted family. A believe that perfect rest by the south stasis.

People stood on the page, waving to the incoming, black-angle pen. Fog steams up off the field. The south seal is ashore. Mass is immense on spaces. A grammar of colors. I picture warm language. The Satie of connect. Field steams to fog. Specific I call the loss in my family. How do we recognize the habitat of a new rhesus. Example in the negation to shake loose incorrect constituent. One coleus, canvas from several skylights of the upstairs, or barnwood. Chance is the market.

The dream of undefined descriptive grapefruit. Sound sealed you. What do one pulls. A specific language, hushed, reserved for the bedroom. This dream brings. Said his house was advanced. The real of syntax is not in world. I formed our city in the stove. The art of the flight divining birds. The sun's need amid what brings only a dull write. The morning urine forms, the foam readily dissolves into the city. In home, there are many wife. Death and delight have been the fate of geeks.

Considerations of Representability

Language is the fireplace.
                        The lower the envelope
the higher the sound.
                    Roaches of the stove.
                                    House
the block, block the house.
                        The grapefruit is not the
dream of the awareness which it represents.
                                        A
geek's I suddenly expected to delight.
                            Former home
are life here.
            Pants in which leg pulls.
                            Great forms
of urine dissolves in the east foam.
                            Summer, we
dream, is foghorns song.
                        These are only birds and
have no other art.
                Loss of write, loss of need.
                                    World
from the insect syntax.

Poem swollen from a long development of events.
The ontology of my whatever world.
                            Page of this

and that without read.

Locating "prior" to concept.
A room of news.

Sound of gas kite, warrior, faint
song in the Mylar as I make my breakfast.

The tide
is full of forms.

Blind matches talking in color.
Coming to sensitivity of language with the greatest
information.

Rain as hang-up, as sex of handguns.

As
woman feeding older, his popcorn drifted into
pigeons.

If the object becomes fill, objective forms
become obsolete.

This pastel noise.

The concentric forms a pastel that readily circles.
The recognition coming with self greatest.

Augury
or the wax of matches from the flight of Mexico.
We becomes object by obsolete, objective by
obsolete.

Each one drifted his body on, one older at a
shapelessness.

Headlines from the insect world.
Thought was small carving than the block.

The

bowl of names.

A new rain of loss had form in our
form.

Swollen in a day of volleyball.

I speak the
power of my former truth.

This sound brings in the
gas jets of the water.

World what you full.

More on the definition on their way to certain.
Loomy sailing at air.

Fear of sleep.

Distance arrived
between the small fishing meaning just as the
verification worked its way over the this.

Work bus
sleepers on way.

Choices went sailing through the
genuine language.

This is the page between chosen
and random.

Anything is a many.

The more we put
into the meaning, the less certain we are it this.

The
small fishing of an old sun.

There enters open

window within a world.

Random chosen at random.

Popcorn I sprinkled is sea for many kelp.

Pour cat as glad spray.

The saw gets cruel in that

corner of the circus.

Thing, it is not a hedged idea.

People who run to catch the bus tend to sit at the

front.

Really personal universe.

The turtle play to

cure the snows.

I smell my own breath.

Trapped to

corner the sun for the porch, it snows.

Glad rags

defines bags.

As sense of soil begins to rock, little of

time begins to grow.

Only struggle or us is defines

in so by its conditions.

More eat above the porridge.

Crowd could stone my own mime.

Korea is doors on many.

Past case attention.

                                                              The
morning Phnom Penh falls, the Khmer Rouge
merely walk into the city.
                                        Mereness the degrees
which are not to be mortality.
                                        Diane loves to Arbus
his you.
                        Think on the do of what.
                                        The rim of ages is
dimly page.
                        Only by the clouds, but amid the light.
The undefined is descriptive a catalogue terms.
                                                              This
city, merely falls, walk morning.
                                        A said alias rose up
out of the name.
                        World of the floating.
                                                        Death
should not have destruction.

This action, inevitable in its guilt.
                                        Is this a thought
or language of longer.
                                Ocean who run to catch the
calm tend to perfectly at the never.
                                        Strewn form
and/or order.
                        The wall is never well words.

                                    The

bicycle riders glide through as a regatta.

                                    A rolling

people and down sleeves.

                        Each one pulls his pants

on, one leg at a time.

                    People catch on bus is front for

those who run with what they know to be the sit.

                                        As

if a time, the synonymous glide through the tense.

The poem, remorseful, are a form of progressions.

Boy asks the small, doing down I'm me.

                                Shirt and

tie are not white.

Sickling with the cells about here.

                            World words

make.

            There was fear of locating the concept sleep.

An old grandfather would lay table to bed.

                                This is a

meaning.

                How long does it, did it, take to sense this

data, this then language, this.

                        Nervous head are a

loud system.

                Temperature searches for an back of

whatever there is in the body.

Skates sound.
Low oranges at ten thousand pour highway.
A collective without inward, without turning,
without neglect.

Dark is a glare.

All of same.

The kill in the brain of the ghoul.

Cross-section the
loud headlines of nervous world in head and you get
insect.

As he grew older, his body drifted into
shapelessness.

Value, its other words.

Turning
higher can cause sun to lower your collective
rainbow.

Patterns of objects.

Morning in the dark
wall advances, but thru its sky the glare of the great
east.

Vision ten loss oranges onto a loss.

Which is
dogs, which is bark.

Here the meaning is adequate.
How do the razor decide the day.

I would speak his
photograph on the suddenly by the expected.

This is
a name awareness sentence.

Ontology searches for an inventory of whatever
there is in the world.
                    This is the turned truck.
How do you conversion bird.
                              Rim spring.
A true as things and known as the all.
                                        A first
experience, not existence, of light is the predicated
sigh.
        What if I have goals is not poem.
                                        Fud he
turned.
        Mushroom is a rose, not a cloud.
                                        A specific
blues, gray, reserved for the day.
                                  Clock with a mane
made of not act a not man.
                              Across a present with a
merely instant.
                Proliferation filling the alphabet of
the room.

Existence is our experience of what might have
predicated.

The upstairs is a room of coleus, canvas,
barnwood and news.
                              Specific forget of lepers called
blink.
          A morning in which to use the term Q-tips.
                                                  A
voice that coming part from the brain room.
Presence recognize up off the new.
                              Loose is not
senses but a morning of shake.
                              By spaces I barren a
land in the awesome and we immense.
                              People
incoming sidewalks to stood.
                              This is now an
incorrect life of my themes.
                              The weather smell.
                                                  The
poor cat cant spray.
                    Needle of the diamond to pine.

I omitted warm visits.
                    The spring mass is
languorous, the barren language casual.
Realism is the condition.
                    People stood on the
expression, objectify to the incoming black-clad
insurgents.

How do we recognize the enemy of a
common time.
A geometry of trees.
This is not an
incorrect example of constituent negation.
One
blowfly filling from several parts of the room, or
sky.
Swamp is predicated on gas.
Milky I see the
field in my sky.
Grapes made
to mane.
The rest of stasis.
Haze in the glow to
shake light days sign.

Lion with a mane made of grapes bites a
peach-headed man.
I meet my friend in the market.
Which do you use.
The sun's loss amid family
brings only a specific freedom.
The angle of pen is
not in page.
The rhesus habitat loves you.
The seal
of the south came ashore.

Connect his name was
Thoreau.
The morning Phnom Penh fog, the Khmer
Rouge merely steams into the field.
I picture warm
language.
A grammar of colors.
Example in the
negation to shake loose incorrect constituent.
One
coleus, canvas from several skylights of the
upstairs, or barnwood.

Do City

Great field of fog advances in the east
steams.

Meet of the market.

Physical language are picture here.

A grammar I suddenly follow to colors.

Page from the pen angle.

Barnwood, we maze, is coleus day.

Sneeze in the morning to shake loose
sleeping senses.

The lower the habitat, the higher the
rhesus'.

These are only seal and came no other
guntower.

Context in which miscreants use.

The negation is not the incorrect of
the constituent which it example.

Loss of freedom, loss of family.

Connect the Satie, kill the Thoreau.

Pulls to recognition of pants with the
greatest time.

Sound sealed envelope.

Sidewalk on the side of what.

Bowl of what and write without need.

Dream truth to grapefruit.

Home visit from a former day of life.

Birds as art, as flight of augury.

The city of our new stove.

Sound of geeks jets, water, faint hum in the lightbulb as I make my delight.

Foghorns song brings in dream.

As he advanced older, his house drifted into block.

The urine is foam of dissolves.

If the syntax becomes more, world distance becomes real.

A photograph I suddenly expected to speak.

The world searches with ontology first.

A new sensitivity of information had formed in our language.

The noise of this.

Fog forms the tide of my low rain.

We talking blind about house, block with color.

Each one pulls his sex on, one hang-up at a handguns.

Poem with events end.

Old or the popcorn of feeding from the woman of pigeons.

Mylar was more warrior than the song.

This dream forms in the summer song of the fill.

Read in a page of this.

The concept forms a difficulty that
readily locating.

We form at the small fishing form, just
as the rain worked its way over the loss.
There are small carving within a
thought.
The forearm we put into the
volleyball, the long day we are it swollen.
Pomegranates is a world.
Drifted is the shapelessness between
older and body.
Wax made in matches.
Truth I speak is made for many power.
Grandfather would lay his truss on the
table by the bed.
Object posited at distance.
We went sailing through the gas jets.
The greatest recognition of an old self.
Sprinkled concentric circles atop pastel.
Grains on the bowl on their way to
names.

I could sprinkled my own popcorn.
Any loomy or thing went sailing
through so by its air.
As small of fishing begins to arrived,
village of sun begins to worked.

Open room as world window.

I do a many voices.

The sleepers chose to work the bus.

Posited, it is not a random inserts.

Little verification between the distance.

Learning to put the certain for the definition, it exists.

Chosen random page.

Sealed in an envelope of sound.

The sun gets meaning in that corner of the this.

Genuine language choices us.

Soil above the little of rock.

The crowd is merely a stone mime.

Spray of the cat.

This page ages.

More porridge eat.

A personal universe rose up out of the really.

Not by the sun, but by the porch.

Rags should not have bags.

The thing of idea is dimly hedged.

Saw is cruel on circus.

This breath, my own, smell oranges.

He play to turtle his cure.

All the defines which are struggle to be us.

Page based on built is this for those
who identify with what they know to be the
ages.

Do what and/or think.

Diane loves Arbus, rolling down their
you.

Mortality who run to catch the
mereness tend to sit in the degrees.

Is this a floating or picture of world.

The deserves, past, are a case of
attention.

Morning and city are not falls.

I visit the home of my former wife.

As if a Korea, the many glide through
the doors.

A descriptive catalogue and undefined
terms.

A dull light brings me what I'm amid.

The death is never perfectly fate.

This name, said in its alias.

This progressions for its poem of
whatever there is in the remorseful.

Inevitable oppressor action.

Order of form.

A down without people, without
rolling, without sleeves.

This is a tense.

How white does, did it, take to black
this shirt, this and tie, this.

Small fog at what boy asks me.

This is the distance between meaning
and verification.

Words with the wall about well.

An old ocean is calm perfectly to never.

People are a bus front.

Language worked.

There was park in glide the bicycle
riders regatta.

Temperature, its back the body.

This is a collective inward neglect.

The world in back of the words.

Cells would lay his sickling on the
table by the here.

Fear ten thousand sleep onto a of.

Forearm swollen from a long day of
volleyball.

Which is all, which is same.

How do the head hum the system.

Turning onto can pour you to
thousand your ten oranges.

Data in the dark language shadows,
but thru its sense the glare of the this edge.

Grandfather the loud table of nervous
truss in head and you lay bed.

Shadows of billiards.
Sidewalk the skates are sound.

Ghoul brain.
Other is a value, not a words.
A first weight, not vision, of loss is the
days loss.
Objects are the physical patterns.
How do you criterion meaning.
A day as razor and decide as today.
Lower with a sun made of rainbow
bites a higher man.
What if I believe world is insect
headlines.
Handguns are a sex hang-up.
Across a wall with a great morning.
Photograph speak the expected of the
suddenly.
A specific bark, sentences, reserved for
the dogs.
Sentence I'd name.

We have poems with goals.
By up I rose a cloud in the sink and we
mushroom.
True, it is not a known things.
The oranges truck.

Blues is our day as to what might have
gray.

Little soil above the rock.

Merely moving of present called
instant.

This is not turned but a fud of it.

The alphabet is a maze of coleus,
canvas, barnwood and proliferation.

Clock act up off the not.

This is not an incorrect experience of
predicated existence.

A spring in which to seen the rim
dimly.

Conversion of the tree to bird.

Now I weather the smell in my warm.

The voice of brain.

Black-clad people, incoming from
waving sidewalks of the insurgents, or
stood.

A diamond of pine.

Here we follow the grammar of
colors.

Experience is the existence.

I forget lepers blink.

News stood on the sidewalks waving
to the incoming, black-clad room.

Senses sneeze to shake.

The Q mass is morning, the barren
spaces tips.

Land is mass on spaces.

Recognize in the new to do loose
season presence.

Now do I see the themes of a new life.

This blowfly filling.

The sky rise across field brings only a
dull milky.

The haze of light days signs.

Geometry and light have been the fate
of the trees.

Said his believe was stasis.

Common enemy time you.

The languorous of the casual deserves
language.

The morning lion mane falls, the
peach-headed man merely bites into the city.

A first haze, not glow, of light is the
days sign.

The expression of objectify is not in
degrees.

In Korea, omitted are many visits.

Swamp of the floating gas.

I visited my realism in the strategy.

Satellite Texts

Sitting Up, Standing, Taking Steps

High gray sky. A large wood table with only a green bottle of
"white" Rhine wine atop it (empty). An open umbrella upside
down in one corner of the room. Ritz crackers topped with cream
cheese and, beside them, Crayolas. Gray plastic bottle of lemon
ammonia on its side on the green tile in back of the toilet. My red-
and-black-checked CPO jacket atop a guitar in my rocking chair.
Butter on the knife. Dobermans and Danes. The walk-in and his
cutout. A callus around the ring. Slice of toast on a saucer on a
corner of the wood table. The low fast foreign car. The girl with
green eyes. The venetian blind. One day of Crash City. Water table.
The fatal florist in the forest. The thickness of my mother's ankles.
Poise of the pen. Yellow Buick. The numbers and kinds of irreduc-
ible acts. Cloud shadow on the still bay. Crips and walkies. Black
sock. Extension and the nature of existence. The transfer point.
Red orange. Solidity. Fog. The green felt-top table in the tavern
light. The geometry of cues. His sister. The olive trees of Sacra-
mento Street. Chipped cup. The submarine on the horizon in the
sunset. State of null karma. Undefined descriptive predicate. Little
lobes. Some handsome hands. Statue of a dog with a fish in its
mouth. Something about cowboys in bus depots. The real heat.
Great sloping grove of clover. The bell curve. Woman in a pink
blouse. Amber, ochre. The action faction or the praxis axis. Chaps
tick. Cheesy smell of a dog stool. Hiss of traffic. Sunset debris.
Jackalope. Pudding cups. Bruise on her thigh. Crab grass. Eggplant
in the shape of a face or dolphin. Blue bench. Prairie apple. Albino
with a beard. Hard edge. Pornographic motherhood. Chess people.
World behavior. Knuckle archives. Sausage. Saucer. Long-legged

women on platform shoes, short skirts, streaks of blonde in their
hair, lipstick a deep, deep red. Itch of the coccyx or the cuticle wall.
A net of concrete atop the planet, streets and roads and boulevards.
Oily leather skin of the shopping bag lady. Experimental sheep.
Moldy towel. Hair in a shag, with large white earrings. As tho
under a footbridge. A small man in a big brimmed hat. In a heliport
by the sea wall in the fog. A new white pen to write with. The bus
to the suburbs. A store full of reptiles. Rows of white headstones.
Toll bridge. The eyes of the bus driver in the rearview mirror.
A small mole on the female stranger's upper lip. An old Chinese
woman with black slacks on under her dress. Helicopter, harbor,
filmy morning light. A green suit, a white shirt and a loud tie or
a gray suit, a blue shirt and a striped, quiet tie. Three kinds of
prose. Color films of dead people. Burned-out buses among back-
lot dill weed, Military Ocean Terminal. Deer fetus wine of China.
Pigeons in the eaves of a Queen Anne's tower. All toes of identical
length. Odor of stale soap, bus depot john. Abductor muscles. The
bitterness of women. The problem of truth in fiction. Abandoned
railroad cars on a siding by the rock quarry. Advanced life support
unit. Geometry of the personal. Midget in a large felt hat. Fork lift.
Abandoned industrial trackside cafeteria amid dill-weed stalks. My
droor thing. Corridor of condos. Post-nasal drip. Hot hamster. Sand
in the notebook. A saltwater cave. Eroded ruins. The bend in the
pelican's wingspread. Algae in a tide pool. An old windowless
house of concrete, its door rusted off, with nothing inside it but
odor and an open safe. Pepper on the eggs. Jaws. One of several
small silver bracelets. A thin layer of sand, a coarse film, in my nose
and hair. Under a willow beside the pile of raked leaves, the lawn
mower in the graveyard. Density or sleep. The Paradise Cafe. A

small heap of grey, broken bird wings. Puka shell necklace. The woman with the shawl or the woman with the apple. The angle of the pile of unwashed plates. Red goose shoes. A terrible dirigible incident. Natural gas pipeline. Lubricated prophylactic. Legend of the Pony Express. Midmorning. Dark stools. Rice paper wafer. Longer boat under the bridge. The brown boot. Bananas. This way. A linguistic emulsion. Feedback. Radial tires in the mud. The constant knocker. The bridge of the nose. A location or condition of the mind. Prodder. Curlews and herons in the lagoon at low tide, the red sky of night, sailor's delight, moss on the willow, shoes off, pebbles between toes. Frigate. Ceramic blue star. Briar patch. Friend or lover. The long pier. A system, an argot. The window in the windsurfer's sail. Geese of the lagoon. Long shadows. A field of woven grass. A superficial, professional verbal exchange. Outdoor basketball courts as a form of sculpture. Sharp shadows on the fennel that constitute a description of dawn. Article-starved predicate. World of ski boots. Root beer. Big damp grey dog. Panda plant, ice plant, wandering Jew. Along the coast, on cots, in coats. A warm new storm. Blue ink on a white page between red lines. Words after words. Chard. The loose goose. The late dawn of December. Duck soup. A cheeselike discharge in her vagina. The fat cat's flat hat. Glass beads, tortoiseshell ring. Legendary bladder, legendary weak bladder. Stable, half-supple string of terms and relations. Hang glider. Forgotten sentence. Deep blue dome of sky above still grey plane of water. Between movies, not cinema, not films, not here, between movies. Condo door awning. A not-fat dalmatian. Schizo. Things to know versus things to do. Ochre school bus. The objects of thought, qualities and relations. The chapter on things. Corn row hair style. Shower or storm. Bozos,

yo-yos, turkeys, geeks. Slope-shouldered fuckoff. Henry Africa's.
Curlew, sandpiper, tern, gull, godwit. Swizzle stick. Cuticle. Static
electricity. Mauve. Tow-away zone. Blue mailbox. Cabin cruiser.
Itchy balls. Half-eaten apple. Helen Frankenthaler's newer works.
The Jello word for the day. Spurs. A duck that looks just like
Groucho. Banana-flavored taffy. Mirror image. A fire in the oil
fields. Motown. Spewed shrapnel-like remnants of a helicopter.
Tripod. Cumshot. Certain, possible, impossible. During. Herons
about a boat hull at low tide. Pink crayon, blue crayon. Fat black
dog. Bloody earlobe. Faucets. A field of clover over there. The
towers of the bridge. The pillars. Odor of paper. Orange and green
quilt. Hair in an Afro blowout. Golden saxophone. Key of C. Tail
of an afghan. Vapor trail in a light blue sky. Trace of a vapor trail.
Memory and imagination. New page. A park on a hillside. A valley
full of water, a bay. Green and round and in pain. Toy boat. Kite in
the shape of a moth. Gray day. Slow trombones. Red lines. Gentle
smell of dust. Duck pond by the freeway. Bo Diddley's hat. The
damaged guitar. Expository sentence. More than this. Walnut
desk in food stamp office. Half hour of videotape. Boulevards.
Studebaker. Blue-grey eyes. Not nouns. A series of ankles. An
investment. Phil Whalen's "platter of little feet." His shaved head,
light-colored eyebrows, thin lips, wide ears. The precise odor of
pavement. The fog before dawn. The missing felt-tip pen. The
ability. Kidney beans, pinto. Inherent danger in. Ninth. Lithogra-
phers, associates. Spurs, chaps, myth. The inflamed hangnail. As
big as. Red goose shoes. Watermelon tattoo. Hoosier state. Bean
factory. Wart upon nose. Ice tea. Colorless dawn sky. Sloop. Verb.
One mean mastiff. Tug rope. Slide guitar. Man of no fortune. Worm
time. Macro-. Oat Willie's cappuccino. Towards words. Determiner.

Faucet. Tattoo of a watermelon. Light blue summer morning sky. Swordfish. Seahorse. Recent problems in the general theory of karma. Revisionaries. His class origin versus his class stand. One rim job. Butch. A lad with an Afro blowout. A stinger. Number or doobie. Next to the last. Texaco, Arco, Exxon. Garden Street, Treat Street, Canty Lane, Highland Place. Tamal, Represa, Corona, Stormdrawer, Marion, Butner, Steilacoom, Sandstone, Redwing, Starke. Facials and manicures upstairs. Pronominal anaphor. The staggers, the shudders, the White House horrors. Alcatraz shade and blind. The hustle, the bump. Crash City. Neck, bridge, nut, fret. Meat rack. An attitude towards the verbal. An old man in a straw hat in the shade with a Dr. Pepper. Yellow mustard dispenser. Hotter, more hot. A deposit of red pepper on a lettuce leaf. Horny high school students. The politically conscious meter maid. Charred hill. Dry leaf. Cecil the seasick sea serpent, Rags the tiger. Neighbor. Burnt eucalyptus. The first poem about Kefir. Capitol of North Dakota. Turmoil. The sexually active dental technician's very good friend's larger but younger spaniel. A stairway to heaven. Nancy and Sally and Suzy. Kevin and Kirk. Kevin and Patty. Patty and Andy. Patty and Frank or Darrell. Tony and Roberta. Frank again and Nora and Eric. Richie and Joan and Carol. Aaron and a different Carol. Jesse and Sarah. Maxine or Ashleigh. Jeanne and Peter. Fame as a subject. Fame as an object. Mister tooth decay. Ferry terminal. Quarry. Hobo camp, the ranch. Population. Fluoride. Peonson's bald head (pate). Cops or thieves or cops and thieves. The dry dock. Bison, bison. Blue Capri. Still more pronominal anaphors. Her red fuzzy muff. Ambivalence, an autobiography. Good buddy. Bachelors together. Hoop, rim, backboard. Fine white smoke of a grass fire just east of San Quentin on the first day of July.

Forgotten things. The headmaster's daughter. Low in tar. Mucous. The red scooter. Almond mask. His sock. Each new first time. Description, an invention. Slice of life pie. Marigolds. White white jumpsuit. Echoes. Concentration camps by the name of Bantustans. Clarinet. At first. The day before Barbara's birthday, two before Chuck's. Brown or red brick. Blue toothpaste. On stage. Ferry terminal. Four-day week. Interpol or Cointelpro or Burns. Namibian difficulties. The recent unpleasantness between Japan and the U.S. List lover. Trailer park. Underpass. Tuesday, a.m. What, alarm, ceiling, clock, dull light, urine, toothpaste, blue shirt, jeans, water for coffee, bacon, eggs, soy toast, phony earth shoes, bus, another bus, typewriter, telephone, co-workers, salad, ice tea, more co-workers, bus, ambulance on freeway, another bus, a beer, chicken, rice and squash, today's mail, feces, TV, glass of Chablis, darkness. Rare delta fog. Plywood, fiberboard. Couch, divan, chesterfield, sofa. String of silver elephants on a chain about her neck. Her inevitably turned-up Levi cuffs. The moderately successful wage slave. Morning in North Beach, Sunday in Chinatown. Locked bumpers, a problem in front of Rincon Annex, inside WPA murals of the working class, back from Ghana at forty. The tease. Sky-blue wall of the racket club. Space cowboy. The cotton rings around the mountain, bum rhythm, the limp, the gimp. Googoo dada dada. P soup. For the entire family. 2 Disney smash hits. The All ★ Game. Two ponies in a brick-red trailer behind a brown pickup with a bale of hay in the back. Bush jacket from China. Names of the cross streets. A restful orange. A restful orange bridge. The water, the haze, the sky, all blue, a line drawing. Or not blue but grey or gray. All the same. Industrial park. Heliport. Saliva. Canal at low tide. Pompadour sheriff's yacht by the curious name of

Bijou, a year's wages. Shade over shade over shade. The curl of the ear. The tongue behind the teeth behind the lips, at the entrance of the throat. Remainder of a cigar. Calm blue eyes. Bells and chimes and wooden drums. Straw horse. Off-white piano. High hat. Blue couch. An old pair of Frye boots. Summer. The sun. High gray sky.

BART

Begin going down, Embarcadero, into the ground, earth's surface,
escalators down, a world of tile, fluorescent lights, is this the right
ticket, Labor Day, day free of labor, trains, a man is asking is there
anything to see, Glen Park, Daly City, I'm going south which in my
head means down but I'm going forward, she says he should turn
around, off at Powell, see Union Square, see Chinatown, last day
of the season so they say, visualize tourists, worms in a salad, wife
speaks no English, Czech perhaps, Soviet, Polish, is this the right
ticket, carpet of the car is yellow, orange, green, red, blue woven
 in also, going faster now, lights flicker now out the windows, dark
there, not flicker but we pass them so quickly, didn't realize this
station was underground, 11:30 Glen Park, we surface, cloudy
day, these windows are dirty, should I get off here, should I wait,
forget about Balboa Park, is it there, does it exist, does it exist for
a reason, pen is blue for a change, a possible difference, a man
about my age with razor-cut hair, old women, I get off, Daly City,
go down concrete stairs, into the interior again but not really, the
ticket *is* wrong, means I'll spend 75¢, okay, pay more attention, the
vagueness of the landscape here, a large parking lot and beyond it
houses, nothing special, this is where they keep the families now,
upstairs to the platform, this one to Concord, a man, his wife, two
sons, one daughter, another man in a tweed hat, is that what you
call a fedora, not really, Arthur Jackson please call the station agent,
taking a long time to get under way, doors close, I feel the motion
first in the small of my back, my butt, car hums as it moves, you
can hear the air-conditioning, another world when you come out
she sez, look at those houses, big dumpsters in supermarket parking

lot, we're above it all, but now going down again, Balboa Park, second time, car stops, nobody gets off or on, money's available, we'll prove it, says Wells Fargo, poster of a stagecoach, this is an act, this is deliberate, parallel to the freeway, apartments very square here, you don't think of it as the City but it is, go into the world and describe it, the father talks with his youngest son, rest of the family is silent, more people get on, no one gets off, 11:59, moves quickly now, other conversations not loud enough for me to hear them, voice on the public address system sez 24th Street, no one is waiting but we stop, bought this notebook just for today, months ago, bought this pen just last Friday, today's Monday, Kathy Tobin and Shelley have pens just like it, 49¢, stiletto point, man gets on with a racing form in hand, looks apprehensive, you always see stress in everyone's face, it's in their eyes, how they hold their mouth, as if it took an effort to keep their lips in control, from contorting, you don't need to know them, any day, especially after work, Civic Center, 12:08, car's half full now, a longer stop than usual, no one's tried to sit next to me so far, Ev sez I wear my hair like a wild man, it puts the straights off, three older people stand and wait to get off, that man with the hat, carpet is mostly a yellow blend on this car too, fat woman with two boys, she shouts at them to sit down, I see my reflection in the window, an act of description, hand writing, good thing I don't get carsick, back now at Embarcadero, more people on, this has a different rhythm than buses, Duncan writes on them, anthology of literature scribed on public transit, man sitting next to me now, had to put my book bag on my lap, move my Argus C3, gray hair, balding, wears a green sweater, realize I'm underwater now, the bay, we all are, you too, move at 80 mph, now that boy's talking to his mother, America is beware

of microwave ovens, I'm wearing my phony earth shoes, beginning
to show their age, harder to write with the book bag in my lap,
alters the angle, the surface, Oakland now, rail yards, Military
Ocean Terminal, postal station for incoming foreign mail, where
 I'd be if I hadn't quit, 8 years ago this month, every cell in body
different now, that woman's still ordering her children, just her
form of conversation, boxcars, seatrains, above the ghetto, sunnier
here, the symbol of Mack Truck is a bulldog, Tribune Tower on
the left lost now amid office buildings, into the earth again, you
can hear metal scraping, forget the air-conditioning, this train des-
tined for Concord, man with the green sweater gets off, wanna ride
backwards somebody sez, more young people on the car now, man
in front of me seems to have gone to sleep, red tile at 12th Street,
blue at 19th, Japanese tourist, this is the familiar part to me now,
way to Berkeley, more scraping as the car turns, I anticipate the
nature of future stops, Pill Hill to the right, cluster of hospitals,
with the inevitable parasites, chem labs, funeral homes, why call
them parlors, remember waiting at MacArthur Station at twilight
one night with Acker, sunset just before the rainfall, blacks in pith
helmets are taking Polaroids of one another, now a woman sits next
to me, her probable husband next to the man in the yellow shirt
who wakes and goes back to his Chronicle, sixth of September,
Grove-Shafter Freeway to the right, now they move to sit together,
can I find my mother's place from here, no, take my jacket off, get-
ting warm, Rockridge, 12:30, beautiful homes then below ground
for a minute, how is a tunnel thru a hill the same or different from
one underground or underwater, suddenly remember nights of stay-
ing up high to scribble verbatim thots as poems, 1964, Ginsberg-
esque or so I thought, I didn't think when that ordering mother

got off, college-age couple there now, arms about one another, description implies a relation, the dry hills of Orinda, at the end of a summer drought, John and Ann used to live at the top of that hill, house is still there, we used to visit often, my mother's older sister, her husband almost as old as her father, my grandparents never approved, trees and low hills, suburbs to the east, country once, when we're "outdoors" above ground I can't see myself in the window, that's where the world is, condo-like office buildings, new life in Lafayette, a girl, age 10 at the most, in a bright pink jumpsuit is standing on the platform, waiting to go the other way, hot rods on the freeway beside us, 24 East, man in the yellow shirt is reading TV Log now, there's a cemetery, I notice a ring on his left hand, for a long time we've been turning slightly to the left, in Walnut Creek you can see Mt. Diablo, it's the mountain here as much as Tam, more parking lots, more condos, why didn't some-one just shoot old Henry Ford, is housing contingent on transporta-tion or vice versa, only in our time have people begun to live away from their work, what it does to the psyche, how large is your turf, my triangle the City, Berkeley, Marin, plus of course parts of Sacra-mento, Pleasant Hill now farther than I've ever gone before, nearing end of line, 12:47, streets without sidewalks, with trees, affect the rural, swimming pools, patterns of colored gravel, a power mower for every home, tanned fat men in shorts, so here's where they keep all the trains, dozens of them, grey sluglike things, flat brown countryside, I get off at Concord, no place to sit down, clock says my watch is slow, lots of motorcycles in the parking lot, voice on the speaker system says don't ride bike on the platform, crowd begins to thin out, I find a bench, old men still wear puka shells out here, women in pastel pantsuits, that's a shopping mall a block away, the parking lots merge, four state-college-type jocks sit down on a nearby bench, woman walks by with three children, one in her arms, says of the car as she passes, it looks pretty full, it does, same one I got off of waiting to go back, do I want to drink that Fresca now, perfect summer weather here, so often I've noticed that people who grew up in the country work in the suburbs, service the people who work each day in the city, train pulls out and suddenly I see the whole west side of the valley, train engineers wear blue jumpsuits, slight breeze, woman comes by saying Steven, Steven, someone walks by with a transistor radio playing Spanish, scowls at us, couple with a baby talks to me, how often do they run, this one's crowded, standing room only, I get a spot but I'll have to ride backwards, woman in dark glasses tells her daughter to sit in her lap, she doesn't but takes a seat to herself, sobbing softly, blonde girl, 4 maybe, leans over her seat, watches me write this, guy sits next to me almost lands on top of my camera, has an "army" haircut and a brown paper bag, what is described forms a place, all words aim at that, I'm more cramped now, jacket, book bag, Argus in my lap, my left hand rests on the case of the Argus, holds the notebook, red cover, white pages, my wrist beginning to ache from the controlled act of writing, these aren't tourists, they're locals riding around as if they were, travel plans of the working class, now we're down to standing room only, 1:19, going backwards exerts a pull, San Angel Road, you could type towns by the kind of street signs they use, color, how much information they put on them, etc., housing tract, ranch-style school grounds, an orchard, someone says he's a native of San Francisco, Pleasant Hill and lots of people want to board, the couples in the next seats have introduced themselves to each other, he designs restaurant décor, we pass Palmer School, lots of vans, campers, minibuses out here, condos in the distance, a few eucalyptus, yesterday at this time I was basking in the center-field bleachers at Candlestick Park, Montefusco halfway to a four-nothing shutout, man came up to us wearing bones in his ears, wanted to look at our field glasses, cameras, offered us a hit of coke, smack, grass if we wanted, we didn't even if we did, he showed us the coke, it was yellow, that was yesterday, it doesn't exist anymore, Lafayette and still more people get on, it's an event, ride BART for a day for a quarter, Labor Day is a day of rest, of description, is a relationship of words to place, nearing Orinda, voice sez her name is Jennifer too, Upper Happy Valley Road, Acalanes, Mt Diablo Blvd, I'm growing older in small units, by the minute now, new information modifies my history, losing weight too, 30 lbs since June, should these things have seat belts, air bags, one of the women standing is overweight, beside her is a beautiful daughter, she too looked like that once, assumption, my ears pop, we're back in Oakland, in the Montclair section, then Rockridge, train on the far platform on its way to Concord, money's available, we'll prove it, sez Wells Fargo, older houses now, this town is black, run by whites, I get off at MacArthur, decide to sit in the sun awhile, drink my Fresca, have to shove thru mob of boarders to do it, not as hot here, my whole body is feeling the motion, it puts a stress, a pull on every organ, wobble a bit or stagger, sit cross-legged at end of platform, realize I haven't had a cigarette today, trying to quit again, Camels left on my desk at home, man in a yellow shirt on the platform looks like my idea of a Navajo, has that broad face and crewcut particular to my image of that, wearing cowboy boots as well, Fremont train pulls in, I'll let it pass, want to finish my Fresca, take a few photos, get the motion

out of my body, one way to see the bay, even see the City from here,
1:59, I'm only half done, is that it, an act, something done deliber-
ately, of description, which means place, but of travel, meaning
place shifts, alters, speech chain Möbius strip, had not expected
the crowd, but that's alright, this blue ink is lovely, a pleasure to
watch, jotting, is what I do, wander around the platform, take
photos, speaker system sez slight delay on the Richmond-bound
line, which is exact opposite of one I'm waiting for which arrives
as I write this, jammed it seems as I wait to board, but not really,
just people waiting to get off, an act of writing without let up,
downtown Oakland now, can't even find the Tribune Tower, then
underground again, all these cars have identical rugs, realize that
I was wrong before, it was a five-nothing shutout, I forgot Gary
Alexander's homer, his very first, in the eighth, up into the rightfield
bleachers, 12th Street, more people get on, have to stand now, kids
getting on one train, get off, get on another, repeat the performance,
an act of endurance, calling each other names, you're stupid, etc.,
should we get off at Fremont, a long way from there yet, they run
down the aisle onto the next car, another group follows, a small
girl is eating a saltine, the woman I'm sitting next to is her mother,
in front of me a woman with gray hair, a permanent, in a red jacket,
man standing in the aisle holding onto the handrails pulls himself
up off the floor of the car, feet swing forward and back, Lake
Merritt, woman next to me, across the aisle, wearing a pale green
suit, above ground again, pass Richmond-bound train, quick gray
flash and it's gone, East Oakland, Polymir, a big Monkey Wards
store, Melrose Ford, church spires, Fruitvale, people get off, not
on, for once, hear a voice say "I'm sorry," Jimmy Carter for Presi-
dent '76, blue sign painted (crudely) on side of apartment building,

oomaloom, Michael, thinking of you, down below the carbarn
for the AC Transit buses, Oakland Coliseum across the parking
lot, CSB Construction, Sunshine Biscuits, Fun Games Inc., PACO,
water tower, Standard Brands, homes built just before the war,
green, pink, light blue, yellow, another train to Richmond, just
the facts, ma'am, just the facts, San Leandro, more people get off,
woman in a red wheelchair sits in the aisle, a field of greenhouses,
homes, now more affluent-looking (not very), now less, Bay Fair
shopping center, crowd is thinning, means either people are tiring
or they don't want to go to Fremont, less wealthy and intriguing
than Concord, homes not that poor, tho, small boats in the drive-
ways, Hayward, large blocks of apartments, a school in the blue
and green, Grand Auto, apple trees, willows, 2:46, never was this
far before, a golf course, dry fields, another BART carbarn, I change
seats, rooms to sit by a window, hawk in the sky, hills to the left
grow higher, still dryer, a large playground, Union City, grain mills,
auto-wrecking yards, Pacific States Steel, this isn't so far from San
Jose, a small lake with water, I'm the only white left on this car,
tourism is different to different peoples, train stops before we get
to the station, people stand, stretch, kids dash up and down aisles,
whooping, parents not caring to stop it, Japanese man asks me if
this is Fremont, people get on, I see that the woman in the wheel-
chair is Indian or Pakistani, children are crying or whimpering
in español, sign on a hillside says Niles, where they used to make
silent movies, westerns, my grandfather would ride his motorcycle
out from Berkeley to watch them, fingerprints on these windows,
black smudges like a grease pencil, black man in a turban wanders
about the platform, a little girl comes up and makes a face at me,
friendly, my right lens is scratched, a slight blur, need a new pair of

shades, also new trousers, new jacket, we move again, pass a stable, kids shout caballos, a lake, then homes, this world is foreign to me, an act of description, old railcars, I beams, a school or hospital off in the distance, we stop, a woman gets on chewing blue gum, a yardful of transformers, PG&E, old homes, weathered, wooden, no lawns, just dirt, these tracks constantly bordered with cyclone fence topped with barbed wire (and I only just noticed), girl in a pink dress cries, a vacant lot, full of refrigerators and stoves, South Hayward, 3:13, woman with the gum gets off, others get on, I've seen hundreds, thousands of people, only one I've recognized, an old man in the CP, we merely nodded, a helicopter going in the other direction, this will be the longest stretch of riding yet, to Richmond, or maybe not, grove of apple trees, in Hayward I can see Mt. Diablo from another angle, nobody gets on or off, the sign for no smoking is a burning cigarette behind a red barred circle, the sign for no trespassing is the outline of a hand, in which the thing described is constantly moving, I can never hope to know all these lives, Honda Civics, bugs, Fiats, my brother and I would go with our grandparents each Sunday for a "ride in the country," which meant Grizzly Peak Boulevard, or out the Arlington or down to Lake Merritt, Golden Grain Spaghetti plant, more greenhouses, where people work takes up nearly as much space as where they live, but you forget about it, those become empty spaces, an old man with bright blue socks runs along the platform to get on, San Leandro, I flex my writing hand to ease the pain, see a young man is watching me intently, trying to figure this out, AJB Linoleum, nothing but blacks on the streets below, then more plants, one for yeast, billboard in Spanish, Longview Fibre, sky a very light blue, two teenage boys in identical white baseball shirts with green

sleeves walk by, going by the carbarn I realize all those buses have
numbers painted on their roofs, I see in the distant hills the Greek
Orthodox Church and the Oakland Mormon Temple, getting closer,
lumberyard, chopped Harley, what I describe is what comes to me
in words as I look out the window, miss all the rest, can't even write
it all, Fruitvale, the big Chicano family gets off, Texaco, Shell, patio
furniture says a sign, distributors of Hartz Mountain, into the earth
again, an act of endurance, hand writing, hours without letting up,
to see if one can, man in front of me has a shirt the orange of sher-
bet, his wife, I make these assumptions, a blouse of light purple,
only he gets off, 12th Street, she doesn't, still more people get on,
standing room again or almost, third time I'm at 19th Street today
and not the last, woman over there has a pair of crutches, man
sitting beside me wears an off-white leisure suit, Pill Hill, a collec-
tion of overpasses is often beautiful, curving masses of concrete,
MacArthur Station, a crowd mobs in, people complain of the heat,
this station the key to the system, many people standing, now an
older woman in a heavy sweater sits by me, how can you describe
people when you can only see surface features, Grove Street, I
see the Berkeley Campanile, the Claremont Hotel, the old portable
classrooms of Merritt College on wheels now, the campus to be
torn down, Ashby, into Berkeley for the first time today, I hear
somebody ask someone else her name, people get off at the down-
town station, I've only talked once all afternoon, more people get
off, few tourists left, there are only three more stops to Richmond,
above ground on Gilman Street, neighborhood where I grew up,
houses I've lived in, Solano Avenue, a game of baseball in Feeney
Field, the bar in the circle of the no-smoking sign goes from upper
left to lower right, an act, homage to you Jack, oomaloom, one

word after another, tennis courts, a man and a boy walk thru an empty parking lot, gulls sleep on a football field at a high school, another carbarn for AC Transit, I get off at Richmond, it's windy, I put on my jacket, 4:04, I can see Mt. Tam, Point Richmond in the distance, somebody's taking my photograph, two older couples are sneaking cigarettes behind a sign, younger people just do it, who cares, teenagers run up and down the platform, slap the car windows, board and get off, giggles and shouts, the quality of light is just beginning to change, late afternoon means earlier now, mid-September, I try to figure how many stations I'll go by today, 71, couple in front of me is just starting their trip, they decide to go to Concord, she takes a Dramamine, a family gets on, all the kids have chartreuse turtlenecks with their names on them, we go by an old trailer park, another lumber yard, new condos on the west slope of Albany Hill, on my left my old high school, thru a thin haze barely see the outline of the City, no Golden Gate, a dozen kids dark down the car, others follow, cooler now, they got off daddy a kid sez to another, kids now running in opposite direction, still find tourists in Berkeley, the car crowds in a hurry, I'm feeling weary now, wish my ears would pop, a small woman with a thick accent sits beside me, two young people, a couple, are with her, they seem to really like her, she wears a yellow dress, a copper bracelet, there's a motorcycle parked on the freeway, the City more visible from Oakland, but not very, I get off at MacArthur to transfer, my hand hurts, I wobble walking, a woman comes up, asks me what I'm doing, we discuss writing, she wants to try it "sometime," asks me am I writing things, I shrug, I don't ask her name, the Daly City train comes, I get on, it's so crowded I have to stand, I keep writing, I'm much more conspicuous now, people are staring, I can't hold on and write at the same time, I nearly fall, I'm going to have to stand all the way back, we'll be back under the bay in a second, 80 mph, a man watches me write this, I remember what Einstein said when asked to explain the theory of relativity in 25 words or less, what time does the station get to the train, it's coming, Embarcadero, my writing is a scrawl, an act of description, I'm describing these people who watch me, madras shirt, curly gray hair, here's the station, I get out, sit down, I can still feel the pulling forces, I am about to board the slow upward path of the escalator, thru the ticket gate with the wrong ticket, then back up to the street level, earth's surface, then home, 4:51, 9.6.76.

NEW CALIFORNIA POETRY

EDITED BY	Robert Hass Calvin Bedient Brenda Hillman Forrest Gander

Designer: Janet Wood
Text: 10/15 Sabon
Display: Akzidenz Grotesque Extended
Compositor: BookMatters, Berkeley
Printer and binder: Friesens Corporation